שַׁעֲרֵי בִּינָה ב׳

GATES OF UNDERSTANDING 2

To Alan & Barbara
In friendship
Larry

פִּתְחוּ־לָנוּ שַׁעֲרֵי־בְרָכָה...

Open for us the gates of blessing . . .

בָּרוּךְ אַתָּה ,יְיָ, מְבָרֵךְ הַשָּׁנִים.

Praised be God who blesses our years.

—FROM THE LITURGY

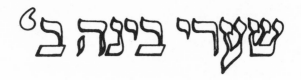

GATES OF UNDERSTANDING 2

Appreciating the Days of Awe

A companion volume
to
SHAAREI TESHUVAH: GATES OF REPENTANCE

LAWRENCE A. HOFFMAN

Notes to *GATES OF REPENTANCE*
by
CHAIM STERN
with
A. Stanley Dreyfus and Lawrence A. Hoffman

CENTRAL CONFERENCE OF AMERICAN RABBIS

5744   New York   1984

LIBRARY OF CONGRESS CATALOGING IN PUBLICATION DATA

Main entry under title:

Gates of understanding (Sha'are binah)

In English.
Vol. 2, published by the Central Conference of American Rabbis.
Includes bibliographical references and index.
Contents: 1. A companion volume to Shaarei tefillah, Gates of prayer.
2. Appreciating the Days of Awe, a companion volume to Shaarei teshuvah, Gates
of repentance.
  1. Prayer (Judaism)—Addresses, essays, lectures. 2. Reform Judaism—
Addresses, essays, lectures. 3. Reform Judaism—Liturgy—Addresses, essays,
lectures. 4. Siddur (Reform, Central Conference of American Rabbis). Gates of
prayer. 5. Mahzor. High Holidays (Reform, Central Conference of American
Rabbis). Gates of repentance.
  I. Hoffman, Lawrence A., 1942-   . II. Central Conference of American
Rabbis. III. Siddur (Reform, Central Conference of American Rabbis). Gates of
prayer. IV. Mahzor. High Holidays (Reform, Central Conference of American
Rabbis). Gates of repentance. V. Title: Sha'are binah.

BM660.G37   1977   296.7'2   77-23488
ISBN 0-916694-34-8 (v. 1)
ISBN 0-916694-84-4 (v. 2; pbk.)

Copy editing and publishing services provided by SPECIAL EDITION,
P.O. Box 09553, Columbus, Ohio 43209 (614-231-4088)

Contents

Acknowledgments

WRITING A BOOK about liturgy is always a labor of love. But composing this volume has been particularly so, because of the generous help and warm support I received from so many colleagues, all outstanding in their knowledge of Jewish tradition and their love for the Jewish People.

Rabbi Herbert Bronstein, my successor as Chair of our Liturgy Committee, proved ever willing to share his time and offer advice.

Rabbi A. Stanley Dreyfus, always my teacher, added immeasurably to this volume, by reading its drafts and correcting its errors. He is awesome in his ability to combine both knowledge of and love for the Jewish tradition, mastery of our Reform liturgical heritage, and poetic facility with the English language.

Rabbi Joseph B. Glaser has been a friend whose unfailing wisdom, both Jewish and general, sustained me throughout the entire project. The book would not have been completed without his gentle insistence that we provide for the needs of a knowledgeable Jewish community.

Rabbi Stuart Geller and Rabbi Eric Hoffman added immensely to the final manuscript, by reading successive drafts with great care and offering many excellent recommendations. I am indebted also to valuable suggestions made by Rabbis Harvey Fields, Jordan Pearlson, David Polish, William Sajowitz, and Daniel J. Silver, and by student rabbis Connie Abramson and Yoel Kahn.

Rabbi Chaim Stern has already proven himself to be a gifted poet and sensitive soul, whose love of Jewish literature shines forth from virtually every page of the *Machzor* to which this book is a companion. In addition, he is the primary compiler of the Companion Notes (Part Two). The character of Reform worship will have been determined in large part by this one man.

Rabbi Deborah Zecher enhanced the value of the Companion Notes with careful and caring research.

Rabbi Elliot L. Stevens directed this, as he does all Conference publications, with painstaking diligence

To whom should this work be dedicated? Clearly, its intent transcends the artistry of any single life. It reflects the searching minds and loving hearts of generations of rabbis whose diligent commitment to Jewish study has long been my ideal. Let this book, then, be dedicated to all my students whom I love dearly, and for whom I research, write, and teach. This book is theirs.

LAWRENCE A. HOFFMAN

Introduction: How to Use This Book

This is the second volume in the series *Gates of Understanding*. Volume I accompanied the daily, Shabbat, and festival prayerbook (*Gates of Prayer*); Volume II describes our liturgy for Rosh Hashana and Yom Kippur (*Gates of Repentance*). Both books are designed for reference purposes.

Volume I had five distinct parts:

1. Whence We Came—a series of short essays describing the origins of Reform worship;

2. What We Believe—several theological essays, each relating specifically to prayer and often explaining the theological assumptions behind one or another of the Shabbat services in *Gates of Prayer*;

3. How We Worship—discussions of the environment of prayer: the music, the synagogue, and the psychological disposition of worshipers;

4. The Liturgical Message—a summary statement of the process of prayer and the role of the worship experience in defining Jewish identity;

5. On *Shaarei Tefillah*—short descriptions of the theological uniqueness of each of the Shabbat services, notes indicating the derivation of each prayer in the volume, and the official lectionary (table of scriptural readings) now in use within the Reform Movement.

Volume II contains three parts:

1. A Worshiper's Commentary—unlike the Companion Notes (Part Two), this commentary provides a running account of each service in *Gates of Repentance*. It provides background information on the history and theology of the prayers, by bringing together insights from Jewish tradition and from modern scientific study. Along the way, we include much necessary information about Jewish liturgy, generally, to enable interested lay readers to appreciate the liturgical subtleties peculiar to the Days of Awe. Thus, we discuss such matters as the nature of the Jewish calendar, music in the service, basic service structure, the use of specialized worship garb (*kipa* and *talit*), the origin of synagogue poetry, and the like. As much as possible, we avoid technical vocabulary, footnotes, and other features typical of scholarly apparatus; this is, above all, a religious

1

commentary for worshipers. Rubric headings and page references to *Gates of Repentance* precede each discussion, and cross-references are given to relevant data elsewhere in both volumes of *Gates of Understanding*.

2. On *Shaarei Teshuvah*, Companion Notes to *Gates of Repentance*—brief scholarly apparatus detailing the history and intent of each specific liturgical entry in *Gates of Repentance*.

3. Index—the Index allows readers to look up any liturgical or liturgically related topic covered in this volume, for example, *Akeda*, Cantor, Confession, Music of the Liturgy, *Piyut*, *Talit*, *Tefila*, etc.

Readers desiring an overall understanding of the significance of their new liturgy should read the summary essay "The Liturgical Message" in Part 4 of Volume I.

Part One

A Worshiper's Commentary to GATES OF REPENTANCE: *Appreciating the Days of Awe*

Introduction to the Commentary

The title for this part of the book ("A Worshiper's Commentary to *Gates of Repentance*") has been selected deliberately. Obviously, it accompanies the specific High Holy Day liturgy contained in *Gates of Repentance*; but beyond this fact lie two additional perspectives that the title ought to suggest.

First, this is a commentary. As a form of expression, commentaries enjoy high regard in the history of Jewish literature. It has always been the Jew's assumption that the written word contains within it untold depths of insight that must be elucidated by running comments. The best example is the Bible itself. Even before it was canonized, rabbis were composing explanatory extensions to the written text, fleshing out the literal account with details that went far beyond what the biblical authors had in mind when they constructed the books of the Bible in the first place. These original commentaries to the biblical text, or *Midrash* as they are known, were themselves outfitted with commentary through the years. Other commentaries by later medieval Jews were eventually printed in the margins of the biblical texts themselves, as it was assumed, by then, that without the commentaries, one must necessarily fall short of understanding even the most elementary lessons buried in the text.

In this way, a Jewish library is made up of commentaries on basic texts, and then commentaries on commentaries, and even commentaries on commentaries on commentaries. In our case, the basic text is the liturgy, and we happily adhere to age-old Jewish precedent by providing at least this first-order commentary to it.

Our first perspective, which is to carry on Judaism's "commentary tradition," must be modified by a second: this is a commentary *for worshipers*. Elsewhere in this book (Part Two), we have supplied the scholarly apparatus that passes for knowledge in today's scientific world. That is, should our readers wish to know those details essential to a scientific comprehension of the origin and development of a given prayer, they should consult the notes in Part Two, not this commentary. Some of that information will be found here, too, but only when it fulfills criteria other

5

than the systematic supplying of data pertinent to a prayer's history. The information presented in this section pertains only to the act of worship.

Putting it another way, we can say that this commentary differs from the Companion Notes in the same way that traditional Jewish commentaries differ from scientific notation. Scientists treat the material they study from a perspective of neutral objectivity. They observe and describe; they rigorously avoid any personal entanglement with their subjects. Traditional Jewish commentators, on the other hand, were passionately committed to the texts they read. If they wrote commentaries to Torah, it was so that Jews might better understand the word of the living God; when they penned commentaries to prayerbooks, they hoped to make prayer come alive, as worshipers struggled to address their Maker.

Though not mutually exclusive, these two perspectives adopt separate routes to "truth." For the scientist, truth is often still regarded as the discovery of what exists in some presumably objective world of facts "out there." For the religionist, truth is both broader and narrower than that. It is broader in that legends, stories, and ideas are as important as empirical facts; they, too, enrich the process of religious growth, so they, too, deserve to be included in a commentary claiming to discover meaning buried beneath the surface of a prayer's text. But it is narrower also, inasmuch as some factual data—the date of a prayer's first appearance in manuscript form, for example—may turn out to be utterly irrelevant to the act of worship and are best avoided in a commentary designed to further worship's ends.

In sum, in contrast to the scientific Companion Notes (Part Two, pp. 157–231), what follows is a religious commentary, not unlike those our ancestors have been compiling for centuries as Judaism's legacy to the life of the spirit. To be sure, this commentary speaks in the accent of today's world; for example, it is, we trust, neither "preachy" nor polemical, to note but two rhetorical styles that have characterized some commentaries of the past. In our day, we prefer discussions of history and theology, and we seek enlightenment regarding the ways in which our text either continues or discontinues tradition—and why. What follows is a service-by-service and, often, a prayer-by-prayer, religious commentary on the new Reform liturgy for the Days of Awe. It should unlock the messages that lie behind the *Gates of Repentance* so that worshipers may better fathom the depths of the age-old yet ever-new prayers of our people.

The Services of a Machzor

Technically, *Gates of Repentance* is a *Machzor*, as opposed to a *Siddur*. Until the 15th century or so, Jews bound all the prayers for the whole year in one volume called either *Machzor* or *Siddur*. The title *Siddur* comes from the Hebrew word meaning "order" and refers to the fact that the book contains an order of prayers. The name *Machzor* is derived from the word meaning "cycle" and so, informs the worshiper that the prayerbook with that title holds all the prayers necessary for the yearly cycle of holy days. By the 1400s, however, we find people complaining that the liturgy had grown so much that they could not carry the heavy prayerbooks to the synagogue. As a result, the services were bound into separate volumes. In the Ashkenazic world of Northern Europe, the daily and Shabbat book was called a *Siddur*, while the name *Machzor* was reserved for the liturgy of holidays (*Regalim*—that is, Pesach, Shavuot, and Sukkot—and *Yamim Nora-im*—that is, Rosh Hashana and Yom Kippur).

The Table of Contents (*Gates of Repentance*, p. vii) lists the services that will be found within this *Machzor*. By comparing it with the contents of a traditional *Machzor*, one can learn a great deal about Reform Judaism generally, and Reform Judaism today, in particular.

Traditionally, our calendar begins in the evening, so that each holiday has first an Evening Service (*Arvit* or *Ma-ariv*), then a Morning Service (*Shacharit*), and, finally, a late Afternoon Service (*Mincha*) that precedes the Evening Service of the next day. In addition, holidays feature a service called *Musaf*, meaning "additional," and Yom Kippur is unique in that it ends with a Concluding, or *Ne-ila*, Service.

A glance at the Rosh Hashana Table of Contents reveals two facts immediately. To begin with, the practice of praying three times each day is no longer acknowledged as universally possible within Reform Judaism. For better or for worse, the Afternoon, or *Mincha*, Service is missing here, as it has been since the first edition of the *Union Prayer Book* (1894). Secondly, *Gates of Repentance* differs from its antecedent *Union Prayer Book* in that it contains two sets of services for Rosh Hashana. Partly, this is an extension of the principle of providing alternatives for a Reform

7

constituency that we now know to be far from homogeneous in nature. In 1894, Reform Jews sought uniformity in public worship and for their new prayerbook. They accepted as their prayers only a small fraction of the totality of prayer material that the Jewish tradition offered. By contrast, today's Reform Movement is committed to recapturing the entire depth and breadth of our tradition, and, in the spirit of true liberal religion, it offers different samplings of tradition blended judiciously with modern readings, so as to give alternative, but equally acceptable, portraits of authentic Jewish existence. This is particularly evident in *Gates of Prayer*, where we provide ten Friday night Shabbat services, each with a different theological or thematic approach (see *Gates of Understanding*, Volume I, pp. 171-176, for a discussion of each theme.) But we see the same commitment to variety in this volume as well. Congregations may choose from two Rosh Hashana services, and people who celebrate two days of Rosh Hashana may elect to use both, thus widening their spiritual horizons on the second day. (For the reason behind keeping two days rather than one, see this commentary's introductory remarks to Evening Service II, below, pp. 25-28.)

Three aspects of the Yom Kippur Table of Contents demand our attention. First, unlike Rosh Hashana, we still have an Afternoon Service (*Mincha*) here. It is assumed that Reform Jews fast on Yom Kippur, spending the whole day in the synagogue. There is no reason to end the services at noon, since people will not go home for festive repasts as they do on Rosh Hashana.

Secondly, we notice a separate listing for the Memorial Service. We shall deal with this service in detail later (pp. 146-149), but for now we should note that this is one instance in which Reform Judaism has creatively expressed a contemporary spiritual need in such a way that other branches of Judaism have emulated our example. Traditionally, there is no separate Memorial Service in the liturgy. At best, there is a short set of prayers called *Yizkor*, which is inserted just before replacing the Torah in the Ark. Some readers may recall a time when worshipers whose parents were living were asked to leave the synagogue at *Yizkor*, in keeping with a folk belief that Satan would be tempted to give them reason to mourn if they were found among mourners. But Reform Judaism rejected this superstition. It saw the value in an extended Memorial liturgy. Particularly in this post-Holocaust age, we yearn for a fitting memorial for the six million victims. The result is a separate Yom Kippur Memorial Service, expanded in this latest Reform *Machzor* to voice our anguish over the six million martyrs of our own time.

Our final general observation concerns the Yom Kippur Additional Service. We have seen already that holidays have traditionally included a

Musaf, or "Additional" Service, and that we follow tradition on Yom Kippur by presenting prayer material for the whole day, from morning to nightfall. One might conclude, then, that our Additional Service is the *Musaf* service. This conclusion would be both right and wrong.

At issue here is Reform Judaism's somewhat ambivalent relationship to the ancient sacrificial system that once characterized Jewish worship, a system which it both respected and rejected. Reform Jews respected the abstract idea of serving God, having, as they put it, a Priestly Mission (see below, pp. 39-40, 42-43, and 81-82); consequently, they called their synagogues "temples" and generalized to the whole Jewish people the sacred charge that had once been vested only in the priests. We are all a priestly people with a sacred mission to serve God's ends, they said. At the same time, they rejected the very notion of animal sacrifice, along with the special elevation of one class of people, the priests, who alone had been considered fit to present offerings to God; they took issue with the Orthodox practice of praying that God might restore the sacrificial cult at the end of days.

It happens that *Musaf*, more than any other service, retains the ancient connection to the Temple cult. To begin with, the *Musaf* service was fashioned around a theology that laments the fall of the Temple, while blaming the Jewish people for that fall in the first place. The Temple was destroyed, says the *Musaf* service, because of our sins, so that we now live in exile, awaiting the time when we can return to Zion, rebuild the Temple, and begin sacrificing once again. (In this connection, see also pp. 141-142 below.) In the meantime, we present to God our prayers, which are the offerings of our lips, and in place of the festival "Additional Offering," we offer an "Additional Prayer," describing in words the exact sacrifices we would offer with our hands, were we to have the opportunity.

Needless to say, both the contents of this *Musaf* service and the very idea that we include it only because we cannot offer an additional animal sacrifice were objectionable to Reform Jews. Also, unlike the other services, very little novel material was added to *Musaf*, so that once the sections relevant to sacrifice were deleted, very little else remained. So *Musaf* has generally been left out of American Reform prayerbooks. Thus, the new *Gates of Repentance* includes an Additional Service but does not label it as *Musaf*. Its contents are almost entirely novel (as we shall see), because the model of the traditional *Musaf* service has continued to prove unacceptable to us.

Our commentary will go through two alternative services for Rosh Hashana evening and morning. For Yom Kippur, we will work our way from the well-known Evening, or "*Kol Nidrei*," Service to *Ne-ila*, the Concluding Service, stopping to look inquiringly at Reform Judaism's

9

own creation—an extended Memorial Service—and at the Additional Prayers, which constitute a modern version of the ancient *Musaf* tradition. We shall see also that, although we have eliminated the Rosh Hashana *Mincha*, or Afternoon Service, the Afternoon Service for Yom Kippur is probably the highlight of our entire *Machzor*.

Rosh Hashana Evening

General Comments

Determinants of a Service

The character of a service is generally determined by three elements: the music, the non-musical features of choreography (that is, the "how" of prayer, the way the service proceeds), and the felicity of the English readings. We have discussed music and choreography in *Gates of Understanding*, Volume I (see pp. 27-37, 115-127, 146-150, and 159-163) and need not go into detail here. Two obvious illustrations make the point well enough: it is its music, the *"Kol Nidrei"* chant, that makes the Yom Kippur Evening Service memorable; and Rosh Hashana morning is recalled favorably on account of its choreographic peculiarity, the blowing of the *shofar*. (For discussions of the *"Kol Nidrei"* and the *shofar*, see pp. 96-104 and 114-118 below.)

English Translations or English Paraphrases

What can we say now about the third determinant, the English? At issue is our usual expectation that English renditions should follow the Hebrew in an exact word-for-word translation. That way, worshipers may "know" what the Hebrew means; they have the sense of saying the "real" prayers, albeit in translation. But, contrary to this "common-sense" notion of what English prayers should be, Reform prayerbooks have consistently introduced new versions of the vernacular that, at times, have had only tangential connection with the Hebrew passages they accompany. These free translations—or, better, paraphrases—of the Hebrew text's theme are the third determinant of a service's uniqueness and deserve our attention at the outset of our commentary.

What gives us the right to introduce our own English interpretations instead of literal translations of the traditional Hebrew? Primarily, we do so because in the very first few centuries of our people's prayer life,

11

the precedent for novelty was established. Contrary to popular belief, the Rabbis of the first few centuries of the common era did not require adherence to established immutable prayer texts. Instead they preferred to balance the regular and anticipated wording with a delightful mixture of verbal surprise. Rote recitation is boring after all, and, whatever prayer should be like, it should not be boring! So the Rabbis enacted the following principle: the service should follow carefully a fixed structure that would consist of a series of given themes succeeding each other in predictable order; but, at the same time, this dependable thematic progression was to be expressed at each and every occasion with novel wording freshly selected by those charged with leading the service. The structural fixity (or *keva*, in Hebrew) was thus balanced by linguistic creativity (or *kavana*). So, the first thing to be said for our inclusion of a variety of English paraphrases of the Hebrew is that, far from constituting a deviation from tradition, this practice marks a continuation of Rabbinic Judaism's earliest model for prayer. (See also below, p. 121.)

Thus, *Gates of Repentance* is both traditional and Reform: it insists on the same creativity that the earliest Rabbis demonstrated, sometimes translating their Hebrew literally and sometimes utilizing a new English prayer that reflects their theme in a novel way.

Rubrics

Each of the basic liturgical units or building blocks of the service is called a "rubric," a word related to the prayerbooks of the Roman Catholic Church, where, traditionally, each new prayer or unit of the service may be introduced by instructions printed in red ink. A rubric is, thus, any specific liturgical unit that originally might have been set off by "ruby" printing. Each service is composed of a progression of rubrics.

Structure of the Evening Service

Our Evening Service has two major rubrics: the "*Shema*" and its accompanying benedictions (pp. 24–29 in Service I, pp. 54–59 in Service II), and the *Tefila* (pp. 30–39 in Service I, pp. 60–68 in Service II). The official call to congregational prayer (the "*Barechu*," p. 24, or p. 54) introduces the "*Shema*"; a silent prayer (p. 38, or p. 68) and a special prayer for the Days of Awe, "*Avinu Malkenu*" (p. 40 or p. 69) follow the *Tefila*; and a reader's *Kaddish* (p. 29 or p. 60) divides the two rubrics from each other. We find also a group of introductory prayers (pp. 17–24, or pp. 49–53), which set the mood and prepare us for the two important rubrics that follow, as well as some concluding prayers (pp. 43–48 and 73–75) to round out the service and draw it to an end.

So the service's structure can be summarized rather easily. Both in Service I and in Service II, we follow the Rabbis' admonition to adhere carefully to the structural integrity they prescribed. In both cases, we have:

1. introductory, or preparatory, prayers that set the mood;
2. the "*Shema*" and its accompanying blessings, introduced by the Call to Prayer ("*Barechu*");
3. a Reader's *Kaddish* to divide the "*Shema*" from the *Tefila*;
4. the *Tefila*, followed by private prayer and "*Avinu Malkenu*"; and
5. concluding prayers.

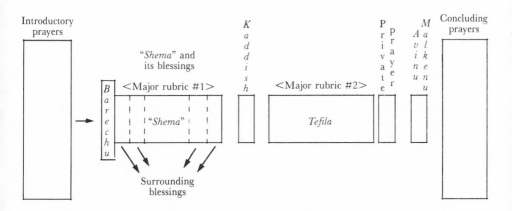

We will look at each item in turn, but first we must note how the two services differ from each other. As we saw above, a service receives its essential character by virtue of the uniqueness of its English readings, its music, and its choreography. Unlike the fixed text, the music and choreography are largely in the hands of each congregation's planners; these are the ways that each worshiping community plays out the liturgical script, so to speak. The script itself, however—those unique sets of English readings that determine the character of the services in *Gates of Repentance*—is beyond the control of local congregations. Congregations have to choose between alternative evening scripts, and they would do well to devote considerable attention to the fact that the two Evening Services are really quite different from each other.

Service II is a bit more creative than Service I. The reason for this is that, rather than randomly mixing novel English versions with literal English translations, our *Machzor* generally adopts the principle of using either literal renditions or free paraphrases, but not both, for each rubric taken as a whole. Thus, Service I employs creative English readings for the first main rubric, the "*Shema*," but then translates the following rubric, the *Tefila*, rather literally. In Service II, the reverse is the case. There, the "*Shema*" is translated literally, whereas the traditional themes of the *Tefila* are rendered freely. Simply because the *Tefila* is longer than the "*Shema*," Service II contains more creative material. We begin our commentary with the more traditional Service I.

Evening Service I
Preparatory Prayers (pp. 17–24)

The opening prayer immediately following the optional lighting of the candles sets the mood of Rosh Hashana. In keeping with the traditional slant of this service, we begin the evening worship with an Eastern European, 17th-century prayer-poem called "*Hineni.*"

"*Hineni*" was intended as the cantor's opening supplication in the *Musaf* service. This was the service in which the prayer-leader was expected to reach new heights of artistry and spirituality in the presentation of Israel's prayers to God. The prayer cannot be understood without examining the role of the *Chazan* in our prayers.

The Cantorate is a venerable institution. The term *Chazan* is known to the earliest rabbinic records, around the turn of the Common Era. The man occupying the role, however, was not yet charged with the primary function of singing the liturgy. He was just a general synagogue official whose duties included matters as diverse as sweeping the sanctuary, on the one hand, and engaging in religious debate with non-Jews, on the other. By the fifth century, however, the basic prayers began to expand, as special poetry called *piyutim* were added (see p. 77 below). By the Moslem period (seventh century and onward), the liturgy was so large that only experts could master it, particularly because it was still not fixed, but instead, changed with every service, as new poems and embellishments were added. Thus, there developed a highly trained class of cantors who composed and sang complex synagogue poetry.

From the very beginning, these cantors were vested with great spiritual responsibility. Not simply talented artists, they were entrusted with the awesome responsibility of assuring the very efficacy of prayer. Every Jew could cry out directly to God without an intermediary, of course. Nonetheless, the sacrifices had once been offered by specially designated priests who represented the people, and at least one major rubric of prayer, the *Tefila*, was viewed as the substitute for the sacrifices that were not possible once the Temple had been destroyed (see pp. 9 above and 79–80 below).

Thus, the *Chazan* took on the role of representing the people before God during the *Tefila* and came to be called the *Sheliach Tsibur*, literally, the agent—or representative—of the congregation, a term we still use. Unlike the priests of the Temple cult, the office of cantor was not hereditary. The synagogue was a democratic institution—at least insofar as men were concerned—where merit depended on knowledge and personal piety. Any mature man could be the *Sheliach Tsibur*, so long as he could be trusted to present the *Tefila* appropriately before the Most High. But as synagogue poetry and the desire for artistic excellence became common, the *Sheliach Tsibur* came more and more to be a professional cantor who was judged on his voice, his musicianship, his composing and repertoire, his knowledge of Judaism (particularly the meaning of the prayers), and his personal piety.

Despite many changes in the role of *Chazan* during the following centuries, the awesome task of representing the community of worshipers before God was always considered primary. Only in fear and trembling could a cantor approach the *Amud* (the lectern) whence his prayers might rise to heaven; and this was particularly true on the Days of Awe, when even the most reverent Jew could not help but be aware of the fact that no one is free of sin.

This sense of inadequacy as he undertook his most holy task on the most holy days of the year is what prompted an unknown cantor in Europe to compose "*Hineni*." As the cantor begins our first High Holy Day service, he or she (now women, too, are cantors, of course) pleads with God (p. 19), "Behold me, of little merit, trembling and afraid, as I stand before You to plead for Your people, O gracious God. . . . Let them not be put to shame because of me. . . . Sinners though we are, let our prayers come before You, innocent, sweet, and pleasing. . . . "

Was "*Hineni*" in the old *Union Prayer Book*? Yes and no. Few Reform congregations had cantors in 1894, when the first edition of the *Union Prayer Book* was published. The role of representing the congregation before God had been assumed by rabbis who read most of the liturgy in what were increasingly labeled as "Reader" parts. So "*Hineni*" itself was not included in the old Reform *Machzor*. But worshipers will remember the "Rabbi's Prayer" said before the open Ark on Yom Kippur Eve. There, facing the Torah scrolls, just before "*Kol Nidrei*," the rabbi voiced a plea equivalent in every regard to the "*Hineni*" prayer, "May my people not be put to shame because of me." (A similar prayer is in *Gates of Repentance*, p. 247.)

So our return to the traditional "*Hineni*" illustrates our continuity with both Reform and pre-Reform traditions. Having rediscovered the *Chazan*, we prefer having the Hebrew text before us. An exquisite chant accompanies it after all. But, like our Reform precursors, we feel free to change the text slightly, and to place it in our worship where its original purpose will be better served. Though composed for the beginning of the *Musaf* service in traditional worship, we have repositioned it here, so that for us, it now introduces the Days of Awe with an appropriate mood of awe.

The opportunity for a striking liturgical introduction to Rosh Hashana continues with the juxtaposition of modern poetry and then, two traditional proclamations (pp. 20–23). "We Will Not Forget You" (pp. 21–22) is an abridgment of a poem by the contemporary poet, Hilary Mindlin, which invokes the compelling call of Sinai still echoing through the centuries of time, as "the ancient desert dream we keep." Then (p. 23), in testimony to keeping the Jew's "desert dream" even now, we proclaim the Sacred Assembly of Rosh Hashana, first in the words of the Torah (Lev. 23:24), and immediately afterward, in two verses from Psalms (81:4–5). Both selections speak of blowing the *shofar*. In an earlier draft, our *Machzor* provided for the sounding of the *shofar* here. But the *shofar* is traditionally reserved for Rosh Hashana day, and the suggestion that we add a *shofar* blast to the Evening Service proved too revolutionary a change for the committee charged with preparing *Gates of Repentance*. Still, as we argued in *Gates of Understanding*, Volume I (pp. 146–150 and 159–162), the choreography of prayer is as important as the words that compose the prayerbook script. This is nothing less than a sacred drama that engages us all as actors. Those congregations wishing to blow the *shofar* either before or after the biblical proclamation in the middle of page 23 are free to do so.

The "Shema" and Its Blessings

The "*Shema*" and its blessings follow (pp. 24–29). We have already seen how this entire unit is one of the two main rubrics that make up the Evening Service, and how creative paraphrases rather than literal translations constitute the substance of this rubric in Service I. Our comments on the content of the traditional Hebrew versions are best delayed until we get to Service II (where the "*Shema*" is translated literally). In the meantime, we can address two questions that people have regarding our liturgy.

First, though the words *blessing* or *benediction* are used regularly, both here and in our liturgy itself, we have not explained what these terms mean. Second, we should stop to see how our printed titles of blessings, such as the capital letters in the middle of pages 24 and 25, have been chosen.

Blessing and benediction are the same thing. These are two English translations of the Hebrew *Beracha*, by which we mean a specific literary genre of prayer. In fact, the *Beracha* is the one prayer genre most favored by the Rabbis who shaped the liturgy in the first two centuries C.E.

Most of us are familiar with "short blessings": for example, "*Hamotsi,*" which we say before eating, or the blessing recited before lighting Sabbath or festival candles (see the middle of p. 17). These are simple, one-line expressions of praise for God who has done something for which we are grateful (brought forth bread from the earth), or charged us with a given commandment (to light the Holy Day lights). What makes them blessings, however, is not their content, but their form: they begin with a standard style, "*Baruch ata, Adonai eloheinu, melech ha-olam,*" "Blessed is the Lord our God, Ruler of the universe . . . "; and they end with the specific virtue for which we give thanks (for bringing forth bread from the earth, for creating the fruit of the vine, etc.).

But these short blessings are not the usual sort that one encounters in public liturgy. Synagogue prayers prefer long blessings which share some formal characteristics with the short ones, but which have their own peculiarities as well. Most significantly: though long blessings may or may not begin with a "*Baruch* . . ." ("Blessed . . . ") clause, they always end with one. And this concluding "*Baruch*" line always summarizes the theme of the long blessing it ends. Thus, a long blessing may run on for paragraphs or even pages, but its contents are always easy to ascertain simply by skipping ahead to its final sentence, which begins with "*Baruch ata, Adonai*" ("Blessed is the Lord . . . ") and then concludes with the act of God which the benediction discusses and for which we give thanks. This final summary line is called a *chatima*, literally, a "seal" for the benediction. The usual English word is "eulogy" or just "conclusion."

In traditional prayerbooks, it is most difficult to separate the text into its constituent benedictions. Editors rarely print them with any regard to their structural differentiation. Yet, as we saw above, the liturgy is composed essentially of a progression of independent themes, many themes constituting separate blessings. Hence, in their failure to divide blessings from one another, traditional prayerbooks give the mistaken impression that our liturgy is a haphazard compilation of unrelated prayers. It is that mistaken impression that *Gates of Prayer* and *Gates of Repentance* seek to correct, through a careful printing of the text in a layout specifying the beginning and end of benedictions and the theme that each blessing traditionally sets forward.

This leads us to the second concern: the titles of the blessings we use in our *Gates* series. Most blessings have traditional Hebrew titles to express their themes. These are regularly printed in the right-hand margin of the text just before the blessing begins. When literal translations are included (such as we shall find when we get to the *"Shema"* and its blessings in Service II), direct translations of these Hebrew titles are placed opposite them in the left-hand margin. For example (to cite two benedictions of the *Tefila*, which we shall discuss shortly), pages 36–37 contain three blessings entitled (in Hebrew) *Avoda, Hoda-a,* and *Birkat Shalom,* and these are accurately translated in the left-hand margin opposite them, as "WORSHIP," "THANKSGIVING," and "PEACE," these being the English equivalents of the Hebrew and literal translations of its themes.

But we have seen already that the early liturgy favored free-flowing paraphrases of the required themes rather than slavish repetition of single versions of them. So our English is often not a literal equivalent of the Hebrew, and when this is the case, we do not label the English prayers with exact English equivalents of the Hebrew title. Rather, we select one phrase from each such English paragraph, which seems to summarize the particular thrust of that unique treatment of the traditional theme. This summarizing phrase is printed as the English "title." So creative prayers are prefaced by traditional Hebrew titles expressing the mandatory theme and by corresponding excerpts from the English text drawing attention to the specific way in which the theme has been presented.

For a discussion of the basic ideas in the *"Shema"* and its blessings, see below, pp. 29–40, and *Gates of Understanding,* Volume I, pp. 16–17.

The Tefila

Having postponed a full discussion of the first major rubric, the *"Shema,"* until Service II, we arrive now at the second one, the *Tefila.* In Service I, it is supplied, generally, with relatively straightforward translations of the Hebrew passages. The titles of the benedictions that constitute the *Tefila* convey a good idea of the string of concepts that this ancient rubric contains.

The *Tefila* extends from page 30 to page 38. It consists of seven benedictions, labeled:

1. God of All Generations (p. 30),
2. God's Power (p. 31),
3. God's Holiness (pp. 32–33),
4. The Holiness of This Day (pp. 34–36),
5. Worship (p. 36),
6. Thanksgiving (pp. 36–37), and
7. Peace (pp. 37–38).

Our focus is the specific ways in which the themes of the Days of Awe are reflected in the *Tefila,* but because one form or another of the *Tefila* is said every day, we should pause first for a brief consideration of this prayer for ordinary days. Then we can see how its weekday form is expanded or otherwise altered to fit the unique context of the High Holy Day season. (Further discussion of this rubric can be found in *Gates of Understanding*, Volume I, pp. 17–18.)

When we come to our analysis of the "*Shema*" and its blessings, we shall see that they stand essentially as a creed: they state a set of Jewish beliefs. By contrast, the *Tefila* (which is our subject here) is normally petitionary. Having expressed one's faith in God by reciting the "*Shema*" and its blessings, the worshiper now turns to God with requests. On a regular weekday, the *Tefila* contains nineteen blessings, the middle thirteen of which are devoted to listing the matters we ask God to grant: discernment, pardon, health, justice, and so on.

But these middle thirteen petitions are lacking in the *Tefila* for the High Holy Days. On Shabbat and on all Holy Days, including the High Holy Days, asking for personal or communal benefits is considered inappropriate. Both Shabbat and the Holy Days are likened to a taste of the world to come, when we shall lack for nothing, when, at last, evil and suffering of every sort will be conquered. The world to come—or the messianic age, as it is sometimes known—is referred to as "the day that is entirely Shabbat," or "the day that is totally good" (i.e., totally *Yom Tov*). Thus, the first three benedictions and the last three benedictions are constant: they are said daily, on Shabbat, and on Holy Days. But the middle petitions drop out on the latter two occasions, and, instead, we insert a special, fourth blessing, which is called "The Holiness of This Day," and which elaborates upon the theme of the specific day in question. Thus, it is "The Holiness of This Day" (pp. 34–36) that portrays the unique flavor of Rosh Hashana.

The most striking discovery one comes across upon reading through this blessing, is that the day is never referred to by the term *Rosh Hashana*, "New Year." Indeed, if one reads the Bible, one finds that this was not originally the New Year at all, but the seventh month of the year that began at Passover. It is not referred to as "New Year" until the first or second century C.E., and even then, it is only one of four new years. Just as today there is a fiscal year, a school year, a calendar year, and so on, rabbinic society conceived of several beginnings in the year, and Rosh Hashana was only one of them. But the others were tied to institutions rooted in socio-economic situations that were changeable, while Rosh Hashana was indissolubly linked to the unchanging concerns of the human spirit. It inaugurated the Days of Awe, which culminate in Yom Kippur itself. Unlike the other "new years," which eventually lost their importance, Rosh Hashana refused to fade away with the passing of time.

So our blessing properly ignores the chance circumstance that this day

19

is one of the new years in the Jewish calendar. The momentous weight of this Holy Day is derived from the fact that it is the Day of Remembrance. The benediction begins with that fact (middle of p. 34) and ends with it (concluding line on p. 36). The congregational reading at the bottom of page 34 expands the idea. We pray that on this day, remembrance of us may rise to God on High, that we may be blessed with a renewal of life. It is the renewal of life, not a calendar year, which should occupy our attention!

A lengthy consideration of the doctrine of remembrance can be found later in this book (see pp. 93–96 and 98–99). For now, however, it is necessary to note that important ideas do not exist in isolation. Precisely because they are monumental concepts, they evoke other, related concepts, which, when taken together, shed light on each other. Judaism does not present independent ideas so much as idea-complexes, bundles of ideas that strengthen our grasp on reality, allowing us to see the same phenomena from different perspectives.

Thus, the concept of remembrance is but one side of a multifaceted conceptualization of the universe. It is only one idea of an idea-complex. Remembrance implies a certain relationship between God and Israel, such that God is prepared—perhaps, even obligated—to bring us, God's people, to mind annually. To be sure, this whole notion must be described metaphorically. We do not mean that God is a person who remembers the way people remember. But human language is all we have, and, with all its drawbacks in defining divine-human relationships, we must try to use it to suggest those ideas for which we stand. Thus, we speak of God as remembering Israel.

But, the principal reason God remembers us is that God has made an eternal covenant with us. At Sinai we accepted the Torah as our obligation, while God promised, in turn, not to abandon us. So, on this Day of Remembrance, God brings us to mind in the capacity of covenant partner. Life is renewed for us, not simply biologically, but spiritually: life with purpose, life with meaning, life with dedication, life devoted to the covenant and its promise of a better world brought about by God and humanity working in partnership. As we renew life, then, we renew the covenantal relationship, recalling its origins at Sinai and its vision of the final messianic day (see also pp. 99–100 below).

"Uvechen"

Our messianic vision is the subject of a famous insertion in the High Holy Day *Tefila* called *"Uvechen."* The word *uvechen* means "therefore," so that the insertion constitutes a sort of a threefold summary judgment on what the covenantal relationship with God implies. God is the Monarch who has created the world and selected Israel to carry out a mission of bringing to fulfillment the hope of world harmony. The first paragraph (middle of p. 32) asserts that "Yours is the majesty," and prays for that day when all humankind will "become a single family, doing Your will with a perfect heart." So far, our focus is universal good, which we see as appropriate for a world conceived by a single divine will.

But the second paragraph narrows the focus. As the chosen people, endowed with a mission to strive for a realization of the vision expressed in the previous paragraph, Israel now prays with particularistic concern for "Your people," for "glory to those who revere You," and for blessing for our Land of Israel and the City of Jerusalem.

But these benefits sought for ourselves are only to presage the universalistic final hope, "the light of redemption for all who dwell on earth." Then, concludes this prayer (p. 33), "The just shall see and exult. . . . Violence shall rage no more, and evil shall vanish like smoke; the rule of tyranny shall pass away from the earth."

Thus, the "*Uvechen*" insertion presents us with the first of many instances in our liturgy where Judaism's balance between universalism and particularism finds typical expression.

Tefila Emendations for the Days of Awe

Before leaving the *Tefila*, we should make note of five small High Holy Day alterations in this prayer, which serve to restate different aspects of the primary idea-complex of the Days of Awe. Renewal of life finds repeated emphasis. In the first blessing (p. 30) we pray, "Remember us unto life, . . . inscribe us in the Book of Life." The image is Rabbinic, portraying a book in which all our deeds are recorded. God reviews the record, and, we trust, not finding us wanting in the balance of good and evil we have wrought, enters our names in next year's Book of Life, so that we may begin again. But God is not dispassionate in this concern with Israel's destiny. The second blessing (p. 31) reminds us that God is compassionate: "In compassion You sustain the life of Your children." As the Rabbis expressed it, God overlooks our first sin. Humans sin; if they repent, they are pardoned. Again, in the penultimate benediction (p. 37), we return to the image of the Book of Life. The Hebrew asks that we be "inscribed" for life; the English is rendered, "Let life abundant be the heritage of all the children of Your covenant." And finally, in the closing lines of the *Tefila* we add the wish, "Inscribe us in the Book of Life, blessing, and peace."

The related idea, that today we celebrate God's sovereignty over creation, finds its emphatic affirmation in the conclusion to the third benediction in which God is praised specifically for being a holy Ruler (p. 33). The regal image is deliberately selected for the Days of Awe. Normally, this benediction ends with God being described more generally, not as a holy *Ruler*, but as a "holy *God.*"

"Whose presence gives life to Zion and all Israel"

This conclusion to the blessing for worship (p. 36) well illustrates the development of the Reform Movement during the last century. In the traditional prayerbook, this benediction asks God to accept our prayers, but at the same time it wistfully recalls the days before the Temple was destroyed and asks God to re-establish the sacrificial cult. Utilizing the biblical image that supposes God's actual presence in the Temple at the place of the offerings, the benediction concludes, "Blessed is the Lord, who returns the divine Presence to Zion."

This conclusion was offensive to many Reform Jews. They found the sacrificial cult objectionable to modern thought. They denied that the Jewish people is in exile and, instead, saw a positive purpose in living in the Diaspora; they could not accept the myth of a personal messiah who would redeem them from exile, carry them off to a restored Jerusalem, and rebuild the Temple for sacrifices again.

Reform rabbis thus looked for a more appropriate way to conclude this blessing. Fortunately, Jewish tradition, it will be recalled (see above, pp. 11–12), once favored many options for the wording of each theme, and out of the many ancient versions that once existed for this prayer, an alternative to the one found in the traditional prayerbook had survived. Some people once ended this prayer by saying, "Praised be Thou, O Lord, whom alone we serve in reverence." This alternative version was preserved in the Palestinian Talmud and was known liturgically to Ashkenazic Jews who said it during the High Holy Day services. Reform Jews simply extended the normal Ashkenazic High Holy Day practice and began using this conclusion daily throughout their *Union Prayer Book*. Thus, they were able to maintain a traditional prayer rubric with an equally traditional conclusion; yet, by replacing the daily conclusion with the High Holy Day version, they remained true to their theological principles.

In recent times, however, the traditional Hebrew conclusion for weekday use began to take on new meaning. Though we Reform Jews today still agree with the pioneers of our movement in insisting that we are not in exile, waiting for God to reinstitute life revolving around the Temple cult, we are also the generation blessed with sharing in the miraculous rebirth of the State of Israel. The idea that God's presence returns to Zion after centuries of the Land's virtual demise, reflects the reality of our love for Zion. But Zionism within Reform ideology differs from secular Zionism in that, for us, any state—even a Jewish one—is incomplete without the guiding hand of God. So, even though our *Machzor* might well have remained consistent with the Ashkenazic practice of a thousand years by maintaining the optional conclusion ". . . whom alone we serve in reverence," we sought instead in this case to exercise again the Reform imperative of drawing upon tradition, insofar as tradition is consonant with our principles and satisfies our contemporary search for meaning. The present volume includes the version which depicts God's return to Zion, but translates it creatively as: ". . . whose presence gives life to Zion and all Israel."

This translation implies an affirmation of Jewish life in Israel and the Diaspora, equally. Consonant with our traditional Reform perspective, we maintain that God's presence in the Land of Israel remains unrelated to the fact that the sacrificial cult there has ceased. God is present in Zion and in Jewish life everywhere.

"Avinu Malkenu"

"Avinu Malkenu" is a liturgical highlight of the Days of Awe. We say it during the Rosh Hashana Evening Service, and then four additional times before the closing blast of the *shofar* at the end of the Yom Kippur *Neila* service. For many, it would hardly be Rosh Hashana or Yom Kippur without *"Avinu Malkenu."* Two anecdotes illustrate its enormous popularity.

The first story involves the way in which Reform editors have determined how much of the traditional *"Avinu Malkenu"* text they would include in their prayerbooks. Though a lengthy petition today, the prayer began as only one line, the last line of the prayer as we have it. Its author is said to be Rabbi Akiba (second century C.E.), who composed his words at the occasion of a drought. It is told that his supplication for divine mercy, even in the face of humankind's apparent paucity of goodness, brought rain. Through the centuries, that one line attracted others, until a lengthy litany was built up. Since it was easy for different verses to become attached to the poem, more than one final version found its way into the printed texts that comprise the official liturgical rites of Jews around the world. But all rites have some verses in common, and these are generally recited in the same relative order.

The editors of the *Union Prayer Book* compiled their *Machzor* in the 1890s, but in an effort to pare the traditional service to a manageable length, they were faced with far too many verses, many of which they

23

found to be redundant or even theologically offensive. So, they selected only those traditional verses which they liked best, and then rearranged them into what appeared to be a more logical or aesthetic sequence. The editor of *Gates of Repentance*, too, wanted only the finest selection from among the traditional verses. Though generally contented with the *Union Prayer Book* version, he decided to add one or two verses, but while he was at it, he also decided to restore the original order, so that the Reform Movement's *Machzor* might be congruent with those used by the rest of the Jewish world.

What neither he nor his committee took into consideration was the immense folk appeal of the Reform text as it had appeared in the *Union Prayer Book*. Actually, the appeal had nothing to do with the text itself. The people's fondness for the text was rooted in its music, specifically in the one composition by the contemporary composer, Max Janowski. Overnight, it seemed, his setting for *"Avinu Malkenu"* had caught on sufficiently to become a genuine Reform tradition across the United States and Canada. One could not change the order of the verses without ruling out the possibility of retaining the Janowski melody.

The committee quickly saw the importance of music for worship. The editor added the extra verses, but relegated them to the end of the prayer, thus leaving the lyrics for Janowski's music intact at the beginning. Thus, choirs and congregations can still sing the Janowski music without difficulty.

The second anecdote illustrates the Reform attitude toward Jewish law. Jewish codes of law rule against the recitation of *"Avinu Malkenu"* on Shabbat. Its verses seem to approximate petitions too closely, and we have seen how ordinary petitioning is prohibited on Shabbat (see p. 19 above). But Orthodox congregations keep two days of Rosh Hashana; so if they omit *"Avinu Malkenu"* because one of those days is Shabbat, they can still say it on the other day. Reform Jews, however, keep only one day (for reasons that are explained below—see pp. 25–28), so they would not have another opportunity to say the prayer. What should be the Reform position on saying *"Avinu Malkenu"* on Shabbat?

Reform rabbis have answered that it is better to disregard the letter of the law in this case, allowing the people to say a favorite prayer which they otherwise would miss. A similar problem arises with regard to blowing the *shofar* on Shabbat. Tradition bans it, not because there is anything wrong with blowing the *shofar* then, but because one might inadvertently carry it to and from the synagogue on Shabbat, and carrying on that day is prohibited by Jewish law. Reform Jews blow the *shofar* on Shabbat, just as they say *"Avinu Malkenu"* then.

Much more could be said about *"Avinu Malkenu."* For a simple folk prayer that grew through the ages, it contains a great deal. First, there is the very repetitive use of *Avinu* ("Our Father") and *Malkenu* ("Our King"). These two divine epithets, current from early times onward, represent two opposite, yet complementary, attributes of God. God is the merciful Parent, and at the same time, the just Ruler. The world is balanced, says the Midrash, between absolute compassion and rigorous application of justice.

Secondly, note should be taken of Rabbi Akiba's original petition, "Be gracious and answer us, for we have little merit." Literally, the Hebrew states starkly that *"ein banu ma-asim,"* "We have no [good] works [to our credit]"; that is, we are seemingly not deserving of God's compassion. This statement is striking because one often reads that Judaism never taught the doctrine of humankind's complete dearth of meritorious achievement. Normally, one associates that idea with the classical Christian doctrine of original sin and the lack of works (as they call good deeds). Christians, not Jews, have developed a specialized theological vocabulary in which divine grace, freely offered to sinning men and women, figures so prominently.

It is possible that Akiba was deliberately exaggerating. Perhaps he was overcome by the long and futile effort to end the severe drought; or, he may have been drawing on the literary style of his day, using an overstatement that no one then would mistake for literal accuracy. But he may have meant what he said, "We have no good works"; and if so, it would seem that Judaism and Christianity were once very close in their respective doctrines of human virtue. Akiba, too, believed that people are, by nature, undeserving of God's favor, though, of course, later Jewish thinkers modified this extreme position. At any rate, to this day, our liturgy here proclaims that in the end we rely on God's grace, for *"ein banu ma-asim,"* "We have no [good] deeds."

The consequences of Akiba's extreme view did not go unnoticed in the writing of *Gates of Repentance.* On page 512, the same *"Avinu Malkenu"* reappears, the last time now, until next year; however, it is rendered in a slightly different translation. Instead of "Be gracious and answer us, *for* we have little merit," we find, "Be gracious and answer us, *even when* we have little merit."

Evening Service II

We have already noted that a second Evening Service will be of particular use to congregations that observe two days of Rosh Hashana.

Before turning to the service itself, therefore, we may appropriately

25

pause here to explain the principle that lies behind the decision by some congregations to keep but one day, while others celebrate two.

The discrepancy of practice is to be found in the nature of the Jewish calendar, which is both solar and lunar. We tend to think of a year as solar, in that every year begins and ends at the same time relative to the position of the earth and the sun. A solar year, thus, corresponds to one complete rotation of the earth around the sun, and when the earth and the sun reach the same position vis-à-vis each other, a new year begins. Jewish years are both lunar and solar: lunar in that they are built upon a succession of lunar months, but solar too, in that we add periods of time (leap years) to insure that seasons will not occur at inappropriate times relative to the position of the sun.

But the months are lunar: that is, every month begins with the new moon, and lasts as long as it takes for the moon to circle the earth. The average time for the moon to complete its rotation—and, therefore, the idealized average time for each lunar month—is roughly 29½ days. So twelve such months (that is, one year's worth) will total only about 354 days, some eleven days shorter than what the solar year demands. Eleven days alone do not matter much, but eleven days multiplied by several years do. Passover, for example, a spring festival, would fall earlier and earlier, reaching the middle of winter before long. So we add some time to the calendar every so often, to prevent the lunar year from falling further and further behind the solar year.

To restore the balance between solar and lunar cycles, we apply a mathematical formula that adds an extra month to seven of every nineteen years. That is why Rosh Hashana falls at a different time each solar year, beginning in October, but eventually falling back to early September. At that point, we declare the next year a leap year, adding a whole month to make it last longer. By the time we get to next Rosh Hashana, it will be a month later, in October again. But the next Rosh Hashana after that will again fall eleven days earlier. A succession of these "normal" years will continue until, eventually, the New Year again threatens to arrive far too early (in August, perhaps), whereupon an extra month will be intercalated into the system, thus making a leap year, as we start all over again.

Originally, however, the system was not governed by mathematical computation. Instead, people depended on actually sighting each new moon. Lunar months, as we said, last an average of 29½ days, so the new moon would be seen after either 29 or 30 days. When people saw it, they went to the rabbinic tribunal in Jerusalem which officially proclaimed that the new month had begun. So it was possible for each new month to fall on either of two possible times, the 30th or the 31st day since the last new moon had been sighted, depending on when the moon was seen, and there was no way to know in advance which of the two days it would be.

Once the court made the determination, it faced the difficulty of notifying the Jewish communities outside Jerusalem. At first, we are told, a series of bonfires was lit from Jerusalem outward to signify that the new month had begun, but after a while, people resorted to a less ambiguous means of spreading the news: messengers. It happens that most Jewish holidays fall near the middle of the lunar month, some, in fact, exactly on the full moon; so by then, many communities—and certainly all those in the Land of Israel—would have been informed of the actual new month date by the messengers. For outlying communities in the Diaspora, however, messengers would not have arrived in time for people to know whether the month had begun on the first or the second possible day. And thus began the custom of keeping one day for the holidays in Israel—where everyone knew the exact day of the new moon—but keeping two such days in the Diaspora—where people knew the day had to be one of the two days, but did not know which. Even after a publicized mathematical system of computation was operative, so that people could know in advance when the new moon arrived, religious conservatism resulted in the Diaspora still keeping its two days. In the last century, when Reform Judaism emerged, one of the first things Reform Jews did was to end the anachronism of keeping two days for holidays in an age when we no longer depend on eye-witnesses and long-distance runners.

Rosh Hashana, though similar, was not the same as other holidays in this regard, inasmuch as it is the only holiday that falls on the first day of the month. There was, thus, no time at all for witnesses to ascertain the new moon and then for messengers to run anywhere, even within Jerusalem itself. Work, therefore, had to cease on the eve of the first potential day of the New Moon, and Temple worship had to begin under the assumption that the court eventually would announce that the new moon had been spied the night before and that the New Year had in fact begun. When that happened, the Jerusalemites finished celebrating the day, and by the time night fell, one day of Rosh Hashana had been kept.

But a problem occurred when it turned out that the new moon had not been seen the previous night. This put the people of Jerusalem in an awkward position: they had marked that day as the New Year, only to find out at the end of it that they had been wrong. They had no option now but to keep the next day too, and to consider the previous day's observance an error, or, technically, to maintain the legal fiction that the two days together were like keeping one long day.

One can readily see that outside Jerusalem, people always kept two days of Rosh Hashana. Messengers were unable to get to them until both days had been over. They had to wait a long time to discover what the court had decided, and whether, therefore, it had been the first or the second day of celebration which "counted" as the actual New Year's Day.

Thus, it became customary in the Diaspora to observe two days of holidays, including Rosh Hashana; while in Jerusalem, two days of Rosh Hashana alone seem to have been kept sometimes. I say "seem to" because, in fact, only the second day in such a case was really Rosh Hashana; the other was an unavoidable error. That is why Reform decided to keep only one day of Rosh Hashana, too. Clearly, except when such an error was retroactively determined to have occurred, only one day of celebration was the rule, even in Jerusalem; and our mathematical computation prevents such an error today. On the other hand, some people note that regardless of the theory that insists on there being only one day, two actual days of Rosh Hashana celebration always took place in the Diaspora and (unlike other holidays) was frequently the rule *de facto* even in Jerusalem; so these people conclude that Rosh Hashana is different from the other holidays and deserves two days of observance.

In sum, most Reform Jews do not add an extra day to Rosh Hashana. In Israel, on the other hand, Rosh Hashana occupies two days. This, however, is the result of medieval immigration into Israel from Europe. It was the large number of European settlers who brought their custom of keeping Rosh Hashana for two days that resulted in Israel's present practice. From the time the mathematical system was introduced in the fourth century until after the Crusades in the 11th and 12th centuries, Palestinian Jews kept one day only of all holidays, *including* Rosh Hashana.

At any rate, for those Jews who distinguish Rosh Hashana from the other holidays, *Gates of Repentance* has two Rosh Hashana services. The second day need not be a carbon copy of the first.

Preparatory Prayers (pp. 50–53)

This introduction to Rosh Hashana Eve should be compared with the parallel unit for Service I (pp. 18–24). Instead of the traditional *"Hineni,"* we have a composite reading from Psalms (p. 50) emphasizing our dependence on God. The following reading (Psalm 121, p. 51) is a continuation of the *Union Prayer Book* tradition, and appeared also in Service I. But here it functions as a continuation of the theme of depending on God, since "I lift up my eyes to the mountains. . . . My help will come from the Lord." In Service I, it functioned not as a reminder of our need to rely on God, but as a continuation of the theme that was there underlined, i.e., Creation, since God (says the psalm) is "Maker of heaven and earth."

Thus, we can add one more way in which the two evening services differ from each other. Service I begins with the theme of Creation (a major idea for these Days of Awe, as we shall see below, pp. 102–104). Service II, our subject at the moment, commences with an emphasis on reliance on God. That sense of human finitude leads us to take stock of the year gone by in "In the Twilight" (pp. 51–52), and the last lines of this prayer also introduce the idea of Creation in this service: "May this Rosh Hashana, birthday of the world, be our day of rebirth into life and peace. . ." (p. 52).

The same biblical call to sound the *shofar* that we saw above in Service I occurs here, too, offering the opportunity actually to blow the *shofar* as the Ark is opened (see above, p. 16).

The "Shema" and Its Blessings

We saw above that the "*Shema*" is the first of the two main rubrics for the Evening Service. Inasmuch as the more traditional treatment of the "*Shema*" occurs in Service II, we delayed the consideration of the idea-complex marking this rubric until now.

The "*Shema*" represents the Jewish creed: it is what Jews have believed about God. As such, it belongs to the earliest stratum of our multilayered prayerbook. The "*Shema*" itself (p. 56) is biblical and was once used as part of the Temple cult. By the first century C.E. it had made its way into the synagogue service and was recited twice daily with its accompanying blessings. In the morning, there are two blessings said before it, and one after it. In the evening, an additional blessing is appended at the end, so that there are two before and two after.

Because it is a creed, the "*Shema*" should be approached from the perspective of belief. Its first and best-known line ("Hear, O Israel: the Lord is our God, the Lord is One") affirms Judaism's central tenet. When we take the Torah out of the Ark, we rise and recite together "the watchword of our faith," as a sort of pledge of allegiance to its principles. The "*Shema*" is the most direct statement of the monotheistic ground on which Judaism is based.

But acknowledging Judaism's monotheistic basis is not enough. Monotheism alone does not distinguish Judaism from other great religions that also assert the fundamental unity and uniqueness of the divine. Christianity and Islam are obviously monotheistic, both being offshoots of their Jewish "parent." But so, too, are the Eastern religions. True, they often appear to Westerners as containing room for many gods. But adherents of these faiths would quickly accuse Western observers of mistaking outward appearance for inner reality, if they were to make the mistake of imputing polytheism to the great religions of Asia.

So we should ask: Granted the Jewish insistence on one and only one God, what kind of God is this God of Judaism? How does the God whose existence we Jews posit differ from the God of other faiths? It is this question that the blessings of the "*Shema*" answer.

Look, then, at the benedictions surrounding the "*Shema*" (pp. 54–55 and 57–59). Their themes are listed in the marginal titles:

1. Creation,
2. Revelation,
3. Redemption, and
4. Rise Up to Life Renewed.

The last theme, obviously, differs from the first three. It is actually a prayer for living safely through the night and owes its existence to the symbolic similarity between sleep and death (an association that may have been especially poignant to our ancestors in antiquity). The last blessing is, thus, a petition for the continuity of meaningful life when we awaken, and is added only at night. The other three blessings, however, are standard both day and night, and as a group they provide the prayerbook's classical statement of Jewish theology: in short—our God created the world; revealed the Torah to a chosen people, Israel; and, having delivered Israel from bondage once, promises again and for all time to redeem them (and the world in which they live).

Creation (pp. 54–55)

Jews have always taken it as axiomatic that God created the universe. This belief has generally been expressed by the phrase "creation out of nothing." According to the Midrash, God first created Torah, which was then used as the design for the universe. So the world is planned, designed, logically ordered, and systematically arranged.

But even as Jews have insisted on the divine origin of the world, they have generally not demanded that the Creation accounts in the Book of Genesis be taken literally. The Rabbis held the principle that the stories in the Torah do not follow the laws of chronology, or, as they put it, "There is no 'earlier' or 'later' in the Torah." So how long the creation process took, exactly how it occurred, and similar questions, were held to be essentially unanswerable from the biblical pages alone. At best, these were relegated to the rarified discussions of philosophy and mysticism. In the second century C.E., for example, "Creation Doctrine" (*Ma-aseh Be-reshit*) constituted a field of expertise for a very few mystical adepts who dared to face issues of ultimacy, unlimited by safe and sure boundaries of everyday consciousness. In the Middle Ages, philosophers and mystics alike vied for a comprehension of the process that even today takes the breath away, as we, too, struggle to understand not just how a creative order came into being, but even the awesome fact that it did at all—that there is something rather than nothing. Maimonides (d. 1204), for example, was even willing to consider the possibility that raw matter, out of which the universe was formed, might be as infinite as its Maker. So, he posited a theory by which God is seen as the world's Creator, in a deeper, non-temporal sense: everything other than God is dependent on something else for its sustained existence, so that the whole universe is a lengthy chain of interdependent entities; except for God. God is (by definition) the sole entity upon which all else ultimately depends, but which Itself depends on nothing, such that if all created matter were to die, only God would still remain untouched.

Not every classical Jewish doctrine fits harmoniously with the contemporary state of scientific knowledge, but the Jewish view of Creation does. That is because this Jewish tenet is neither scientific nor unscientific in the first place. The "scientific" details were always matters of conjecture, so that one could side with Maimonides or not, proclaim a mystical sense of Creation's secrets, or avoid the study of "Creation Doctrine" completely. The Jew's interest in Creation as a manifestation of the divine touches not upon scientific truth or falsehood, but upon the values implicit in the world. And by definition, values are beyond the ken of science.

So, Jews insist that the universe is valuable because it is intrinsically and indissolubly linked to God. It is ordered according to divine blueprint, the Torah. Its rules cannot be meaningless, and human life here must not be empty of purpose.

Our God is, first and foremost, a Creator.

Revelation (p. 55)

Our second blessing preceding the "*Shema*" asserts the Jew's faith in revelation. Revelation, like Creation, can be understood in different ways, however; and here, too, we come across the recognition that every one of those interpretations exists not in an ideational vacuum, so to speak, but as part of a bundle of related ideas, what we called above (p. 20) an idea-complex. So we should look briefly at some of the explanations Jews have had for revelation, and at the relatively unchanging idea-complex that underlies them all.

Revelation, broadly understood, is the process by which God and God's will are known to humans. This the Bible takes for granted, as any casual reader of the Bible can testify. God regularly addresses people, informing them of their duty, and clarifying the nature of reality. Thus, ultimate truth is knowable, for biblical men and women, only insofar as they remain open to God's revealing word about their world.

But the Bible is not the work of one author, or even of one generation. So, this reasonably simple conceptualization of God's revelatory activity must be modified, depending on what part of the Bible we are describing. Sometimes God speaks through prophets, as in the eighth century B.C.E., for example, when we find people such as Amos and Hosea who are the special recipients of God's messages. Even before that, monarchs, like David and Solomon, relied on similar agents of God's word who saw it as their task to correct the kings whenever they went astray. But a specialized class of prophets is not always assumed. Sometimes God carries on conversations with people who are not prophets: Cain, for example, when he kills his brother Abel. So the way in which God reveals the divine will to people varies, even within the Bible, as does the nature of the message presented and even the time, place, and vehicle of that message. What does not change is the firm belief that the message is there to be known, and that life is meaningless without our finding out what it is.

Prophets present a peculiar problem to their society, however, in that it is hard to decide whether we can trust their word. They may be lying or suffering delusions, or just misinterpreting. Even when prophecy was at its height, and there were certain accepted behavioral symptoms by which true prophets were recognized from false ones, prophets were still regularly opposed by the powers-that-be whose policies they decried, or by other would-be prophets who claimed to have equally decisive, albeit contradictory, divine messages. Thus, a new stage in the history of revelation was reached when one specific revelatory message, the Torah, was canonized as the central word of God, given at one unique and historic event: Sinai. Thus, in the fifth century B.C.E., the era of Ezra and the return from Babylonian exile, a single Torah came into existence as the accepted record of God's will, and from then on, Judaism was a religion of the book. All religious debate would, henceforth, be theoretically settleable by reference to the one book which we call the Torah.

Who, however, would be the determiners of the Torah's meaning? No book is without ambiguity, especially one with such diverse material, compiled over the course of ages, so long ago. Jewish society was then established as a theocracy, its leaders being priests, like the famous Ezra, who is himself often credited with the Torah's canonization. In fact (to anticipate this commentary a little), one of the *Haftara* readings that we offer for Rosh Hashana morning is the biblical account of Ezra's reading the Torah publicly to the people (pp. 132–134). Surely, it is no surprise to find that the Torah itself, which Ezra and his priestly group composed, vests the final interpretation of the Torah in priests. So, for many years, it was the priests who established God's revelatory messages for Israel. Our people had moved from a system of direct revelation to revelation through Torah, and from prophets to priests.

But it was the Rabbinic age that left the most lasting stamp on our doctrine of revelation. Rabbis, no less than priests, derived their understanding of God's will from the Torah. But they also canonized other literary works into what we call the Prophets (*Nevi-im*) and the Writings (*Ketuvim*), which, together with the Torah, now constitute our Bible. God's direct revelation was thus extended further than Sinai, to the prophetic age, and even beyond. The last prophet is known to us as Malachi (literally, "My messenger"), whom the Talmud and modern scholarship date in the fifth century B.C.E. But even a century or so later, an anonymous author tells a story of Job, whose questions about the goodness of the universe receive a direct reply from God (Job 38). And 200 years after that—in the middle of the second century B.C.E.—someone wrote the book of Daniel to illustrate the virtue of faithfulness to God even under such duress as the Jews suffered at the hands of Antiochus during the Hasmonean revolt (which we recall annually at Chanuka). Daniel, too, receives communication from God (Daniel 2:19).

But the Rabbis were equally certain that in their day *direct* revelation had come to an end. They declared prophecy to be over, and, by their very act of biblical canonization, ended the possibility that someone might write, or even uncover, yet another source for direct apprehension of God's will. It was this issue of revelation that divided Jews from the early Christians, because for Christianity, God had not ended direct, prophet-like discovery of the divine will. Christians said that later knowledge was available through Jesus, its content recorded in a new set of holy books called the New (as opposed to the Old) Testament.

For the Rabbis, though, even patent miracles were declared out of bounds in the determination of God's will. A famous anecdote in the Talmud pictures rabbis locked in debate over the ritual purity of a particular kind of stone oven. Convinced of his opinion, one of the protagonists invokes miracles to prove his case. He makes a tree change location; water flows backward in his defense; the very walls of the academy in which he is sitting tilt inwards, threatening to annihilate the debaters—all this, to demonstrate dramatically God's endorsement of a particular legal opinion. But his opponents are adamant. Miracles are no guarantee for truth, they maintain, because the will of God is now known only by a majority vote on the meaning of the Torah. In our case, the majority voted the other way, so even without any equally substantiating miracles on their side, they defeat the miracle worker. The story ends with God chuckling in heaven and declaring happily, "My childen have defeated me, my children have defeated me."

Thus, it was now rabbis—not priests, prophets, or miracle-workers—who maintained the key to revelation. Technically, their every insight was contained within the words of the written Torah, but to this stark statement, barely believable as it stands, they added a corollary. When Moses received the written Torah on Mt. Sinai, he also received from God an oral commentary revealing its true meaning. Thus, the written Torah is inexplicable without the oral commentary. It now became the Rabbis' task to determine the content of that oral amplification which—they believed—had been inherited from Moses by Joshua and subsequent generations, up to and including themselves. So revelation was now a book plus a commentary spun out by the process of rabbinic study and argumentation, until a decision could be reached in any individual case.

We said at the outset that this commentary follows the traditional Jewish means of defining God's will; and that a Jewish library has commentaries, and then commentaries on commentaries, and so on *ad infinitum*. What we meant becomes clearer now. Ever since the Rabbis, the Jewish mind has approached the apprehension of God's truth through successive commentaries built on past strata of yet other commentaries, all of which are theoretically assumed to belong to the never-ending corpus of oral law.

In this assumption, we Reform Jews differ not at all from the Orthodox. We, however, would find it difficult to hold that our every statement today actually derives literally from the single revelatory event at Sinai, when the oral law in all its unfolding wisdom was first revealed. Instead, Reform Jews have tended to speak in terms of ongoing revelation, some indefinable process by which God's will is regularly made known anew to each and every age. Implicit here is the notion that truth itself is not permanent, unchanging, and immutable, but, instead, alterable, part of the same process of change and development that scientists assume with regard to evolution in general.

For Reform Jews, then, revelation is Torah-based and consists of both written and oral traditions. But God's will is knowable not only to the Rabbis of old, but to us as well, and our discovery of truth makes no less a demand on us than does some ancient statement garnered from a venerable tome of some bygone time and place. Let me quote from the "Centenary Perspective," the latest statement of Reform Jewish belief, a document voted on and accepted by Reform rabbis meeting in convention in 1976:

Torah results from the relationship between God and the Jewish people. The records of our earliest confrontations are uniquely important to us. Lawgivers and prophets, historians and poets gave us a heritage whose study is a religious imperative, and whose practice is our chief means of holiness. Rabbis and teachers, philosophers and mystics, gifted Jews in every age amplified the Torah tradition. For millennia, the creation of Torah has not ceased and Jewish creativity in our time is adding to the chain of tradition.

Though short, our prayer on revelation (p. 55) alludes to the Rabbinic conception of revelation described above. But the Reform interpretation quoted from the "Centenary Perspective" is equally evident: God (we read) has taught us "Torah and Mitzvot, laws and precepts," and we obligate ourselves to study them so as to understand their meaning for our life. By Torah and its associated laws, precepts, and *mitzvot*, we mean the oral elaboration on the written word. But that elaboration varies with every generation's studied views, as revelation continues here no less than at Sinai; for (as the opening and closing lines of the first English paragraph remind us), God's relationship with Israel is eternal.

The benediction on revelation both begins and ends with the related idea of divine love. With this observation, we move to a consideration of the idea-complex in which the prayerbook's rehearsal of the Jewish doctrine of revelation is embedded. Clearly, the knowledge of God's will is not the same sort of thing as the knowledge of the fifty states in the United States of America, or the ten Canadian provinces. Leo Baeck once wrote, "To observe and explore the world is the task of science; to judge it and declare our attitudes toward it is the task of religion. . . . Religion measures experience in terms of intrinsic values." Divine revelation differs from every other sort of discovery in that revelation posits a religious measure of things. We already observed in our prayer on the theme of Creation that, "The Jew's interest in Creation . . . touches not upon scientific truth or falsehood, but upon the values implicit in the world" (above, p. 31).

And the values enter, we now understand, with Torah, which coexists with Creation to point the way for the world that ought to be, not just the world that is. The idea-complex, of which revelation is a part, is a picture of a world where God has displayed the essence of divine love by guaranteeing meaning in what might have been a meaningless cosmos. The gift of Torah and the manifestation of divine love are interdependent concepts. And, finally, there is the Jewish people whom God has selected as the chosen vehicle to carry the promise of Torah into an otherwise barren world, proclaiming throughout history that which is (to quote Leo

Baeck again) "the distinctiveness of Judaism, which it has passed on to the rest of mankind, its ethical affirmation of the world."

Our second statement of belief surrounding the "*Shema*" thus follows on the first. Having proclaimed the existence of an ordered cosmos, we now posit its meaningfulness. In this idea-complex, regardless of how one understands the process of revelation, the fact of revelation remains. God has chosen Israel, charging it with the teachings of the Torah, and in so doing, God has demonstrated divine love, for the Torah is none other than the key to finding meaning within existence.

Another word must be said about the inclusion of the idea of "love" in the idea-complex of revelation. Its presence here is obviously not accidental, as it occurs in both the first and the last lines. In fact, as we said above (p. 17), the last line of a blessing (the *chatima*) summarizes the blessing's main theme; so one might even get the impression that this benediction is not about revelation of Torah at all, but about God's love. Actually, we now understand that God's love and revelation are two intertwined parts of the same idea-complex. Thus, to speak of one notion is to allude to the other simultaneously. Still, we should wonder about the reason behind the decision to synopsize the idea-complex with that aspect which mentions love, rather than what might seem to be more obvious, that is, the aspect which mentions Torah.

This verbal preference seems even more worthy of investigation when one considers that there is a parallel blessing over revelation in the morning (see pp. 169–170), and it, too, ends not with "Torah" but with "love"— "Blessed are You, O Lord: You have chosen Your people Israel in love."

What we have here is the classical Jewish equation between justice and mercy, law and love. People today may not immediately appreciate the distinction between these ideas, or the philosophical significance of binding them so indivisibly together, but we shall see that the ancients did, and it was against the backdrop of antiquity that the Rabbis made the decision to connect these two conceivably opposite characteristics in the first place.

Though the era generally known as the Common Era (C.E.) is often thought of as the "Christian Era," its first two centuries were hardly Christian at all. What we know of Christianity until the fourth century indicates that the Church was a relatively small, struggling entity whose mission to the Jews had failed, and which had consequently turned to non-Jews to fill its ranks. Only in retrospect, then, can the era be entitled "Christian."

But neither was the era Jewish. If anything, it was "Gnostic," a term applicable to a variety of religious groups in the late Hellenistic world, which emphasized the distinction between light and darkness, and frequently went so far as to assert the existence not of one but of two deities—

a "good" god of light and an "evil" one of darkness. Not all Gnostics were dualists, to be sure, and, in fact, both Judaism and Christianity were influenced to some extent by Gnostic ideas. Jews, for example, regularly celebrate the distinction between light and darkness (see the Creation benediction, last line, p. 54, and top of p. 55, or the *Havdala* blessing, p. 527), and they once even decorated mosaic floors of synagogues (for instance, Beth Alpha in the Galilee—you can still visit it) with a picture of the sun in the center; and early Christian art depicts Jesus as a sun, since, for them as for Jews, the sun was paradigmatic of light, which stood for truth and goodness. So both Judaism and Christianity made primary distinctions between the two realms of light and darkness, though, unlike many Gnostic cults, they never went so far as to sacrifice their monotheism for the dualistic principle of a different god for each of the primeval realms.

A further claim of most Gnostics was that the good god of light was not the direct creator of the universe. Creation had come about, they claimed, through the work of the evil god, who had further blemished human life by saddling humankind with so-called divine laws such as the Torah. The Torah, then, was described as issuing from a severe god of darkness, who could be characterized as anything but loving. Love was seen as the exact opposite of Torah, because love was the primary quality of the good god of light.

It was this Gnostic dualism which our blessing sought to overcome. For Jews, there can be only one God, responsible both for the love that binds people together and for the law that puts limits on what they can do. Hence, the blessing's idea-complex deliberately combines God's selection of Israel "in love" with the giving of Torah—law—as the visible sign of that love.

It may even have been a specific Christian form of Gnosticism that our blessing sought to contradict. In those early years, when Christian doctrine was still being formulated, some Christians identified the God of the Old Testament with the Gnostic god of evil. The antithesis was said to be the New Testament's God who sends Jesus with a new covenant based solely on love.

In this early Christian view, law and love are necessary opposites: the absolute strictures of law are the basis for Judaism, and the corrective emphasis on love is the foundation for Christianity. In response to this far-reaching claim, our blessing regarding God's revelation asserts that the Torah, which establishes law on earth, is equivalent to the finest demonstration of God's love. God shows love by making the very institution of civilized law possible. Without the existence of law to govern human relationships—whether in the international arena, individual countries and communities, or specific relationships between two human beings (e.g., marriage)—we should be unable to maintain love at all.

This supposed ideological conflict between love and law would be of historical interest only, were it not for the fact that an audience of millions will recognize it as familiar Sunday morning television fare. Though responsible Christians knowledgeable in Bible would deny the divisive contrast between an "Old Testament" of vengeful law, and a "New Testament" of gracious love, many avid fundamentalists still preach this as their gospel. So the closing message of our benediction regarding revelation rings with relevance as much as ever. Our God, we say, guarantees the very possibility of love precisely through the establishment of law.

Redemption (pp. 57-59)

We have seen, then, that our God creates an ordered cosmos and, through what we call Torah, provides it with meaning. According to the third of the *Shema's* benedictions, God also redeems. And, like the parallel concepts of Creation and Revelation, Redemption, too, is open to several definitions.

Religiously speaking, another word for redemption is "salvation," but Jews tend to avoid that word, because by now it is heavily laden with Christological connotations. A synonym, one that is preferred because its political denotation is easily pictured, is "deliverance." So God redeems us, saves us, delivers us—but from what?

The notion of redemption is prevalent throughout our prayers. We have already come across it (see discussion of "*Uvechen*," pp. 20-21 above). Here, it is God who is described as the Redeemer, but elsewhere in the traditional liturgy, a personal messiah is assumed to be the redeeming figure sent by God. The idea of God's sending a descendent of King David as the messianic savior has been difficult for Reform Jews to accept; we have preferred to democratize the dynastic messianic expectation, in the form of a messianic age in which all humanity may share actively as instruments of redemption. So, in messianic prayers—e.g., the first benediction of the *Tefila*; see Hebrew, p. 60—Reform liturgy has generally substituted the word *ge-ula* (redemption) for *go-el* (redeemer). That means that we have retained the idea of divine redemption, even though we have denied the traditional imagery of personal messianic intervention at the end of days.

The question still remains: What is it that we are to be delivered from? The first part of our prayer (middle of p. 57) says explicitly that we are to be saved "from the hand of oppressors, . . . the fist of tyrants." So the political connotation of the word "deliverance" is appropriate. It is underscored by the familiar ending to this benediction, the *"Mi chamocha,"* or Song of the Sea, which is the thanksgiving laudation offered to God by the Israelites when they were released from Egypt. In its paradigmatic form, then, deliverance is what God wrought for our ancestors at the time of the Exodus.

But through the ages, the identity of the tyrants from whose fist Jews might be delivered became less and less specific. Redemption came to refer to deliverance from oppression in general. The word lost historical concreteness, becoming, instead, an ahistorical term. In fact, for most of the Middle Ages, Jews were largely unconcerned with the historical times in which they lived. Instead, they fastened their gaze on the *end* of history, treating history itself as merely something to get through until the coming of the messiah, when history as they knew it would cease (see below, pp. 140–142). They would be in a post-historical age, a Time-to-Come (*Olam Haba*, in Hebrew). Redemption was that divine act which would end all of history, along with history's endless succession of oppressors; it was evil itself from which Jews expected God to deliver them.

This valiant optimism despite all vicissitudes in the medieval chronicle of Jewish life stands at the center of the meaningfulness that our previous benediction posited. Talmudic debate never firmly determined the nature of this anticipated Time-to-Come, and Maimonides (d. 1204) suggested that the proper Jewish approach was to eschew useless speculation on the matter and, instead, to work diligently to fulfill God's will so as to hasten its coming. Later, by the 16th and 17th centuries, mystics were avidly claiming that every single *mitzva* which a Jew fulfills is somehow connected to the process of *Tikun Olam*, "the reparation of the world." Reform Jews clothed the same Jewish optimism in a new metaphor: a Jewish Mission, the bringing of a life rooted in ethical monotheism to the four corners of the world, when, at last (to cite a prayer we will consider later—see p. 144) "All the world shall come to serve You,/And bless Your glorious name,/ And Your righteousness triumphant/ The islands shall proclaim" (p. 448). So the idea of redemption has remained constant, though its specific metaphorical means of expression has altered with time.

Jewish ideologues of modern times have often found fault with this traditional approach, charging that it has generated political passivity. For, if redemption lies beyond history, it must also lie beyond the political process that determines history. In the 19th century, the most severe critics were some of the early Zionists who postulated the need for autoemancipation, that is, the doctrine that Jews take their fate into their own hands, so as to end their plight by working within the historical framework of real, day-to-day affairs. More recently, the historian-philosopher Hannah Arendt has echoed this verdict on Jewish history, charging the Jewish people with a chronic self-inflicted "disease" of "worldlessness," living in a fairyland of make-believe, instead of grasping the political process and using it for their own ends. Certainly, in our time Jews have re-entered history—forcefully, and with a passion.

On the other hand, the unfettered optimism in humanity's own ability to rescue the world from woe seems nowadays to be less and less tenable. One is reminded of Leo Baeck who retained his optimism throughout his incarceration in Hitler's death camps (see note 12, p. 163). Like other Reform Jews, he was committed to a life of ethical behavior. And explicitly, he grounded his faith in a better future on the fact that "the path of this life comes from God and leads back to God." Reform Judaism today would agree. Political action is necessary; we cannot afford the debility of "worldlessness"; but without faith in a religious reality that transcends the world as we know it, there is little reason to believe that tomorrow will necessarily dawn any brighter than today.

Hence, the significance of our final statement surrounding the "*Shema.*" However we conceive of God (for various views, see *Gates of Understanding*, Volume I, pp. 41–102), we claim bravely in the face of history itself that human history is not capricious. There is a divine purpose, underwritten by a divine Author who created a world, revealed Torah (its blueprint), and promises redemption in the end.

Particularly is this final promise evident in the Days of Awe, which Baeck called *messianic* holy days. On Rosh Hashana, the *shofar* is sounded. Its blast recalls the time it was blown at Sinai, thus calling us to awaken to our earthly task of working to fulfill the world's promise (see English paragraph, p. 139, a citation from Maimonides); but it also anticipates the end of days, when the *shofar* is pictured as being blown once again, this time, heralding the realization of the Jew's messianic vision (see pp. 148–150).

The three tenets of Jewish faith contained in the *Shema's* blessings are evident also in the *Shofar* Ritual, especially in Service II (pages 209–210 and 215–217), the more creative version of this rubric, where explicitly, the novel English of the service and even its thematic titles open with Creation and close with Revelation and Redemption. (See also below pages 96–102.)

Concluding Prayers (pp. 42–48 and 71–75)

We saw above that our service consists of introductory (or preparatory) prayers, then two main rubrics called the "*Shema*" (and its blessings) and the *Tefila*, then concluding prayers. We used Service I to study the preparatory prayers, comparing them at the time with those of Service II (pp. 14–16 above). Service I alone was our basis for looking at the *Tefila* (pp. 18–23 above), while we postponed the blessings of the "*Shema*" to our consideration of Service II (pp. 29–40 above). Of the concluding liturgy, we looked only at the "*Avinu Malkenu*" (pp. 23–25 above).

Both services contain four other concluding prayers, however: *Kiddush*, "*Aleinu*," *Kaddish*, and "*Adon Olam*." They differ from "*Avinu Malkenu*" in that they are said throughout the year, not just on the Days of Awe. But something should be said about them here.

Kiddush

In the section on the *Tefila*, we saw that the middle benediction proclaims the sanctity of the day. The *Kiddush*, with which we end the Evening Service, performs the same function. The presence of festive wine proclaims the joy inherent in Rosh Hashana; the *Kiddush* wording announces this day's uniqueness, calling Rosh Hashana *Yom Hazikaron*, the Day of Remembrance. Rosh Hashana is known by other names also: *Yom Hadin* (Day of Judgment) and *Yom Teru-a* (Day of the *Shofar* Blast), for example. But we shall see later (pp. 94–96) that the idea of remembrance best captures the spirit of the Jewish New Year.

An extended form of this blessing, generally performed just as we sit down to dinner, constitutes the familiar home *Kiddush*. It, too, is a ritual to declare the day's sanctity. As Rosh Hashana begins, it is customary to light holiday candles and eat apples dipped in honey, symbolic of a sweet year (see *Gates of the House*, pp. 51–53).

Traditionally, the home celebration accompanied the moment of sunset, as Jews measured their days by actual observation of day and night. Men would go to synagogue services just before nightfall and afterward return home to find that their wives had lit the home candles and had dinner prepared. Then the husbands would chant the *Kiddush*. Most Reform Jews, however, prefer to celebrate both home and synagogue ceremonial together with family and friends, and, at the same time, to break down the stereotypical role limitations of men and women. Thus, today, the home rituals of candles and *Kiddush* take place over Rosh Hashana dinners that may have been prepared by men and/or women; while the blessings and kindling of lights, too, are not necessarily the province of only men or women. Similarly, after dinner, everyone attends services together, and all share equally in the worship service.

41

"Aleinu" (pp. 43–45 and 72–74)

The "*Aleinu*" has been used to conclude services since the beginning of the 14th century. But it was composed originally with a more specific purpose in mind: to introduce the blowing of the *shofar* on Rosh Hashana day. (We still sing it there, using a special melody, and differentiating it from the daily recitation by calling it the "Great *Aleinu*" (see below, p. 101).

"*Aleinu*" combines the particularism and universalism that we encountered first in the "*Uvechen*" prayers (see above, pp. 20–21). God has chosen this particular people, and charged it with the task of bringing about the messianic age of universal peace and harmony. This task is what we Reform Jews call our "Mission" to work in partnership with the Creator of all to achieve universal redemption from evil. These two poles of the particular and the universal are clear in the traditional version of the "*Aleinu*," which can be found on p. 43 in Service I. God is "the Lord of all, the Maker of heaven and earth" (universal), who has "set us apart from other families of earth, giving us a destiny unique among the nations" (particular). The prayer then concludes with the universal theme again, at the bottom of the page.

By contrast, the version on page 72 (Service II) skips over the particularistic message. We read there only of God's mastery of heaven and earth. Reference to the selection of Israel as a chosen people with a "destiny unique among the nations" has been omitted. It is this rendition of "*Aleinu*" that the old *Union Prayer Book* presented. Consistent with the liberal principle of providing alternative understandings of controversial prayers, our *Gates of Repentance* has reclaimed the traditional "*Aleinu*," placing it in Service I, while reserving the familiar Reform wording for Service II.

Behind the Reform version there lies a story of many centuries. In short, the traditional *Aleinu*'s clear statement of Israel's particularity was seen at times as being too strident. By the time the modern age dawned, the following line had already been omitted: "They [that is, the other peoples of the earth] bow down to emptiness and vanity, and pray to a god who cannot save." (With a few exceptions, this line has not been restored even in Orthodox prayerbooks.) But even without this offending sentence, the "*Aleinu*" remained a sensitive issue, often misunderstood as a blatant anti-Christian diatribe. In 1655, for example, when the Dutch Jew, Manasseh ben Israel, petitioned Oliver Cromwell to admit Jews to England, he followed up his argument by composing a pamphlet that explicitly denied this notion. Still, Reform Jews in the 19th and early 20th centuries, both here and in Europe, remained understandably sensitive to the possibility of such a misreading. They were convinced that Christians no less than Jews were destined to play a role in bringing about a messianic age. Elsewhere, especially in the earlier prayerbooks on which the *Union Prayer Book* was based, they made it clear that their vision of ultimate universal harmony still left room for a special Jewish aptitude for bringing about redemption from evil—what we called above the "Jewish Mission" (see above pp. 39–40 and 42); but in this prayer, at least, they emphasized the consensus binding all good men and women of faith, not the uniqueness of the Jewish fate. American Reform Judaism was particularly adamant about identifying with the common American vision of universal justice, so the traditional "*Aleinu*" was edited until it no longer included the particularistic aspect of Jewish theology. So, the *Aleinu*'s claim of the uniqueness of Jewish destiny was absent from official American Reform liturgy until *Gates of Prayer* was composed in 1975.

Why should the particularism of the "*Aleinu*" once again be restored to this prayer, at least in one of the two options presented here? (Our *Gates of Prayer* actually provides four choices; see pp. 615–621, and comments in *Gates of Understanding*, Volume I, pp. 154–155.) To begin with, as we saw above regarding the music to "*Avinu Malkenu*," and as we shall see below (pp. 114–118) with the melody to "*Kol Nidrei*," how we sing a prayer is not an irrelevant consideration. Often, our attachment to prayers depends more on their music than their words. And, unlike philosophical treatises, prayers are not purely rational entities that exist without reference to the people who recite them. Indeed, it is debatable whether prayers that are not prayed but are, perhaps, read as poetry or world literature, or (all the more so) buried in books that are no longer even consulted, are still prayers at all. If the "*Aleinu*" is to maintain its hold on Jewish consciousness, such that it remains a passionate Jewish prayer for ultimate deliverance, it is not without significance that more and more Jews are rediscovering traditional melodies with which to sing it; and while with difficulty, one can fit the traditional melody to the Reform version in Service II of *Gates of Prayer*, one cannot do so without destroying the meter of the Hebrew lines, and, in fact, even without mispronouncing the words by accenting the wrong syllable. So, unless the particularistic message of the "*Aleinu*" is offensive to us, its traditional text ought to be retained on musical grounds alone.

More important is the fact that for many in the post-Holocaust generation, the message of Israel's unique historical destiny is anything but offensive. As early as 1171, Jews emphasized this prayer's assertion that Jews have both enjoyed and (sadly) suffered through a history that can only be described as "unique among the nations." In that year, the Jews of Blois in France were charged with killing Christians for ritual purposes.

This is one of the earliest instances of the blood accusation in our history, though it would be made time and time again, the latest example on a national scale being in 1911 when Mendel Beiliss was so accused in Czarist Russia. A contemporary chronicler of the Blois massacre relates that Jews died while singing the *"Aleinu."* (See *Gates of Repentance*, p. 434, where that chronicle has been included as a reading for the *Avoda*; and see below, p. 144.) So, too, after the Holocaust, it seems appropriate to many to affirm that Jewish history is not meaningless, that even in our suffering, we assert what is obvious to all, i.e., the uniqueness of Israel's story among the nations, as well as that which may not seem so apparent, i.e., the positive evaluation of that uniqueness by Jews who still bear witness to our covenant with God and to our mission in the world.

The first half of the *"Aleinu"* ends with the congregation saying that it bows the head and bends the knee in acknowledgment of our God's sovereignty (middle of p. 43 or p. 72). Traditionally, Jews actually do bend their knees and bow at the waist as they recite this affirmation. Until this point, we can safety say that we have the "original *Aleinu*," the prayer that was composed some time before the year 200 C.E., as an introduction to the blowing of the *shofar*, and was then later repositioned to serve also as a daily concluding prayer.

The background to the second half of the *"Aleinu"* is more complex. It is best known to us by the familiar biblical messianic vision with which it ends: "On that day the Lord shall be One and His name shall be One." In the Bible, these words are attributed to the prophet Zechariah, who was among the emigres returning to Judea after the end of the Babylonian exile (sixth century B.C.E.). But, in fact, we do not know who spoke this familiar line, nor even when he lived, since the section in question (Zech. 14:9) is actually by an unknown author, whose words of prophecy were mistakenly appended to the genuine messages of Zechariah. Most scholars think our unknown prophet lived sometime after Zechariah, possibly as much as two centuries later; others believe he came earlier, well before the Babylonian exile occurred. Our problem is that without knowing when and where he lived, it is very difficult to know what he meant by the words before us.

The context seems to be an apocalyptic vision of the Day of the Lord. The whole world will battle Jerusalem, and God will lead Israel in defensive battle. The world of nature will be torn apart as the Mount of Olives splits in two, until eventually, God will triumphantly enter Jerusalem and be acknowledged as the one true God of all. We, thus, arrive at the universalistic recognition by all humanity that our God is One, that is, the *only* One; God's name alone shall be invoked as divine.

A glance at page 44 or 72 indicates how far we have removed ourselves from the violent vision that once prompted this universalistic hope. The English paragraph leading up to the concluding prayer that "The Lord will be One . . . " (on p. 44) is taken almost verbatim from the traditional *Machzor*, where it had been added to the "original *Aleinu*" by the ninth century at the latest, and probably several centuries earlier. The Rabbinic tradition had already taken the Zechariah vision out of context to omit the warlike piety that was once the context of the line. Apocalyptic thinking is not unknown to rabbinic texts, so, had they wished, the Rabbis might well have included a militaristic perspective in our prayers, particularly here, where they could simply have quoted Zechariah at greater length. But apparently, they made a conscious effort to be selective. They retained the messianic hope that one day God's reality would be perceived by the whole world, but omitted any suggestion that others might be brought to this understanding by force.

Reform Judaism has maintained this non-violent perspective on history, as the more contemporary introductory paragraph (p. 72) indicates. This was a favored section in the old 1894 *Union Prayer Book*, so, with some emendations in the English style and the omission of sexist language, it is reproduced here.

So our concluding prayer "*Aleinu*" ends on a universalistic note that replaces biblical apocalypticism with the wish that the day of the universal recognition of God will be achieved by peaceful means.

Let us return for a moment to Zechariah's striking imagery. To indicate the universal acceptance of God's reign, he says: "On that day the Lord shall be One, and His name shall be One." Could this bold description of God's unity, existing only in the future as a potential reality, be taken more literally, so that it reveals some deeper insight? What can it mean to say that God's name is not yet One?

Though most medieval commentators (the well-known Rashi, who lived in France in the 11th century, for example) understood the biblical text according to the plain meaning which we have described so far, others were sufficiently struck by its extreme metaphor to suggest deeper layers of significance. Generally, speculation centered on the meaning of God's name becoming One. It was suggested that, originally, knowledge of God was available in a single "ineffable" name, which was God's true appellation. That was the name represented by the tetragrammaton, the four-lettered name of God which Jews do not pronounce. When we come across it, we say "*Adonai*," even though the four letters (*Yod, He, Vav,* and *He*) clearly must stand for something else. The 12th-century Provençal scholar, Rabbi David Kimchi (known popularly as RaDaK), thus suggests that the fate of God's name mirrors the fate of the world's condition. The ineffable name was revealed to Moses, and entrusted to the priests. But we humans marred the world with evil, and the pure name of God seemed no longer appropriate. Instead, we learned to use many different names for God, each standing for a different divine attribute. But, at the end of days, says RaDaK, God's reality will be applauded universally; all the attributes will once again be recognized as indistinguishable components within God's essential unity, and we will be able to return to God's single real name again.

Medieval mystics went even further. They maintained that our fragmented world is paralleled by a fragmentation of the divine. According to their imagery, if (as is the case) the intended harmony of the universe has been disrupted by evil, then the very unity of God is fractured. Our task is to bring about a reparation of the universe by slowly ending the world's woes. When the final day of messianic harmony dawns, it will be seen that the world's divisiveness and antagonisms have given way to wholeness and harmony. Only then will God be One.

In modern times, too, sensitive souls have seen deeper meaning in the possibility that God is not yet One. Henry Slonimsky (d. 1970) explained the tragedies of life by denying what had been an assumed philosophical axiom for centuries. Practically every Jewish philosopher of note took it as obvious that God, being perfect, must be all knowing, as well as all powerful. How, then, could a perfectly good God not make use of that divine omnipotence to prevent, say, the Holocaust? Slonimsky answered by denying that God was all powerful to begin with. God, like men and women, he retorted, is in the process of growing. God and the world of creatures grow together, dependent on each other for progress. "Maybe God and perfection are at the end, and not at the beginning," he wrote.

> Maybe it is a growing world and a growing mankind and a growing God, and perfection is to be achieved, and not something to start with.
> Our own prophets and prayer books seem to have had an inkling of this fact. At culminating points in our liturgy we say in a phrase borrowed from one of the last of the prophets (Zechariah 14:9), "On that day He shall be One and His name shall be One." On *that* day, not as yet, alas, but surely on *that* day He shall be One, *as He is not yet one.* For how can God be called One, i.e., real, if mankind is rent asunder in misery and poverty and hate and war? When mankind has achieved its own reality and unity, it will thereby have achieved God's reality and unity. Till then, God is merely an idea, an ideal: the world's history consists in making that ideal real. In simple religious earnestness it can be said that God does not exist. Till now He merely subsists in the vision of a few great hearts, *and exists only in part, and is slowly being translated into reality.*

(*Gates of Understanding*, Volume I, p. 76)

The Kaddish

The *Kaddish* is certainly best known as a prayer that is said by mourners. Even Jews who rarely stop to pray can count on the fact that they will probably be called on to recite this prayer as mourners—all too often. Like the "*Aleinu,*" it was composed early in our history, before the year 200 C.E. It is one of the few prayers we have that were written in the vernacular of the time, Aramaic, rather than the more usual language used for prayers, i.e., Hebrew. The symbolic significance of the *Kaddish* can be seen when one considers that, even though its original language was the vernacular, we today would rarely replace the Aramaic with English. This very intransigent insistence that we use every syllable of the original text testifies to an exception from the normal liberalism with which Reform Jews approach their prayers. This deviation from our usual attitude probably derives from the fact that the *Kaddish*, after all, is associated with death; and even the most liberal among us tend to emphasize a heightened conservatism in matters related to death.

Interestingly, the *Kaddish* was not associated with death until many centuries after its composition. Its original theme, like that of the "*Aleinu*" which it now follows, was the celebration of the ultimate coming of God's sovereign realm. Throughout the prayer, God is described as our Sovereign who is to be praised. God will some day bring to pass the divine realm of absolute justice and righteousness, instead of the mundane world that contains more than its share of tragedy and torment for the humbled and the poor of the earth.

The *Kaddish* is very similar to the prayer Christians call "The Lord's Prayer," or "Our Father." The latter name is derived from the first two words of that prayer, wherein God is addressed as "Our Father." (Christians borrowed this term of address from their Jewish background. Compare, for example, our prayer "*Avinu Malkenu*" or "Our Father, Our King"; see above, pp. 23-25 for discussion.) The former title is used because two of the books in the New Testament, the Gospels of Matthew and Luke, picture Jesus (who is "the Lord" to Christians) telling his disciples that they should pray using the words of this particular prayer. So it is, literally, the prayer mandated by "the Lord," or "The Lord's Prayer."

Since "The Lord's Prayer" and the *Kaddish* are so similar, it has usually been claimed that they must be somehow related. Since it seems unlikely that the Jewish community would borrow a well-known prayer from the community of Christians, which contained apostates from Judaism and which claimed to have usurped the Jews in their position as the chosen people of Israel (see above, p. 37), people have argued either that Christians simply continued the practice that they had known from the days when they were Jews, or that both Rabbis and Christians borrowed a prayer which was said by some other Jewish sect. In the case of "The Lord's Prayer," Jesus was either referring to a rabbinic prayer (perhaps the *Kaddish* itself) with which he, as a Jew, had already been familiar, or he was quoting a prayer used by some other Jewish sect, which he had heard and liked.

It is more probable, however, that neither the *Kaddish* nor "The Lord's Prayer" goes back all the way to the time of Jesus. The New Testament is probably mistaken in assigning the Christian prayer to him, and there is no need to assume that our equivalent prayer must be at least that old.

Crucial to our solving the riddle of the *Kaddish*'s origin is the insight we gained earlier about the freedom with which individual prayer themes were expressed. We said then that even though the order of themes that constitute a service was mandated, the ways in which given themes were actually carried out in any given service were left to the creativity of individual prayer leaders. (See above, discussion of *keva* and *kavana*, pp. 11–12.) Thus, when we see two prayers such as "The Lord's Prayer" and the *Kaddish*, which are so similar, we need not assume that the wording of either one was so set in those days that identical versions would be known and quoted by people everywhere. Since there was still no prayerbook, so that neither prayer existed in a final prayerbook form, there is no reason to believe that either one is dependent on the other. It is more likely that the theme of God's sovereignty was generally known to Christians and Jews, both of whom adapted prayers expressing their longing for the "coming of the Kingdom."

This theme became particularly popular between the two wars against Rome (70 and 135 C.E.). Both of these wars were justified with reference to God's sovereignty. The war of 70 was begun by a sect of Jews known to us only as the "Fourth Philosophy." In their claim that God alone is the true Sovereign, they implicitly denied the imperial claims of Roman rule. The second conflict, the Bar Kochba revolt, actually receives its name from the leader, Bar Kochba, who was greeted as the messiah, that is, as the earthly monarch representing the real Ruler of the Universe, God. So, both "The Lord's Prayer" and the *Kaddish* were probably composed shortly after the war of 70, as attempts to address the political-theological problems inherent in the belief in the sovereignty of God. By these prayers, both Christians and Jews maintained that God indeed would bring the hoped-for messianic realm. Either in addition to, or even in place of actually fighting Roman tyranny, both communities were urged to pray for its end.

But what sort of prayer for the demise of the Roman rule was appropriate? On this question, the two religious communities parted ways. The Gospels picture Jesus telling his disciples, "When you pray, you must not be like the hypocrites; for they love to stand and pray in the synagogues and at the street corners, that they may be seen by others.... Rather, when you pray, go into your room and shut the door and pray to your Father in secret.... " (Matthew 6:5-6). Thus, the early Christian community emphasized private (as opposed to public) prayer and saw the realm of God arriving because of the personal nature of the relationship between God and God's people. God would reward the faith of individuals.

The Rabbis, on the other hand, paid relatively little attention to private prayer. (For a fuller discussion of private prayer, see below, pp. 82-84.) Though Jews were encouraged to address God at all times, it was the specifically mandated times of public prayer assembly that God was said to prefer. The Rabbis did not favor hypocritical praying any more than did Jesus, but as part of their attempt to perfect public worship, they inserted the *Kaddish* into every public service.

More than that, they made the *Kaddish* a conclusion for a session of daily study, which included also an accompanying midrashic sermon of hope. Services thus ended with the study of God's word, a homiletical message which emphasized the prophetic promises of comfort even in the face of great adversity, and then with the *Kaddish*, which asserted the Jew's belief that the coming of God's realm was assured. Because the sermon was in the vernacular, so too was the *Kaddish* which concluded it. Christians and Jews, then, shared the hope of "the coming of the Kingdom," but they differed in this: for Christians, the realm would come because of individual faith; for Jews, it would arrive on account of communal faithfulness to God's word, which the community studied daily so that its message might be known and acted upon.

The *Kaddish* is the best testimony to the Jewish insistence on hope for a better tomorrow and to our linking of that hope to the *mitzva* that we claim is equal to all the others combined: the study of Torah. (See our prayer to that effect, p. 90.)

Through the years, the *Kaddish* became more and more popular. A fourth-century Babylonian rabbi says that in times of woe, the world would collapse were it not for this prayer of consolation. Subsequent generations began using variations of the prayer as a sort of punctuation in their services. Rather than reserve it for the end of a study session (which, in any case, was no longer part of the daily prayer regimen for most people), they used it elsewhere in the service to divide major rubrics from one another. Thus, a lengthy Reader's *Kaddish* ended the *Tefila*, and a shorter Reader's *Kaddish* introduced the "*Shema*" and its blessings. And by the eighth century, for reasons we do not know, one *Kaddish* was reserved for recital at funerals.

Until *Gates of Prayer* and *Gates of Repentance*, which reinstated the Reader's *Kaddish* (see *Gates of Repentance*, p. 98, for example), it was the Mourner's *Kaddish* that Reform Jews knew best. No other *Kaddish* could be found in the *Union Prayer Book*. The authors of the *Union Prayer Book* were simply recognizing the reality that by their time, Jews had forgotten the origin of the *Kaddish*, which they saw now only as a prayer for the departed. The trend toward treating the *Kaddish* solely as a prayer for the dead was evident by the 13th century, when a popular legend depicted Rabbi Akiba saving a dead man from everlasting torture in Hell by locating that man's son, who was subsequently taught to lead the congregation in prayer and to say the *Kaddish*.

It took years for our liturgy to arrive at the point where people felt comfortable saying the *Kaddish* with other people. Instead, they treated the prayer as if every single recitation worked magically to relieve the suffering of that single reciter's deceased relatives. By the 16th century, with the rise of large Jewish communities, codes of Jewish law had to devise priority lists for occasions when more than one person claimed the right to say the *Kaddish*, and the traditional service added the Mourner's *Kaddish* in numerous parts of the liturgy so that large numbers of people could be accommodated, even those far down on the priority list. Only much later did people find that too many people were always present, so that a communal recitation was necessary. We, thus, arrived at the traditional custom of having all the mourners rise to say the Mourner's *Kaddish*, and not just once, but many times, because all the extra instances of the *Kaddish* that had been added to satisfy the old custom of individual recitation were preserved. To this day, in traditionalist services, mourners come early and rise many times to say a *Kaddish*, several of those times coming immediately after each other at the end of the service, in a seemingly redundant way.

In the interests of shortening the service, and thus adding to its dignity, the *Union Prayer Book* omitted all but one *Kaddish*, which all mourners said together. But especially after the Holocaust, it became popular for entire congregations, not just the mourners, to say the *Kaddish* together, in memory of the six million who left no one behind to memorialize them—except us. Our *Gates of Repentance* continues Reform practice by omitting needless repetition of the *Kaddish*; but it restores the Reader's *Kaddish*, which most congregations will want to chant according to the well-known melody accompanying it.

"Adon Olam" (pp. 47-48, 75)

We need only a brief word about the closing hymn, *"Adon Olam."* We end our service as we began it, by singing God's praise. This beautiful poem is usually said to be the work of the 11th-century Spanish poet and philosopher Solomon ibn Gabirol, but, in fact, there is no evidence to support this claim. All we can say of it is that it begins as a philosophical statement of God's unity and majesty, such as a poetic genius like Gabirol might have penned. It ends, however, on a personal note, stressing that this transcendent God of the philosophers is "my living Redeemer, my Rock in time of trouble and distress."

Some scholars think *"Adon Olam"* began as a bedtime prayer, because it ends by noting that "into God's hands I entrust my spirit, when I sleep and when I wake." Whatever its origin, however, it eventually received universal Jewish approval and came to be recited at many and diverse times. In Morocco, for example, Jews sing it at weddings just before bringing the bride under the *Chupa* (the bridal canopy). We follow the practice of the *Union Prayer Book* and include it here as a fitting conclusion to the night of Rosh Hashana.

"Adon Olam" is almost always sung, but to a host of tunes. This has been the case at least since the 15th century when the Maharil (Rabbi Jacob Moellin of Mayence) singled it out on account of its "lovely drawn-out melody." Eric Werner has traced some of the tunes to their roots in popular German folk melodies, including a once-famous "mocking song" called "Expelling the Pope." Thus, for this, as for many other liturgical staples, there is no single "authentically Jewish" melody that must be retained for all time. Still, an English paraphrase ("The Lord of All") has been included (p. 48) so that at least one of the most traditional tunes may be sung with English words or with the Hebrew.

We have now progressed through the Evening Service, stopping to look at all the major rubrics that compose at least one of the services in our liturgy. We have seen how the service begins with warm-up singing, and then proceeds to a creed (the *"Shema"* and its blessings) and a prayer of praise and petition (the *Tefila*). On the Days of Awe, as on every Shabbat and Holy Day, the petitionary aspect of the *Tefila* is omitted. We looked at special insertions in the *Tefila* as well as at the unique *"Avinu Malkenu,"* and ended with a glance at the concluding prayers, which, appropriately, emphasize the Jew's sense of hope and optimism. .

As this commentary continues, we shall have less and less need to speak at such length regarding the prayers we encounter and will be able, instead, to refer to what has been said already. It will be helpful always to keep in mind the essentially unchanging nature of our liturgy's structural parameters. Knowing the basic structure, we know the boundaries of the liturgical "forest." With a few exceptions, from now on we shall be concentrating not on the forest, which we can take for granted, but on the individual prayers, the liturgical "trees" that express the rubrics differently in each service, thus providing the richness of the liturgical tapestry, the novelty and excitement that greet the serious worshiper intent on appreciating the High Holy Day prayer experience.

Rosh Hashana Morning

General Comments

Overview

As there are two services for Rosh Hashana evening, so there are two for the morning. They, too, are differentiated according to the relative creativity afforded each of the two major rubrics, the *"Shema"* and the *Tefila* (for this principle, see above, pp. 11–12). In Service I, it is the *"Shema"* that receives loose paraphrases of the Hebrew originals, while the *Tefila* is outfitted with relatively direct translations; in Service II, the situation is reversed.

The Morning Service is enhanced beyond that of the evening in three major ways, each one of which reveals further differences between the morning alternatives. First, the morning preparatory material is more extensive than the parallel evening prayers. Second, the Morning Service contains the ritual for blowing the *shofar*. Third, in the morning, the Torah and *Haftara* are read. We have incorporated more traditional preparatory material in Service I, which is, in general, the more traditional service. The Torah and *Haftara* material is roughly equivalent, but the normal Torah reading for Rosh Hashana (the *Akeda*, or the Binding of Isaac) is included in Service I, while an alternative reading (the Creation narrative) has been set in Service II. (For discussion of the readings, see below, pp. 90–96.)

Our discussion will, thus, proceed through the various rubrics of each service, as follows:

1. Preparatory Prayers: a) Morning Blessings (*Birchot Hashachar*)
                       b) Poems of Praise (*Pesukei Dezimra*)
2. *"Shema"* and Its Blessings
3. *Tefila*
4. Torah and *Haftara* Readings
5. Service for the Blowing of the *Shofar*
6. Concluding Prayers

To summarize what we said above: in Service I, items 1, 3, and 5 are more traditional; in Service II, item 2 is more traditional. Items 4 and 6 are roughly the same in this regard.

Preparation for Worship

The preparation for worship in the morning is far more extensive than in the evening. In part, this is simply because people have more leisure then, given the time constraints of the traditional Jewish calendar. In the evening, Jews had to get to the synagogue in time to complete the Afternoon Service (or *Mincha*) before the sun set, and their daily work prevented their arriving with a lot of time to spare before beginning their prayers. They came with only a little time available in the waning hours of the daily sun, allotted as much as they could afford to preparing for prayer, and then said their statutory afternoon prayers (*Mincha*). For the Evening Service that followed, their only deadline for ending was the natural desire to get home to their family, but for this service, not a great deal of preparation was required in any case, inasmuch as they were already involved actively in praying, having just completed their Afternoon Service (*Mincha*).

The morning, however, was different. People could arise at a very early hour and allot much time to morning preparation for prayers. They had to finish in time to get to work, naturally, but they could begin as soon as the sun rose. So the Morning Service (or *Shacharit*) became the longest of all the services and was outfitted with considerable preparatory material.

The most important reason for the extensive rubrics preceding the "*Shema*," however, is the nature of the scholars who defined it. We saw above (p. 49) how the *Kaddish* was placed alongside a daily morning study period, and we suggested that its placement there stood as clear witness to the supreme importance of study in the Rabbis' scheme of things. As we saw, there are many *mitzvot*, but the study of Torah is equal to them all. The Rabbis in the Talmudic period, though individualists, agreed absolutely on the need to study God's word, both in its written form (the Bible), and in its oral commentary (the ongoing chain of Rabbinic tradition). Though clearly men of action who led their people successfully through one challenge after another, they nevertheless constituted a distinct class for whom scholarship symbolized status. Those who demonstrated outstanding aptitude for studying God's will and for instituting their own personal piety as a consequence of that study managed to attract many disciples and to amass prestige as a result. In many ways, these rabbis lived apart from the people at large: they prayed with each other, for example, rather than with the masses; they preferred a life of commerce over the dominant economic pursuit of farming; and above all, they were in the habit of generally honing their scholarly skills by memorizing adages of earlier sages, debating each other, lecturing on abstract points of law and lore, and engaging in highly abstruse hypothetical questions, which had no earthly applicability perhaps, but the discussion of which would be rewarded—so they believed—in the world to come.

For these Rabbis, awakening to substantive morning prayer was assumed. People even vied with each other to prove by their conduct at prayer that they had understood God's laws on worship better than their peers. Certainly they took worship seriously, but that very seriousness mandated constant expansion of the prayers they said and steady improvement in the way they said them. Unable to take prayer for granted, they were moved by their consciences to change it regularly. As they believed in a rather extreme individualism, by which each rabbi had to study and then interpret the law according to his own insights, they were prevented from arriving at a system such as we see in the Orthodox community today, where people also take daily prayer seriously, but demonstrate that concern by following strictures laid down by others, rather than by arriving at their own degree of individualism. So, to begin with, the members of the scholar class were highly motivated to get up early and to pray at some length before taking up their occupations in the world of commerce.

Above all, however, was their overriding need to study. The mores of their class demanded it, because God had ordained it. Thus, the Rabbis accustomed themselves to getting up very early in the morning, and, even before engaging in preparatory prayers *per se*, they studied.

But in Judaism, it is not clear where study ends and prayer begins. One reads the Torah to study, but says a blessing first. Or, to take another example: for average Jews, the study of every topic and paragraph in the earliest Jewish sources was never a serious possibility; but surely, the Rabbis reasoned, such people ought to study something. They, therefore, selected certain study passages for daily liturgical recitation by even the most ignorant Jew, who needed only to memorize the passages in order to say them.

Each morning began with three kinds of material. First, there were the study passages themselves, drawn both from the Bible and from its oral interpretation. Second, they had a series of liturgical blessings and accompaniments that bracketed the passages studied (blessings thanking God for giving the Torah in the first place, for example). And finally, as pious Jews, they developed a series of benedictions having nothing to do with study but directly related to natural acts performed by grateful human beings as part of the process of arising: opening the eyes, standing up, getting dressed, and so on. Each one evoked gratitude for being still alive in God's wonderful world. In short, even by the time the Talmud was completed (sometime between the years 550 and 750 C.E.), scholars, at least, had developed an astonishingly large repertoire of study and prayer that preceded the communal preparatory songs and psalms.

Had this repertoire remained the sole possession of rabbis, our service would have been much briefer. But by the ninth century C.E., Rav Amram of Babylonia, the leading authority in what was then the most outstanding Jewish society in the world, decided to pen a list of all prayers demanded of the Jew and to send it as guidance to a new Jewish community in Spain. His effort—known as *Seder Rav Amram*—became the first known comprehensive prayerbook in our history and soon emerged as the basic source to which our own practice to this day is indebted. In his book, Amram assumed that people in his time could not go through the lengthy study sections and their accompanying liturgy on their own at home before coming to the synagogue. So, he included all that home material in his public liturgy. Many prominent authorities have disagreed with that decision—among them, Maimonides himself—but the decision remained. The result is that our morning preparatory rubric is, to this day, composed of two originally separate and discrete units: morning study and blessings, originally said at home, and public psalms and songs designed to prepare the worshiping community for prayer in the synagogue. The former are called *Birchot Hashachar*, or Morning Blessings; the latter are known technically as *Pesukei Dezimra*, or Verses of Song, and in our liturgy, we call them "Poems of Praise."

Morning Service I (pp. 79–162)
"For those who wear the Talit" (p. 79)

Perhaps nothing has been more fiercely debated through the ages of Reform Judaism's development than the propriety of donning special ritual attire for prayer! At issue primarily were the prayer-shawl (*talit*) and head covering (then called *yarmulke*, but now, under the influence of Israeli Hebrew, usually referred to as *kipa*). Both ritual garments deserve our attention, particularly since the debate, though dormant until recently, has once again been joined. Many Reform Jews find meaning in these traditional worship symbols; others charge that their use betrays a subtle move by Reform Judaism "back to Orthodoxy."

We may begin with the Hungarian rabbi Aaron Chorin (1766–1844) who, in 1826, argued seriously for the right to pray with uncovered head.

His idea was only part of a general Reform agenda, which he had first offered in a learned responsum favoring relatively minor liturgical changes in Hamburg (1819). His recommendation did not receive wide favor. Only the Berlin Reform Association followed Chorin's advice; but from its inception, this body had demonstrated itself to be the most radical of Reformers. Its founder, Sigismund Stern (1812–1867), had expressly organized the association as an amalgam of all radical groups, into what he called "a German-Jewish Church." Its prayerbook eliminated almost all the Hebrew. Its first rabbi—Stern had not been ordained—was the noted Samuel Holdheim (1806–1860), known best, perhaps, for moving Sabbath services to Sunday, abolishing circumcision, and viewing Jewish ritual generally as an outmoded vestige from an earlier age when Jews had required visible signs of their distinction from paganism. So in Europe, Chorin's recommendation that head covering be abandoned was honored in Berlin. A smaller community in Soest followed suit after an 1847 address in which the president of the Jewish consistory of Westphalia urged them to do so. The same view was later presented in a scholarly study of the history of covering one's head, written by Leopold Loew, another Hungarian rabbi (1811–1875), who included his essay as part of a lengthy tribute to Chorin. But most Jews in Europe retained the custom of the *kipa*.

In America, however, worshiping with uncovered heads was accepted almost universally as a veritable symbol of Reform, with the result that (as Gunther Plaut summarizes) "perhaps no other innovation of Reform aroused greater opposition than this; no other change stirred so many sentiments." New York's Temple Emanuel had first discussed the subject via a lengthy responsum of its rabbi as early as 1859. In 1928, Jacob Z. Lauterbach reproduced much of Loew's essay, within the parameters of his own responsum which concluded that Reform Jews had every right to worship with uncovered heads, that the entire matter was purely one of custom, not law, and that Jews on both sides of the question should show forebearance toward those on the other side, since "hat on or hat off . . . is a detail that is not worth fighting about. It should not separate Jew from Jew and not be made the cause of breaking the Jewish groups or dividing Jewish congregations."

The *talit* occasioned far less invective. It, too, was banned by the Berlin Reform Association, though it was generally maintained in Europe. In America, it was rarely worn by worshiping congregants, though rabbis frequently donned a *talit*—or a more decorous modern equivalent of one— while leading services. In his "Ritual Directions" with which he introduced his 1866 prayerbook, *Minhag America*, Isaac Mayer Wise summed up the regnant Reform attitude here: "It is no more necessary to wear a

Talith in the temple than anywhere outside thereof. . . . As a memorial, it will suffice that the minister wear it."

Of the two ritual objects, certainly the *talit* is more authentically rooted in Jewish sources. The wearing of *tsitsit* (the fringes sewn on the hem of the *talit*, and the religious rationale for the *talit* in the first place) goes back to a biblical commandment (Numbers 15:39-40), which explains that their purpose is, "You shall see [the *tsitsit*] and remember all the commandments of God and do them . . . and be holy unto your God." Scholars are divided on the kind of *tsitsit* worn in biblical times, but later, by the second or third century C.E., at least, it was common for the scholar class (though not necessarily for the masses) to attach fringes to a large *talit* that extended over the whole body. Wrapping oneself had become a significant ritual act expected of judges before trials, teachers before discoursing on weighty subjects, and rabbis preparing for prayer.

Opinions differed on the extent to which a *talit* might be worn. Some wore it all day, though most did not. In any case, it was generally not worn at night, since the purpose of the *tsitsit* (which were by now attached) was that they be seen, and without daylight they could not be viewed clearly. Palestinian Jews went so far as to omit the last paragraph of the "*Shema*" from their Evening Service, since its primary topic is the commandment to wear and to see the *tsitsit*.

Through the ages, two major changes in the wearing of the *talit* occurred. The first was the introduction of a *talit katan*, a little *talit*, worn underneath one's outer garments. This was an innovation to meet the need of generations who had decided that the *talit* should be worn all day, but who lived in an environment where outward display of such garb would have marked Jews off adversely from the non-Jewish population. The second was the relaxation of the ban against wearing the *talit* at night. All agreed that it should be removed before the Evening Service, with the exception of Yom Kippur (see below, p. 113), but some Sefardic Jews wore it during the afternoon service, at least; and in modern times, both Sefardim and Ashkenazim have favored the reader or the preacher wearing a *talit* even at night, "because of the honor due to a congregation." This latter innovation was known as a custom among some by the 17th century; one hundred years later, it was frequently the established rule.

So, Isaac Mayer Wise's regulation in 1866 was not without precedent. He generalized the wearing of a *talit* by the prayer leader at night to every service. Considering the commandment to wear and to see the *tsitsit* outmoded, and—as a Reform Jew of his time—being hardly able to consider his own wearing of the *talit* an "honor to the congregation," he justified his custom as a "memorial" which, no doubt, he thought would satisfy those in his congregation who might miss the familiar *talit* if they did not see it at all.

The *yarmulke*, on the other hand, has neither biblical nor Rabbinic legal basis. There is no evidence that biblical Jews covered their heads for any other reason except that, as desert dwellers, they needed to protect themselves from the sun. In Rabbinic times, some of the scholar class used headgear, sometimes as a halfway measure to meet the custom of wrapping one's body, sometimes as a mark of special piety (one rabbi in Babylonia remarked that he would not walk even the shortest distance without a hat, since God's presence is everywhere).

Later, in Islamic environs, headcovering was the recommended way for Moslems to distinguish themselves from unbelievers. Moslem tradition described how Mohammed himself had worn it. Especially on religious pilgrimage to a shrine, Moslems were advised to cover their heads. Jews followed suit, copying Moslem religious aesthetics. They, too, now wore hats, and significant personalities such as Maimonides selected the turban variety favored by Moslem nobles. (Incidentally, many Jews also copied the Moslem custom of taking off their shoes before entering synagogues, and Maimonides's concern for Moslem aesthetic sensitivities even extended to his desire to do away with the silent recitation of the *Tefila*, since the masses made noise during it, thus embarrassing Jewish potentates who had to explain the unseemly display to their Moslem neighbors.)

Northern European Jews, on the other hand, had no Moslem customs to observe, and they accepted the practice of wearing hats much more cautiously. Only in the 13th century was it becoming common, and it was still by no means mandatory, even while praying. A celebrated statement on the subject from relatively modern times is a responsum by the Polish Talmudist Solomon Luria (1510–1573), who was asked whether someone suffering from a headache might eat (and say the accompanying blessings) without wearing a hat. Luria responded forthrightly that there is no prohibition against praying with head uncovered, and that he himself might even do so; but in the end, he notes, covering one's head has become a universal Jewish custom, and custom counts for something in Jewish reckoning. He did not want to contradict great rabbis who had gone before him, nor to advise dressing in such a way that observers might be led to the false conclusion that people are in the habit of blatantly disregarding Jewish law. Something that *seems* wrong is, in fact, wrong; inasmuch as people assume that the head must be covered, it would be incorrect to flaunt the opposite practice, thus giving the wrong impression publicly.

Reform scholars, like Lauterbach, later quoted Luria at some length, but disagreed with his conclusion. They were intrigued by the fact that

Luria, one of the mightiest Talmudic scholars of all time, had proven that the whole matter of headdress was *only* (!) a custom and, as such, could, in their opinion, be abrogated in favor of other customs more in keeping with the dictates of modern times.

As far as terminology is concerned: the word *tsitsit* is biblical; *talit* emerged later, in Roman times, as the technical name for a cloak of honor (similar to the Latin *pallium* and the Greek *tharos*). *Talit* is derived from the Aramaic root *tly*, meaning "hang down." The origins of the term *yarmulke* are less clear. Gunther Plaut has argued that it derives from the name applied to a hat worn by Catholic priests at a particular point in the Christian Mass. Sixteenth-century Polish Jews wore hats that looked very similar, so that the term for the clerical hat was applied by non-Jews in their descriptions of the Jews. The Church hat was an *amice* or *armuce* (with the "*c*" pronounced like a "*k*"). A smaller version of that hat, one similar to what Jews wore, was described by the diminutive *armucele*. In time the "*c*" and the "*l*" were transposed, becoming *armulece*, or, eventually, the slurred Yiddish word *yarmulke*. *Kipa* is Hebrew, and can be found among terms included in literature of the first two centuries C.E.

Finally, we should say a word about women who wish to wear either the *kipa* or the *talit*. Authorities are divided on the question of whether women covered their heads in Rabbinic times. If they did, it was only to follow rules of modesty then in effect. They certainly wore no *talit*. By the second century, the Rabbis had ruled that women were exempt from positive religious precepts governed by time; and *tsitsit*, which one must look at (positive) during the day (governed by time), falls into that category. On the other hand, Moses Isserles (the 16th-century Polish authority who rendered the *Shulchan Aruch* acceptable to Ashkenazic Jews) says expressly that if women want to wear a *talit* and even to say the blessing over it, they may do so. Thus, in his Reform responsum of 1971, Solomon Freehof finds no objection in women joining men in the adoption of the *talit*.

Freehof does not argue that the *talit should* be worn, only that in congregations where men wear it, women may do so as well. The issue for him is not only that there is no prohibition against the practice. There is also the positive consideration that "in our Reform movement . . . special emphasis is placed on the equality of men and women." Interestingly, the radical Berlin Reform Association, which took the extreme step of prohibiting the *yarmulke*, argued equally vociferously for the application of the Reform doctrine of sexual equality. This principle of equality had no sooner been enunciated at the 1845 rabbinical conference in Frankfort (see *Gates of Understanding*, Volume I, pp. 25–26), when the association did away with the women's gallery in favor of seating women on the same plane as men.

Given all this information, every Reform Jew will have to determine what his or her position ought to be regarding the *talit* and the *kipa*. As we saw in "The Liturgical Message" (see *Gates of Understanding*, Volume I, pp. 143–146), the structure of our prayerbooks already presents us with a possible stand on matters of this sort, although worshipers are free to accept or to reject that stand along with the prayerbooks in which they are found. What, then, is the structured message carried by *Gates of Repentance*, and how consistent is it with Reform Judaism as described in the last few paragraphs?

Clearly, by its very decision to include ritual garb as optional, *Gates of Repentance* differs structurally from the *Union Prayer Book*. The traditional blessing (predating the year 200) appears on page 79. We recognize that people may now wear a *kipa* too, but because the *kipa* (unlike the *talit*) is rooted only in custom, there is no traditional blessing for it, and no prayerbook space need be allotted to it. But the page begins with the instructions that what follows is "For those who wear the *Talit*," implying that some will do so, and some will not. Thus, the structural message of the new Reform *Machzor* is that the wearing of special worship attire is optional.

At first it would appear that we have here a reversal of the classical Reform position. Such a conclusion would be only partly correct. To be sure, American Reform worship now differs from what it traditionally has been, in that the *talit* and the *kipa* have become acceptable items. But the essence of Reform Judaism was, and still is, its insistence that the eternal verities of religion go deeper than its obvious trappings. Even the Berlin Reform Association, which did away with special worship attire, did not absolutely prohibit covering the head; rather, they voted for "worship with uncovered head," with the stipulation, however, that "the wearing of a black skull cap . . . [is] permitted to individuals." We recall how Lauterbach summed up his epic survey: "Hat on or hat off . . . is a detail that is not worth fighting about. It should not separate Jew from Jew, and not be made the cause of . . . dividing Jewish congregations."

The reality has been, however, that temples which allowed individuals to wear *kipa* or *talit in theory*, often asked them to remove such garb in practice. Even as Lauterbach wrote his summation, "hat on or hat off" was in fact provoking the very divisiveness he deplored. Clearly, the matter went beyond the logic of academic debate. The reader of this commentary now knows all the relevant data that Lauterbach's readers did. Whether these data will be used to harden positions for or against the wearing of *kipa* and *talit*, or to promote a patient acceptance of those on the other side of the issue, is a matter that transcends the facts themselves.

We should recognize that the issue of *talit* and *kipa* is in the realm of symbol (see *Gates of Understanding*, Volume I, pp. 135–139). By invoking the realm of symbolism, we mean that our positions on the wearing of worship attire are deeply rooted in our psyches for reasons we understand poorly, if at all. Yet, we feel so strongly about the matter that we cannot comprehend the rationale of people who differ with us. Discussions are apt to flare into angry debates.

Still, our new prayerbook heralds the fact that the Reform Movement remains open to change, and change in our day implies a willingness to consider a wide gamut of traditional options drawn from our Jewish past. The founders of our movement would have supported our continued emphatic reassertion of Reform ideals, such as the Mission of Israel, the ongoing covenant with God, a religious definition of Jewish identity, and so on. By the same token, they would agree with the view taken by *Gates of Repentance*: wearing a *kipa* or *talit* to enhance the experience of worship does not belong to that critical core of Judaism deserving of argumentation. Pioneering Reform ideologues proved that one could be a good Jew without covering one's head; the statement of our generation is simply the obvious corollary: one does not become a bad Jew if one covers one's head anyway.

Preparatory Prayers

Morning Blessings (pp. 80–91)

In general, this rubric of Service I contains a traditional selection of sources, though even here tradition is balanced by novel poetry and prose drawn from our own time.

For the Blessing of Worship ("Ma Tovu") (p. 80)

The content of this introductory reading makes it eminently suitable for the first prayer recited in the synagogue. In addition, one should note that interesting tales lie behind the first three lines.

The first line is biblical. In Numbers 22, we learn that King Balak of Moab saw how the Israelites had prevailed against the Amorites. Now, fearing similar disaster in his own pending battle with God's people, Balak hires a prophet, Balaam, to stand on a precipice looking down on Israel's tents and to curse them. "I know that whom you bless is blessed, and whom you curse is cursed," he says. But God intervenes. In a humorous interlude, God warns Balaam against accepting his charge from Balak, and when Balaam goes anyway, God sends an invisible angel to turn Balaam's donkey off the road. Poor Balaam cannot even see the angel—though the donkey can—and nothing he does to correct what he takes to be the animal's willful stubbornness succeeds. At last God lets Balaam see the angel and tells him that he may proceed to the Israelite camp, but "only the word that I shall speak to you, shall you speak." Balaam arrives with Balak, and, to the king's dismay, he not only fails to curse Israel, but actually blesses them, with a memorable exclamation, "*Ma tovu ohalecha, Ya-akov . . .* ," "How lovely are your tents, O Jacob, your dwelling places, O Israel!" (Numbers 24:5).

By the 11th century, however, this was not the part of our prayer that fascinated Jewish worshipers. Their interest was diverted to the next two lines, the English of which begins, "In your abundant loving-kindness. . . ." These Jews lived in Germany and Northern France, where medieval superstition was rife. They believed firmly in demons and angels, who prowled the earth seeking opportunities to infect human society. One taboo widely followed was the ban on pointing to anyone, lest the attention of a demon be drawn to that person. (To this day we deem it "impolite" to point.) Yet, Jews needed to ascertain whether a *minyan* was present. Rather than count, thus pointing at each worshiper in turn, they used the next two lines of the "*Ma Tovu*," which, coincidentally, have ten words. One worshiper would say the first word, another would say the next, and so on, until all ten words were completed, and the existence of a *minyan* guaranteed.

Your Endless Blessing (pp. 82–85)

Though little known to English readers, because he wrote in Hebrew, Hillel Zeitlin (1871–1942) is one of our outstanding 20th-century mystical visionaries. Born in Eastern Europe, he received a typical education in Hasidism, which he supplemented by immersing himself in philosophy. He was attracted particularly to such pessimists on the human condition as Nietzsche, on whose philosophy he wrote a Hebrew monograph. More and more he found himself disappointed by secularity, a tendency confirmed by the violent pogroms in Kishinev in 1903. He emerged from them convinced that the answers to life's ambiguities lay not in the rational realm of secular society but in the religious perspective he had studied as a youth, particularly in Jewish mysticism. Until the end of his life—at the hands of the Nazis on the way to Treblinka—he remained a fierce advocate of his newly found faith in Jewish mysticism.

His poem, translated here, speaks of the mystics' sense of the miracle of Creation, the nearness of God, and the age-old desire to sense spiritual renewal, a theme which recommends this poem to us for the Days of Awe.

The Miracles of Daily Life (pp. 85–89)

We reproduce here a selection from the traditional set of blessings said by a person upon awakening. Each benediction speaks of a different daily miracle which we usually take for granted. The religious mentality takes nothing for granted, however: we awaken from sleep (which is like a taste of death) and rediscover how magnificent it is that there should be living beings at all; we look around us, and are overcome with gratitude for the gift of sight; we stand up and thank God for raising up the fallen; and so on.

The two longer blessings on page 87 express our gratitude for body and soul, the former speaking of the awe engendered by considering the incredible workmanship evident in human anatomy, the latter linking our purely physical existence to the vision of inner spirituality.

In the traditional service, men thank God here for not making them non-Jews, slaves, and women. Since the Middle Ages, women, who could not express the last sentiment, were instructed to thank God "who made me according to His will." In one community, at least—in Southern France—we find women saying "who made me a woman," a variation less self-deprecating than the traditional alternative.

What have Jews in the modern age done with these remarkable blessings, which are phrased in the negative, and which cast aspersions on non-Jews, those enslaved against their will, and women? By comparing three different approaches, we can learn a good deal about Reform Judaism, and about two religious alternatives that Reform rejected.

The 19th century forced Jews to come to terms with modernity. One way of doing so was simply to deny that anything had changed. By re-emphasizing one's faith in the Talmud, the Zohar, and the rest of a traditional Jewish library, one could treat the modern world as another blight of human history, which simply demanded more strenuous efforts at uncovering tradition's ageless message. Moses Sofer (1762–1839), known as the Chatam Sofer, best illustrates this approach. Perhaps the most famous arch-conservative opponent of Reform Judaism, Sofer made his mark in the history of ideas by forbidding Reform on the grounds that "innovation [*per se*] is forbidden by the Torah." He found meaning for all traditional practices, our blessings included, in the same texts that had been pored over by rabbis for centuries. Accordingly, he argued that with regard to being born a Jew and not a non-Jew, and a man and not a woman, these blessings were designed to emphasize divine providence. All other peoples find their destiny determined by astrological forces, but Jews alone, he believed, are directed by God. Put another way, he argued that Jews are not governed by natural law. That meant that even the sex of a fetus, though generally determined at conception, might be changed for a Jew any time before birth, if God so wished it. Presumably many men were originally female at conception but had had their gender changed because God wanted more men! The Chatam Sofer's argument is not an answer to the question which modernity poses. Its implicit evaluation of women does not disturb him at all. His tenacious faith in astrology, ancient legend, and outmoded theories of anatomy, clearly at odds with modern science, is something of which he is proud.

Samson Raphael Hirsch (1808–1888), a younger contemporary of Moses Sofer, heartily confirmed his elder's rejection of Reform. But, unlike Sofer, Hirsch took pains to recognize that modernity was not an illusion. As the founder of what we now call Neo-Orthodoxy, an attempt to modernize the Orthodox movement, he had to render the blessings in question acceptable to modern sensitivities. His commentary on them is worth quoting. It displays the same need to find positive meaning in everything traditional that we saw above with the Chatam Sofer, and it bespeaks the same attitude toward women. But Hirsch differs from Sofer in that he feels obliged to lace his interpretation with apologetic, this trait being typical of staunch defenders of tradition in the face of modernity. It is worth noting that the ideological context of his point is none other than the idea of Israel's Prophetic Mission, the same cry for action that motivated those Reform colleagues against whom Hirsch contended. Hirsch writes:

> This is not a prayer of thanks that God did not make us heathens, slaves or women. Rather, it calls upon us to contemplate the task which God has imposed upon us by making us free Jewish men, and to pledge ourselves to do justice to this mission. . . . And if our women have a smaller number of *mitzvot* to fulfill than men, they know that the tasks that they must discharge as free Jewish women are no less in accordance with the will and desire of God than are those of their brothers.

If the Chatam Sofer was on the far right of the religious spectrum, and Hirsch was somewhere closer to the center, Reform Jews occupied the left. They shared Hirsch's desire to modernize their liturgy. But, unlike Hirsch, who was caught in the middle between the uncompromising Orthodoxy of Moses Sofer and the modern world's clarion call for change, Reform rabbis felt no need to justify every bit of tradition. So they solved the problem either by omitting the blessings in question or, where possible, by rephrasing them in words of positive appreciation for what we are, as opposed to what we are not.

Gates of Repentance continues this Reform approach. We thank God for making us free and for making us Jews. We omit any invidious contrast between men and women. Reform Judaism insists that modernity cannot be ignored. It seeks to find meaning in tradition, insofar as that meaning is there: we can and do offer thanks for being free and Jews. But we recognize, without apology, that there are times when the tradition must be abandoned because it opposes principles which we take as prior; in this case, the equality of men and women.

Ironically, we should note that the very three benedictions which Sofer and Hirsch strove valiantly to defend, are not originally Jewish at all, but Greek! When Jews found themselves surrounded by Hellenistic culture, they borrowed a great deal, some things good, such as the format of the Passover *Seder*, which began as a practice by upper-class Greek society of holding festive banquets at which philosophy was discussed. But who merited invitations to these banquets? Only free Greek males. Hence, the Greeks used to thank Zeus for not making them slaves, non-Greek, or women—our very blessings!

"How Greatly We Are Blessed" (p. 89)

Originally, this was part of a much longer section in the *Siddur* leading up to a recitation of the *"Shema."* Inasmuch as the *"Shema"* will be said later in its usual place, however (see chart above, p. 13), it has never been quite clear why it should also be said at this point in the service. Medieval authorities believed that the *"Shema"* had once been banned by the non-Jewish government, so that Jews were forced instead to say it surreptitiously here, as part of the early morning liturgy which the authorities could not observe. When the ban was removed, the extra *"Shema"* remained. We have removed the *"Shema"* from its place here, but retained four lines of the introduction thereto, because they speak eloquently of our Jewish tradition.

Actually, these lines were rediscovered in a musical way by the Reform Movement well before the composition of *Gates of Repentance*. When the president of Hebrew Union College, Alfred Gottschalk, was inaugurated, his friend and colleague, Cantor William Sharlin, composed some music for the occasion. Part of Sharlin's composition was a setting for these four lines, culminating in a triumphant setting for the *"Shema"* composed by Max Helfman (1901–1961). Though the *"Shema"* does not appear here, Sharlin's other lyrics do, and congregations (who know the *"Shema"* by heart, after all) might wish to add the Helfman *"Shema"* here so as to make use of an exciting liturgical musical offering.

For Torah (pp. 89–91)

We saw above that the "Morning Blessings" rubric was composed largely of (1) study passages, (2) liturgy associated with those passages, and (3) blessings relevant to arising each morning. We come now to (1) the study passages and (2) their accompanying liturgy.

Our tradition contains several blessings thanking God for granting us Torah. As we saw (see above, pp. 35–36), the gift of Torah is part of an idea-complex including also the chosenness of Israel and God's love for us. This was the theme of the second of the *Shema's* blessings. Similar blessings, however, will be familiar to anyone who has been called to the Torah. The first benediction a Bar or Bat Mitzvah boy or girl sings, for example, proclaims: "Praised be the Lord our God, Ruler of the universe Who has chosen us from all peoples by giving us the Torah. Blessed is the Lord, Giver of the Torah" (p. 125).

We have spoken already about the concept of *kavana* or spontaneity (see above, pp. 11–12), according to which even from the beginning, the Rabbis felt free to express mandatory themes in different ways, at different occasions. One such theme is this idea-complex of Torah, and given the importance of studying Torah (see above, pp. 54–55), it is no surprise to find the theme in several places in the prayerbook. We have already looked at one such place: the second blessing before the *"Shema."* We will later look at the third place: being called for an *aliya* during the reading of Torah. We now come to the second place—the one referred to above, when we discussed the origin of the early morning study period.

Apparently, the many blessings on the Torah theme were once used arbitrarily, as Jews felt free at any of the three times to recite any of them, or to make up a new one, if they wished. But by the ninth century it became common to assign the Torah blessings to specific locations in the service, with no apparent reason for the choice other than the desire to impose order on the worship experience. Two blessings were reserved for being called to the Torah; some were placed here; another was limited to the *Shema's* blessing at night; and yet another was set aside for that benediction in the morning.

But what happened to all the other blessings on this theme, those which were never officially assigned a place, and as a result dropped out of circulation? For years, scholars had some clue that others existed; medieval books cited versions of blessings that are no longer extant. But the break-through came at the turn of this century, when we located a huge cache of documents, many of them liturgical fragments, which had been stored in a medieval synagogue in the old part of Cairo. In Hebrew, a storage place is called a *geniza*, so these were known as the Cairo *Geniza* fragments.

Further inspection showed that what we had was not one, or even ten, but hundreds of optional prayer texts that had once been used, particularly in ancient Palestine, but that had fallen into disuse as time went on. The final crushing blow to these prayers was probably dealt by the Crusaders who established a Kingdom of Jerusalem which lasted from 1099 until 1187 and continued fighting the Moslems for several centuries off and on. Jews scattered from cities in which they had lived for generations, and instead of continuing their ancient Palestinian prayer practices, they slowly joined the ranks of the majority in their newly found homes, who prayed according to Babylonian practice. We saw above (p. 56) how the Babylonian rabbi, Amram, sent an order of prayer to Spain, in an attempt to inculcate Spanish Jewry with the Babylonian service. In the long run, he was successful. Palestinian prayers survived only as fragments hidden in an attic.

How exciting it was to rediscover this medieval witness to our people's creativity, especially since that creativity was expressed in our homeland, *Eretz Yisrael!* Just as we have reclaimed the Land itself as our ancient heritage, we now wish to reclaim the spiritual culture of that land's ancient inhabitants. So we have included some of this old Palestinian poetry in our *Machzor*. Especially because we are Reform Jews, are we able to do this, since the same openness that allows us to omit the blessing, " . . . who has not made me a woman," (see above, pp. 64–66) permits us also to include material that would not now be acceptable to traditional prayerbooks.

The passage beginning "You raised up a vine . . . " (p. 89) is a *Geniza* fragment. You are praying words that have not been spoken in worship for almost 1000 years!

The two passages, at the bottom of p. 89 ("Blessed is . . . ") and at the top of p. 91 ("Eternal our God . . . "), are two more Torah blessings that are usually said in this place. In our book, they bracket a quotation from the Mishna, which equates Torah with all the other *mitzvot* taken together, and not just any *mitzvot*, but specifically those that have no limitation to them. Mathematicians speak of different infinities, some of them greater than others. In a sense, that is what we have here, virtues which demand infinite attention, *mitzvot* of which one never does enough. "But the study of Torah is equal to them all."

Here too, we have modified the original Mishna, which appears in traditional prayerbooks with various sacrifices included on the list of desirable things for which no limit is set down. We saw above (p. 9) that Reform Judaism denied the continuing validity of animal or grain sacrifice, so we omit those items in our list.

We have now completed *Birchot Hashachar*, the Morning Blessings section which was intended originally for home recitation, but which now forms the first half of the material to be said before the major rubric of the *"Shema."* We turn now to the second half of what we have called Preparatory Prayers, the *Pesukei Dezimra*, or the Poems of Praise.

Poems of Praise (Pesukei Dezimra) (pp. 91–98)

Overview

At the very beginning of the evening service we saw how important it is to prepare oneself for prayer. The section we now arrive at is the preparation rubric *par excellence*. As we saw, it has become the second half of a longer unit, the first half being the Morning Blessings (*Birchot Hashachar*), which have been moved from home to synagogue and which we have just surveyed.

As early as the second century, we find one rabbi saying, "May I be among those who say a daily *Hallel!*" The word he uses, *Hallel*, implies a song or a series of songs (generally, psalms) of praise. It is, in a sense, a generic Hebrew term for such praise of God as can be fulfilled by the selection of any combination of psalms one wishes.

There were many versions of *Hallel* in use then, and some have survived to this day. The most famous is the Egyptian *Hallel*, Psalms 113–118. It receives its name from the beginning of Psalm 114, "When Israel went forth out of Egypt . . . ," and is best known as the *Hallel* we say at the Passover *Seder*. A second *Hallel* is the Great *Hallel*, Psalm 136, which speaks of God's mercy by listing 26 compassionate divine attributes, followed in each case by the conclusion, "For God's mercy is everlasting." The most common *Hallel*, however, is the one to which we now come: the Daily *Hallel*, a series of songs and psalms intended to declare God's praise each morning. From a psychological perspective, it serves, as we said above, as a preparation for prayer, so that after it, we may begin the first major rubric, the *"Shema"* and its blessings.

Though the idea of saying a Daily *Hallel* goes back to the second century, the choice of a single fixed set of psalms to express it is a much later development. The *Geniza* fragments show us the widely diverse customs that were once extant in this commun y or that. Some people said as many as 30 psalms each morning. Others said no complete psalms at all, but only snippets from parts of several psalms—a verse here, and a verse there. In fact, the literal translation of the Hebrew title for this rubric, *Pesukei Dezimra*, is *"Verses* of Song."

By the ninth century at least, the Babylonian custom was to read the end of the biblical book of Psalms as the Daily *Hallel*. That meant that people ended at the last psalm, Psalm 150. The Talmud had professed a particular fondness for Psalm 145, going so far as to declare that the happiness of a share in the World-to-Come awaited anyone who said that psalm three times each day. So the normal Daily *Hallel* became Psalms 145–150. The psalms are biblical, of course, and so, as with biblical readings generally (e.g., the *"Shema,"* the Torah reading, etc.), they were bracketed by blessings relevant to the act of reciting them. The introductory blessing (p. 91) is *"Baruch she-amar,"* which we have called "For Life."

The concluding blessing (pp. 95–98) receives its name from the function of the readings it follows. The psalms have always been intended for singing. So this blessing which follows them is called *Birkat Hashir*, meaning "The Blessing of Song." Just as there were many different sets of psalms used in early times, so there was more than one *Birkat Hashir*. The one we have is cited in the Talmud by its first few words, *"Nishmat kol chai,"* "The breath of every living soul." We have called it "Our Immeasurable Debt to God."

For Life (p. 91)

Jewish thought has always found fascinating the creative potential of speech. Our Torah begins with God literally "speaking" the world into existence, as God says, "Let there be light," "Let the waters swarm with creatures," "Let us make humanity in our image," and so forth. By the fourth century or so (the exact date is uncertain), an anonymously composed book called *Sefer Yetsira*, "The Book of Creation," presented a more complex, even mystical, account of creation, according to which the letters of the Hebrew alphabet come together in various permutations and combinations to create the entire universe. Later still, Kabbalistic mystics posited a creative process that starts with pure thought, then progresses to thought with an object in mind, and finally to speech, out of which actual physical reality is born.

Thus, the benediction we use to introduce the Poems of Praise begins, "Praised be the One who spoke, and the world came to be."

Psalms (pp. 92–95)

The traditional listing of psalms in this rubric is wide ranging. To Psalms 145–150 (see pp. 69–70 above) many other readings have been appended through the ages. We have some psalms intended for daily recitation, and others reserved specifically for Rosh Hashana. Other poetic material post-dates the Bible, but was considered sufficiently attractive by later authorities to warrant inclusion in the list of poems that constitute our *Pesukei Dezimra.*

From all this traditional material, we have chosen to include three psalms as our Poems of Praise.

The first is a series of selections from Psalm 19, which is found not only here, but elsewhere in the liturgy also. Since its central verses speak of Torah, they are included in the liturgy surrounding the reading of the Torah (pp. 154–155). The last verse, "May the words of my mouth . . . ," is immediately recognizable as the familiar conclusion to the silent meditation following the *Tefila* (p. 118, for example). Here, we concentrate on the psalm's opening verses, which continue the theme of the introductory benediction: "Praised be the One who spoke, and the world came to be."

Throughout the length and breadth of Europe, medieval commentators were almost universal in their interpretation of this psalm as attesting to the fact that the universe itself is the best witness to the divine. Abraham ibn Ezra (1089–1164), himself a Spanish scientist who wrote three known works on astronomy, cautioned that those who do not appreciate astronomy will not even understand the psalm. Maimonides (1135–1204), living in Egypt, but grounded in Aristotelian thought from his youth which was spent in Spain, maintained that there is an actual intellect associated with heavenly bodies, such that in their own way, they praise God, just as the first verse tells us: "The heavens declare the glory of God." Rashi (1040–1105), on the other hand, living in Northern France, was unshackled by the need his southern, Spanish, coreligionists felt to find scientific compatibility between the biblical metaphor and medieval philosophy, with the result that he arrived at an interpretation more congruent with modern appreciation. How can "the heavens declare the glory of God" (verse 1), when at the same time "there is no speech, there are no words, no voice is heard" (verse 4)? Rashi answers:

> They do not speak to people, but since their light shines forth for creatures throughout the world, people are moved to speak of the glory of God. . . . "The word pours out day after day" [verse 2] in that every day, the work of creation is renewed. The sun sets each evening, and rises again in the morning, so that people utter God's praise.

RaDaK, that is, David Kimchi (c. 1130–c. 1235) who lived in Provence, midway between northern and southern Europe, summarized the psalm's

71

intent by commenting on the last line of our page: "Their call goes through all the earth, and their words to the end of the universe." This means, he explained, that the performance of the celestial spheres speaks more eloquently of God's reality than all the speech that humans might muster.

Psalm 33, which follows next, continues the theme: "The heavens were made by the word of the Lord. . . . For God spoke, and it was" (p. 94). This psalm goes beyond Psalm 19, in that it deals with creation of human beings, not just the heavenly bodies. Meir Loeb ben Yehiel Michael, better known as MaLBIM (1809–1879) was the chief rabbi of Roumania from 1858 to 1864. He saw the message of the psalm moving from the laws of nature, which are permanent, to the acts of human beings, which are variable. God's greatness lies precisely in the combination of these two opposites, a universe of law and order which we may discover and use, and human freedom to calculate the ends to which nature's laws should be applied.

Moved by the grandeur of the universe (Psalm 19) and our own role within it (Psalm 33), we conclude our Poems of Praise with the traditional final psalm of the Psalter, Psalm 150. Throughout this conclusion, we emphasize the musical abandon that characterizes uninhibited praise. The musical instruments mentioned here were once a part of the Temple cult.

Musical Instruments in Worship

One of Reform's earliest struggles, and, in retrospect, one of its greatest victories, was the reintroduction of musical instrumentation into worship after Orthodoxy had removed it. Because music is critical to our worship, we should pause for a moment to consider in a little more detail the history of using instruments in prayer.

The musical instruments in the Second Temple amounted to a small orchestra, with the equivalent of woodwinds, strings, percussion, and brass. In addition, the Levites constituted a choir. So, Temple music was a combination of voice and instrumentation.

Certainly the earliest synagogues, too, knew music, particularly chant. A great number of the early prayers were sung. We have already discussed the rise of the cantor as a specially trained musician in charge of composing music for the service (see pp. 14–15 above) and then of leading the congregation in prayer. But as far as we know, synagogue worship contained no instrumental accompaniment. Eric Werner has argued that the real reasons for early Rabbinic opposition to musical instruments in worship went beyond their stated rationale, since the Church Fathers of the time demonstrated a similar hostility to instrumentation. But whatever the Rabbis' underlying reasons, it is their stated explanation that lasted—

finding expression, first, in the Talmud and later, in the law codes of the Middle Ages.

In general, the rabbis from the Talmudic period until the Middle Ages advanced several arguments of which two deserve mention here. First, fixing an instrument is among the Sabbath prohibitions, and playing one might lead a person to adjust or fix it, should it break. Second, since we are in mourning for the Temple, music is technically forbidden at all times, unless that music will enhance a *mitzva*, such as a wedding. Though prayer is a *mitzva*, the exception permitting vocal music was not extended to instrumentation. To these two arguments modern Orthodoxy added a third. The instrument most used by early Reform Jews is the organ, which Orthodox opponents characterized as a specifically Christian instrument, in that it was featured also in churches; the Jewish use of the same instrument would, they maintained, be a clear violation of the ban on willfully copying non-Jewish customs.

The absolute ban on music was rarely followed, however. Rabbi Leon of Modena (1571–1648), himself somewhat of a musician and a friend of the Jewish composer Solomon Rossi, wrote at length justifying music in services and urging the general raising of musical sophistication among the laity so that they might better appreciate worship's inherent beauty. But Modena's attitude was not accepted as authoritative. It reflected the culture of Renaissance Italy, where Modena lived, but not the context of the less enlightened European society, where rabbinic codifiers determined which opinions should be accepted as normative Jewish law and which should not.

The debate picked up in earnest as soon as Israel Jacobson, a lay reformer, installed an organ in his synagogue in Seesen, Germany, and publicly displayed his innovation in a formal dedication service on July 17, 1810. Responsa on both sides of the subject followed for many years to come. Orthodox opponents (including Moses Sofer—see above, pp. 64–65) invoked the three arguments listed above. Reform respondents denied that the general ban in theory had ever been observed in practice. They pointed to the great synagogue in Prague, which already had an organ; argued that worship is indeed a *mitzva* which should be enhanced by instrumental music; and denied that the organ *per se* was so inherently Christian that its use would constitute a violation of the law against copying non-Jewish practices.

When synagogues were built in the United States, one of the first matters of concern was the installation of an organ. The Hebrew Union College sanctuary in Jerusalem customarily uses harpsichord and flute accompaniment. Even the guitar is heard these days, as Americans experiment with their own musical idiom.

Our prayerbooks are only settings of lyrics that require beautiful melodies, many of which are still unwritten. We would do well to remember the final psalm of our *Pesukei Dezimra*, with which we launched this discussion. In the Temple of old, people were charged:

> Praise God with *shofar* blast;
> Praise God with harp and lute.
> Praise God with drum and dance;
> Praise God with strings and pipe.
> Praise God with cymbals sounding;
> Praise God with cymbals sounding. . . .

We Reform Jews say that our synagogues have replaced that Temple. Should our praise of God not be equally beautiful?

Our Immeasurable Debt to God (pp. 95–98)

This is the final *Birkat Hashir*, or Blessing of Song, concluding the Poems of Praise section. Immediately following it, we shall say a Reader's *Kaddish* to mark off the end of this rubric and then summon the congregation formally to communal prayer with the *"Barechu."* Inasmuch as, from a traditional point of view, the congregation does not exist in a formal sense until that point, it is customary for the cantor not to lead the prayers yet. But the cantor does anticipate the *"Barechu"* slightly, by taking his or her position on the pulpit at the word *"hamelech"* ("O KING") in the middle of p. 97. This word was chosen by tradition as the cantor's cue because one of Rosh Hashana's primary themes is God's sovereignty (see above pp. 20–21, and below, pp. 96–104).

The "Shema" and Its Blessings (pp. 99–104)

A full discussion of this major rubric can be found on pp. 29–40.

Here in Service I, we supply creative English texts, which, however, deal with the traditional threefold theme of Creation, Revelation, and Redemption.

The Tefila (pp. 104–117)

The *Tefila* is discussed above, pp. 18–23.

The *"Uvechen"* additions and the special High Holy Day insertions (see above, pp. 20–22) recur. In this *Tefila*, we provide translations of the traditional Hebrew. We include also two rubrics that were not covered in our previous discussion, but deserve description here: the *"Unetaneh Tokef"* (pp. 106–110) and the Priestly Benediction (p. 116–117).

"Unetaneh Tokef" (Meditation) (pp. 106–110)

No prayer focuses on the awesome nature of these Days of Awe more intensely than the *"Unetaneh Tokef."* It paints a magnificent metaphor of God the Judge, who examines the record of our deeds in the Book of Life, and makes us pass in inspection, one by one, just like sheep in a flock who walk single file under the shepherd's staff (p. 108). Even the angels are awestruck by the event (p. 107). The prayer continues with a litany of alternative fates (p. 108), and then, at last, the moral implicit in the Day of Judgment is reached. Judaism is not fatalistic. Whatever our record in the Book of Life, we take heart in the fact that "Repentance, prayer and charity temper judgment's severe decree" (p. 109). We emerge from the prayer appropriately imbued with humility, for we must confront our mortality. Our origin is dust, and dust is our end. Only God is eternal.

Small wonder this majestic prayer which so truly captures the serious mood of Rosh Hashana, Yom Kippur, and the Days of Repentance between them struck a familiar chord in the hearts of those who put together our liturgy, so that the *"Unetaneh Tokef"* was included prominently within the prayers of Rosh Hashana and Yom Kippur. Earlier Reform Jews were sometimes uncomfortable with the explicit anthropomorphic imagery of a zealous judging God, the inclusion of angels (in whom modern people do not generally believe), and the precise list of fateful ends awaiting sinners who fail to repent. The prayer was usually edited more than our version here. But even the editors of the old *Union Prayer Book* recognized that the *"Unetaneh Tokef"* is an essential liturgical ingredient for the High Holy Days, and included as much of it as their conscience permitted, especially the conclusion demanding penitence, prayer, and charity.

The *"Unetaneh Tokef"* is outstanding as a magnificent piece of poetry. But since the late Middle Ages, its poetic appeal has been secondary to a folk tale describing the *Unetaneh Tokef*'s composition. Like most folk tales, there are many versions, but they are all much the same, and the following is taken from one of them.

The tale describes a certain Rabbi Amnon who lived in Mayence around the end of the 11th century. Upon being challenged to convert to Christianity, he put off his interlocutor with the promise that he would later appear at court to make known his decision. Overcome with remorse for even having suggested that he might respond affirmatively, he failed to appear at the appointed time, and, as a consequence, was tortured to death by the angry authorities. With his last breath, he is said to have uttered our *"Unetaneh Tokef"*, a prayer which, he said, had been faithfully passed on to him from beyond the grave by an even earlier Ashkenazic rabbi-poet, who had died years before.

Though the details of this story are probably false, there is a great deal of truth to the context in which it is placed. The 11th century saw a reawakening of Christian (and Jewish) piety throughout Europe, its most obvious manifestation being the first Crusade of 1096. The Crusader armies from across Europe came together at a rendezvous in the Rhineland area of Northern Germany. There followed a tremendous massacre of Jews, particularly in two cities where Jewish settlements had existed for centuries, the Jews there having pioneered in medieval commerce and in the development of post-Talmudic Jewish culture. One of those cities was Mayence. (See also p. 85 below.)

Thus the idea of a rabbi in Mayence who was cruelly persecuted is not foreign to the general character of the late 11th century. But this particular story is documented in none of the chronicles of the time, and, in fact, the name of Rabbi Amnon is not even known to us from any other source. He and his fate seem to be pious fictions of folk imagination.

If the *"Unetaneh Tokef"* did not arise out of persecutions in 11th-century Germany, when did it come into being? The answer is that we do not know. But our prayer has many similarities to a Christian prayer which dates from an age when the center of Western culture was still in Constantinople, the capital of the Eastern Church. It is known as the Byzantine period.

The Byzantine period stretches from the foundation of Constantinople under the emperor Constantine, in the fourth century, until the invasion of that city by Crusaders in 1204, nearly nine hundred years later. It is exceptionally significant for Jewish history. To begin with, it was under Byzantine monarchs that the Roman empire was Christianized. Contrary to popular belief, this was accomplished not out of Rome, so much as Constantinople. It was nestled safely in geographic protective custody, so that the barbarians who destroyed the Roman empire actually destroyed only its western half, leaving the eastern half intact. The cultural magnificence of the empire continued in the form of Eastern Byzantium for centuries.

That greatness is evident in massive church construction and extravagant religious literature, penned by poets who created mosaics with words just as the builders were doing with stone. With artistic precision, they combined judiciously selected words and phrases from the entire gamut of traditional religious vocabulary into a glittering poetic mosaic intended for liturgical use. The earliest such poets lived in the fourth and fifth centuries, the most famous (in the Christian world) being a man known as Romanus, who bequeathed to posterity a poem strikingly similar to the *"Unetaneh Tokef"*!

Romanus and the other Christian poets were emulated by a classical school of synagogue poets (called *paytanim*), who applied the aesthetic principles of their time to Jewish liturgy. Their compositions (*piyutim*; sing. *piyut*) are now found throughout our *Machzor.* Like the early morning "*Shema*" (see above, p. 66), *piyutim* were often explained by medieval writers as a Jewish response to persecution. It was believed that unfriendly governments had banned our standard prayers, including the Talmudic material studied daily, so that Jews incorporated the suppressed teachings into complex poetic form where they would go unnoticed. It is more likely, however, that the *piyutim* represent an ongoing, spontaneous, cultural expression by Jews intent throughout the centuries on adding beauty to their prayers. Though Byzantine in origin, the writing of *piyutim* continued sporadically throughout the Middle Ages, especially in the Land of Israel, Italy, Germany, and Spain. Though we do have elegies and lamentations prompted by disasters in Jewish history, these *piyutim* usually reflect eras of peace and prosperity in which poets were free to experiment with the expression of Jewish ideas in novel cultural forms dictated by the dominant aesthetic preferences of one society after another: Christian Byzantium, Moslem Spain, and so on.

Romanus's original creation appears later in a more complex form, whence it entered Christian liturgy; and our "*Unetaneh Tokef*" probably has more in common with the later form of its Christian parallel than it does with the earlier prototype. But whether our prayer comes from the fifth century or from the seventh or eighth is not as important as recognizing the milieu common to both periods. In either case we deal with a Christian world engaged in beautifying every aspect of its spiritual life, a golden age of religion for the Eastern Church, and an equally striking parallel age of Jewish spirituality.

The "*Unetaneh Tokef*" speaks to Jews of every age who gather on the Days of Awe to stand before God, rendering account of who we are and what we have become. In that context, a Hasidic tale reminds us that we are not expected to be anyone other than who we are. We hear that on his deathbed, Rabbi Zusya taught, "In the coming world they will not ask me, 'Why were you not Moses?' but 'Why were you not Zusya?' "

S. Y. Agnon, the late Nobel Prize winning writer, recalled a tale from the same Hasidic milieu, which expands Zusya's teaching.

A king one day grew angry at his son and banished him from the palace. For a while, the prince lived just outside the palace walls waiting to be recalled to his father's presence, but as time wore on he began to despair, and, needing to support himself, he drifted off in search of work. At first, the population treated him in a manner befitting his royal stature; but even that benefit soon failed him, as his fine clothes grew torn and

77

tattered, and people could no longer recognize who he was. When the prince found that his claim to royalty met more and more with skeptical taunts, he stopped reminding people of the honor due him, and eventually, he himself forgot the story of his origins and became a humble shepherd on the top of a mountain far away from the city he had once inhabited.

One day, several years later, the king decided to travel beyond the confines of his palace to view his many subjects. To entice people into the cities where he would visit, he sent a messenger ahead of him announcing that His Majesty might reward loyal subjects by granting their petitions.

The king passed through one town after another, greeting throngs of people who had massed to catch a view of their ruler, and everywhere he went, he found scraps of paper bearing petitions being thrust at him. Most of them he never even read, but he managed at least to glance at a few, including one that arrested his attention instantly. He recognized the handwriting at once. It had been written by his long lost son!

Inquiries quickly revealed that the erstwhile prince was a poor shepherd living only three miles from the city in which the king now found himself. With his heart beating in anticipation, the king quickly changed direction and climbed the mountain to see what had happened to the boy. As he traveled the tortuous route up the mountainside, he recognized how much he regretted his hasty action many years before. If only the boy had been able to grow up in the castle at his father's side! By now he would be grown to manhood. What had become of him?

His reveries were interrupted when his carriage stopped abruptly. He looked out the window, and there, indeed, was his son, still recognizable to a father who memorizes the fine features of his child. But the son no longer remembered his father; he had forgotten even that he had a father somewhere, let alone who that father was. The king lost no time in embracing the young man, and without explaining who he was, asked, "What can I do for you? Just ask, and it shall be yours." The shepherd paused to consider what he had written on the paper, and replied: "All I need is a shelter to protect me from the sun that beats down on this mountain during the day. Beyond that, what could I possibly want?"

Of course the king granted the request. But he knew it was too late to restore the son to his life as a prince among people. He cancelled the rest of his journey and returned to the palace at once. On the way back, he was heard exclaiming through his tears, "My son, my son, he has forgotten who he is!"

The Days of Awe call us to remember who we are; never to forget that, created in God's image, we may aspire to heights undreamed of.

The Priestly Benediction (Peace) (pp. 116–117)

The prayer for peace that normally concludes every *Tefila* is extended in the Morning Service beyond what we say for the service of the night before. A quick glance indicates that the prayer in question is made of two parts, the first running from the middle of page 116 to the lengthy Hebrew paragraph in the center of page 117; and the second constituting that Hebrew paragraph along with its English parallel that follows.

The second part is obviously a blessing, a perfect example of the liturgical literary genre that we described above, complete with a concluding *chatima* (see above, p. 17) summarizing the benediction: "Blessed is the Lord, the Source of peace."

The first half, however, is quite different. Except for the introductory line (p. 116), "Our God and God of all generations, bless us with the threefold benediction of the Torah," the prayer is addressed not to God at all, but to the congregation. The rest of this prayer is a threefold wish for God indeed to bless us; each wish is followed by a congregational response, "Be this God's will!"

This is probably the single benediction offered most often in Judaism, possibly even in the Western world. The late Nelson Glueck, then the president of the Hebrew Union College, offered it at the presidential inauguration of John F. Kennedy. It is known as *Birkat Kohanim*, or the Priestly Benediction.

The Priestly Benediction has a very long history, going back to the Bible (Numbers 6:24–26), where God expressly tells Aaron and his progeny that, as the priests of the Israelites, they are to bless Israel by invoking God's name in this threefold fashion. In the Second Temple, the priests did so, as part of the daily offering known as the *Tamid* (meaning "regular," that is, the regular offering). From the Temple ritual the blessing was transferred to the nascent synagogue service, where it was embedded in that particular portion of the prayers that most closely resembled the Temple *Tamid* offering—the *Tefila* (see also pp. 9, 14 above).

In other words, as the Rabbis understood the *Tefila*, it was a substitute for the Temple cult. In the Temple, people offered actual animals and grain; in the synagogue, they presented "the offering of the heart." As the Talmud puts it (quoting Deuteronomy 11:13): " 'Love the Lord your God, and serve God with all your heart.' What is the service of the heart? One must answer, [the] *Tefila*."

So the *Tefila* became the prayer *par excellence*, because it represented the defunct *Tamid* sacrifice. Many consequences followed from this identification, including the decision to place the Priestly Benediction here in the Morning Service *Tefila*. It was not said in the Evening Service, however, because a *Tamid* had never been part of the evening Temple offering, and, in fact, for many centuries, the evening *Tefila* prayer was treated by many as optional, as there had never been an evening *Tamid* on which it could be based.

The biblical instructions to invoke the Priestly Benediction had been directed at priests, and for centuries, in Palestinian synagogues, only priestly readers, actual descendents of the biblical priests who had received the commandment to bless the people, said these words. In Babylonia, the commandment was generalized to any reader, and we follow Babylonian precedent (see above, pp. 56 and 67–68).

Jewish worship knows of two distinct rituals in which the priests bless the people. The most colorful one is not generally practiced in Reform synagogues, inasmuch as one of our principles has been the abolition of class distinctions based on presumed priestly heritage. We stopped the traditional custom of calling priests (*Kohanim*) to the Torah first, for example. But in non-Reform synagogues, people with names such as Cohen, Kahn, or even Katz (which stands for the initials of the two Hebrew words *Kohen Tsedek*, "priest of righteousness") maintain the historical fiction of tracing their descent back to Aaron, and during festival services they ascend the pulpit to engage in the following ceremony.

While the assembled congregation stands before them, the priests cover their faces with a *talit* and extend their arms over the congregation. The Priestly Benediction is called out word by word. In an undertone, the congregation responds to each and every word by reciting a biblical verse that has that particular word in it. This whole ceremony is known by its Yiddish name, *Duchenen*, derived from the Hebrew word *duchan*, the name for the platform before which the priests of old would stand as they said the blessing.

The practice of *Duchenen* is still a daily phenomenon in Israel. But in the Diaspora, it was long ago limited to holidays. On other days, including Shabbat, it was replaced with another simpler ritual still in use in synagogue services. The *Tefila* is first said silently by the congregation and then repeated aloud by the reader. The Priestly Benediction is not said at all during the silent recitation, but the reader includes it in the *Tefila's* public repetition, by merging the Bible's words of blessing into the *Tefila's* final prayer for peace. This ancient benediction is on the same theme, after all—peace.

Interestingly enough, despite Reform Judaism's denial of class distinctions based on priestly lineage, its ritual has had a fondness for the Priestly Benediction. Since it is biblical, it seemed particularly authentic to early Reformers. Its theme of peace was particularly pleasing. It provided a moving conclusion to the high formality that typified classical

Reform worship.

David Einhorn, who composed the forerunner of the *Union Prayer Book* in 1858 (see *Gates of Understanding*, Volume I, pp. 23–26) was particularly fond of the blessing, because of its theological consequences. We have seen that Reform Jews were taught to appreciate the potential inherent in living as a Jew outside of Israel, in that Diaspora Jews can impart the universal doctrine of ethical monotheism to every nation on earth. This they took to be the religious "Mission of Israel" (see above, pp. 39–40 and 42–43). Einhorn likened that mission to the purely cultic activity that had once characterized an earlier era in Jewish worship. Judaism had progressed beyond that cultic stage and replaced sacrifice of animals with the sacrifice of the human spirit implicit in living lives devoted to God and God's truth. In this sense, prerogatives once limited to those who actually sacrificed the animals—the priestly class—could be viewed now as a spiritual legacy to all Jews, who are called to carry out the "Mission of Israel" by becoming a "light to the nations." This was a bold assertion, which Einhorn drummed home time and again in his prayers. He even called his prayerbook *Olat Tamid* (i.e., The Perpetual Offering), the full name for the *Tamid* offering which we have had occasion to mention as the theoretical paradigm for the *Tefila* (see pp. 14–15 and 79 above). Featured in that book was the Priestly Benediction with instructions that each word be said separately by the reader (as in the ceremony of *Duchenen*) and then repeated by choir and congregation.

This highly dramatic effect was modified in later prayerbooks. In 1896, Einhorn's son-in-law, Emil G. Hirsch, himself a rabbi in Chicago, translated *Olat Tamid* from German into English, hoping to maintain Einhorn's ritual and vision. But the grand metaphor of Israel as a priestly people, committed to perpetual self-sacrifice in pursuit of universal truth and justice, proved too difficult for people to retain. The 1894 *Union Prayer Book* still included the Priestly Benediction, but limited the congregational role to saying *"Amen"* after each of the blessing's three parts. Our *Gates of Repentance* follows the *Union Prayer Book*, but exchanges a simple *"Amen"* with "Be this God's will," the latter phrase being an exact, and very beautifully worded, translation of the traditional response.

Congregations are asked to decide how much drama they wish in this part of the service. Many have decided to recapture the vision of David Einhorn, demonstrating their commitment to Israel's Mission by reasserting the centrality of this Priestly Benediction. Though there are no instructions to stand, these congregations rise anyway, while the cantor chants the age-old priestly prayer for peace, to which the entire sanctuary filled with people reverberates with the sincere wish, "Be this God's will!"

Tradition, incidentally, saw more than just the hope for peace in the

Priestly Blessing. Noticing that God was asked to bless, keep, and be gracious to us, the earliest Midrash to the Book of Numbers (*Sifrei*) attached each separate verb in the biblical benediction to a different act of divine compassion.

> "May God bless you" [means] with physical possessions. Rabbi Nathan said, "Bless you" stands for physical possessions; "Keep you" stands for protecting our bodies from harm. Rabbi Isaac said, "Keep you" means keep you from the evil inclination within you. Other interpretations include: "Keep you"—that is, keep you from the domination of other people. . . . "Keep you"—that is, God will remain [keep] faithful to the covenant made with your forebears. . . . "Keep you"—that is, God will preserve [keep] the messianic end of days for you. . . . "Keep you"—that is, God will keep your soul when you die. . . . "Keep you"—that is, God will keep you in the world to come.

There is deliberate order to the successive interpretations. Our citation was put together with great literary care. We begin with the most obvious and mundane possibility: God keeps our things from being stolen or broken. But by the end we have moved to ultimate concerns of the covenant: life after death, the messianic age, and the World-to-Come.

Meditation (p. 118)

The *Tefila* now concludes with the usual silent prayer, and a suggested meditation that might form part of it. This is a good place, then, to say a word about silent prayer in our liturgy.

Many Jews, particularly those with traditional backgrounds, admit to feeling somewhat uncomfortable with the silence during the private meditation part of the service. Even though they are familiar with the *Tefila* being said silently in the synagogues of their youth, that experience is hardly comparable to the all-encompassing silence of a sanctuary filled with worshipers lost in their own thoughts. The so-called silent *Tefila* is really not silent at all, but said in an undertone by traditional worshipers who hurry through the words of this lengthy prayer, each person going at a different speed. The solemn austerity of classical Reform worship required the elimination of this seemingly undecorous practice. We saw above that the Reformers were preceded by none other than Maimonides, who tried to do the same thing for the same reason (see p. 59 above).

Thus, Reform services represented a certain degree of innovation when their prayerbooks called for actual silent prayer after the *Tefila*. But Reform Jews were not the first to do so. They were returning to a tradition that had once formed the backbone of our prayers, but had been lost for close to 800 years.

When the Rabbis codified the rubrics of the service, they ensured *kavana* (as we saw—see above, pp. 11–12) by allowing readers to phrase themes differently on any given occasion. They also gave worshipers the right to their own silent prayer, spoken directly from the heart. At first, these silent prayers were said after the last benediction of the *"Shema"* and its blessings. At the end of the first century, however, when the new rubric of the *Tefila* was tacked on to the *"Shema,"* in order to make sure that people would attend carefully to it—the *Tefila* was a replacement for the *Tamid*, after all (see above pp. 14–15 and 79)—personal prayer was banned in its old place and postponed to the end of the *Tefila*.

Until the end of the Talmudic period, people felt free to offer, at this point, their own personal words to God. It was common to say a daily confession, to ask for special petitions, or to utter a spiritually uplifting thought. When the Talmud was codified, though, many "favorite" silent prayers of outstanding rabbis were recorded in it, and, because of the veneration with which later generations held these rabbis, people began saying the rabbis' prayers just as the Talmud had copied them, rather than composing their own words of prayer. The first prayerbook, that of Amram, in the ninth century (see above, pp. 56 and 67–68) gives people the right here to say either their own prayer or a specific selection from the Talmud, i.e., a private prayer of a rabbi named Mar, son of Rabina, who lived in the fourth or fifth century. Apparently, of all the rabbis' private prayers cited in the Talmud, Mar's had somehow emerged as the most popular, and 350 years later, almost everyone simply read Mar's prayer. In our time, every traditional *Siddur* includes it, so that, as we saw, in traditional services, no personal, private, silent prayer is said at all.

Our preference is to return to the original practice of asking each worshiper to engage in his or her own private prayer. But we include also meditations of great spiritual geniuses whose words might be said in conjunction with, or even in place of, one's own thoughts. The prayer ascribed to Mar appears on page 38, but each instance of the *Tefila* is printed with a different concluding meditation, so that worshipers have the chance to consider a whole gamut of thoughts relevant to the Days of Awe.

The meditation here is of interest because of its inherent message, but also because it is introduced by part of a poem composed by a non-Jew. Reform Judaism has always been open to truths derived from other than purely Jewish sources, so our inclusion of an introductory line from this poem should not surprise anyone. The poet from whose work it is taken is a Unitarian, Jacob Trapp, and his poem was intended for worship. (For further discussion of non-Jewish worship material, especially as it is reflected in hymns and music, see *Gates of Understanding*, Volume I, pp. 27-30.)

With the final meditation after the *Tefila* we have completed our commentary on the second of the two major rubrics that compose our worship. On the Shabbat (both morning and afternoon), on holidays, and on Monday and Thursday mornings, we also read the Torah, a practice said to go back to Ezra (fifth century B.C.E.). Readings from the prophets (or, in Reform practice, other scriptural writings also—see *Gates of Understanding* Volume I, pp. 272-284) known as *Haftarot* (plural of *Haftara*) are recited on Shabbat and holidays. A liturgy accompanies removing and replacing the Torah in the Ark, so it is the Order of Prayers for Reading the Torah, a new rubric, to which we now turn our attention.

Order of Prayers for Reading the Torah
(pp. 120-137 and 154-155)

Overview

Despite the length of this new rubric, we will have relatively little to say about it in the commentary. That is because most of the matters here are dealt with elsewhere in this book. But a few notes of interest deserve attention now.

Unlike the two major rubrics (*"Shema"* and its blessings, and the *Tefila*), there is no inherent logic to the order of the various prayers one finds in the liturgy surrounding the Torah reading. Obvious exceptions to this generalization are the actual Torah and *Haftara* readings, each of which is bracketed by blessings; and there is some rationale for the specific things said as the Torah is actually removed from the Ark or put back in. But beyond that, we find a combination of various prayers that emerged throughout the centuries, eventually finding their way here.

By and large, the prayers added here have in common the fact that they are communally oriented. Jews have always prayed together to fulfill not only the specific *mitzva* of worship, but also the general one of maintaining their Jewish community. The synagogue was not only a House of Prayer (*Beit Tefila*), and a House of Study (*Beit Midrash*), but also, and not least important, a House of Assembly (*Beit Keneset*). One went to the synagogue to hear the news, to find out who was sick, or just to see and to be seen. In the Middle Ages, in some places, people were permitted to interrupt the reading of Torah in order to announce an injustice that they believed was being perpetrated against them by other members of the community. In other words, though most of the prayers added through time have no intrinsic literary or theological relationship to each other, they are all allied in a common cause of strengthening the internal cohesiveness of the Jewish community.

One therefore finds here:

1. liturgy connected with historical events that the communal memory wishes to retain;

2. prayers linking each individual to the community through the latter's recognition of some individuals in need of healing, of others who have donated to the communal welfare, and the like;

3. petitions for the common good for all present, for the whole Jewish community, or even for the country and government on which the world's welfare depends;

4. prayers of announcement: foretelling religious events about to occur during the week ahead (the New Moon or a wedding, for example), recollecting events just concluded (e.g., individuals thank God for having survived illness) or publicly declaring events going on at that very moment in the lives of this family or that (a Bar or Bat Mitzvah, for instance), and, therefore, happening coterminously in the life of the community as a whole;

5. liturgical declarations of allegiance to the values and beliefs for which the community stands, frequently accompanied by the holding aloft of the Torah, the clearest visible symbol of those values.

Rather than go in order through the next several pages of the *Machzor*, let us consider each of the categories listed above, identifying examples of each.

1. *Liturgy connected with historical events.* Our Reform *Machzor* has transferred the best example of this type of prayer to another rubric, but for illustrative purposes we discuss it here.

In 1096, the armies of the first Crusade set off from France, and a year later stopped in the Rhineland to await the coming of others from elsewhere in Europe. Soldiers anxious for battle fell on the old, established Jewish communities of Mayence and Speyer, decimating their ranks (see also above, pp. 75–76). When the survivors recovered, they remembered their tragedy through a bitter lament recollecting those who had fallen, and wishing swift vengeance upon the enemy at the hand of God. This prayer, *"Av Harachamim"* ("Merciful God"), was said on Shabbat and holidays at that point in the service when the community gathered liturgically around its central symbol, the Torah. Though it is still recited there in traditional services, we have transferred it to a more fitting place (p. 435), as a part of a novel service in our *Machzor* called "From Creation to Redemption" and dedicated toward capturing the total flow of Jewish history (see pp. 138–144 below, for discussion). We have introduced the

"*Av Harachamim*" there with a reading drawn from eyewitness chronicles of the massacre it recalls.

2. *Prayers linking the individual to the community.* These are usually recited at the time a person receives an *aliya*. Originally, the person saying the blessings was expected also to read the Torah. But by early in the Middle Ages, Torah reading had become an art, the mastery of which could not be universally anticipated, so the reading was entrusted to a specially delegated communal reader. Congregants generally were still honored with invitations to go up to the Torah (called an *aliya*, or "going up"), but their role was now limited to a recitation of the Torah blessings. After their *aliya*, just as the individuals were about to go back to their seats, there developed the practice of saying a prayer for them or for any members of their family who happened to be in distress. This prayer, called "*Mi Sheberach*," asks God who blessed our ancestors to bless also the person before us, the members of his or her family who are sick, and so on. In Reform services today, this "*Mi Sheberach*" need not be linked to the receiving of an *aliya*. Rather, the rabbi or cantor announces to the congregation that the prayer is to be said for such and such a person, and the congregation listens intently to the words in English, or perhaps to the chant of the traditional Hebrew text.

The words to this prayer are not in our prayerbook, because the congregation as a whole never says them. But rabbis and cantors have texts with them and are ready to insert the "*Mi Sheberach*" into the service, when informed of appropriate occasions in the lives of their congregants.

3. *Petitions for the common good.* These are found on pages 152–153. The prayer for the congregation is based on a medieval composition that functioned as a communal "*Mi Sheberach*." The prayer for the government is new, but follows a principle of praying for the welfare of the government, which Jews set down in the first two centuries C.E. Liturgically, Jews have included such a prayer for the rulers of their countries at least since the 14th century in Spain. The prayer for the State of Israel is unique to our time, as we pause here to beseech God to maintain the third Jewish Commonwealth.

4. *Prayers of announcement.* Like the "*Mi Sheberach*," personal announcements are connected with receiving an *aliya* and are not included in our prayerbook for public recitation. But the liturgy has special statements to be made by parents of a Bar or Bat Mitzvah, or by someone recovering from illness or escaping disaster. Rabbis and cantors can give congregants the traditional words of announcement for such events, and discuss the relative merit of including them in a service.

Traditionally, the most important public announcement is for a New Moon, which is a minor Holy Day in Judaism. But it is not contained in a High Holy Day prayerbook, for the obvious reason that Rosh Hashana is itself the day of the New Moon, so another New Moon cannot possibly occur during the week following either Rosh Hashana or Yom Kippur. (The announcement is contained, however, in *Gates of Prayer*, p. 453.)

5. *Liturgical declarations of allegiance.* This is the function of the passages recited when the Torah is removed from the Ark or replaced in it. We hold the Torah on high, often walking through the congregation with it, thus displaying our religious "flag," so to speak. On pages 122–123, we announce our intention to follow the tenets of the Torah, we sing the *"Shema"* again (thus noting our primary belief in God's unity and uniqueness), and we proclaim that God gave the Torah to us. On page 154, we put the Torah back, again declaring our faith in God and the magnificence of our Jewish heritage. (Most of the liturgy on page 154 comes from Psalm 19, on which see above, pp. 71–72.)

The last line on page 155 deserves special attention on Rosh Hashana and Yom Kippur: even though it is said at every occasion of replacing the Torah in the Ark, it is emphasized during the Days of Awe. The theme "Help us to return to You, God . . . " is the leitmotif of the High Holy Day season.

In sum, the liturgy surrounding the reading of Torah and *Haftara* promotes bonding. It is a liturgical means of guaranteeing the continuity of a community of Jews who care for each other and who see in each other's existence further evidence of the mission whose fulfilment we take to be our divine task.

Of all the rubrics in our service, this one is probably the least appreciated and the most in need of emphasizing. We ought, once again, to establish a communal focus, to recognize that our very liturgy provides an opportunity for each of us to share the events of our own lives with others in the community, and to discover others present in prayer as distinctive friends and neighbors whose lives touch ours. Perhaps in the context of the High Holy Day solemnity, with the synagogue's massive overflow of congregants, one would be less likely to expect such a personalization of worship. But Shabbat prayer ought to function as it once did, by bringing people together in a warm and caring way around that intrinsically Jewish symbol which has endured through time: the Torah.

"Avinu Malkenu" and the Language of Gender (pp. 120–122)

A full discussion of this favorite prayer is found above, on pages 23–25. But the specific introduction to *"Avinu Malkenu"* which we provide on pages 120–121 of *Gates of Repentance* prompts a discussion of translations favoring masculine language.

Roughly a decade ago, when the Reform Movement began its current liturgical series, authors and editors were just beginning to recognize that their use of language fostered sexual stereotypes. The *Union Prayer Book*, for example, prays "that the day may come when all *men* shall invoke Thy name. . . . [and that] all created in Thy image recognize that they are *brethren*" (p. 71); that we learn to serve our "*fellowmen*" (p. 69); that God "fill the hearts of all *men* with freedom" (p. 68); and that we be respectful "of other *men's* faith" (p. 34). Similarly, we were described regularly as "children of *man*," and God was the "God of our *fathers.*" Linguistically, at least, people who counted were always "he," never "she."

To be sure, people who were raised on these prayers may have been taught that the word "men" in these and other elegant pieces of literature referred to people in general, men and women. Nevertheless, in more recent times we have become aware of the unfortunate conclusion to which such exclusively masculine language leads. Psychological studies indicate that regardless of cultural assumptions regarding the application of the word "men" to refer to women too, readers of passages that contain such masculine referents associate them with males but not females.

Scholars engaged in retranslating the Bible have discovered the same problem. In the standard 1916 Jewish Publication Society translation, which most Jews grew up with in their synagogues and homes, Psalm 1, for example, began with "Happy is the *man* that hath not walked in the counsel of the wicked . . . *his* delight is in the law of the Lord." Did the psalmist really mean that only "men" who prefer God's law to wicked counsel are happy?

In this case, we were actually mistranslating the Hebrew by our slavish word-for-word rendering of the Hebrew original. The editor-in-chief of the Jewish Publication Society's new translation of the Torah (1962), Harry Orlinsky, has noted that the difficulty in Psalm 1 arises from the fact that the Hebrew uses the word *ish* to describe the person who is happy. *Ish* considered alone usually does mean "man." But it does not mean "man" when used in the grammatical structure of Psalm 1:1. When the Bible, as here, attributes to a person an adjectival quality (e.g., "happy") on the grounds that that person does *not* do something (e.g., "walk in the counsel of the wicked"), even when it uses the word *ish* for that person, it does not mean a man only. The Hebrew word *ish* in such cases means collectively, "persons." Correctly understood, the sentence would thus read, "Happy are those [i.e., both men and women] who do not walk in the counsel of the wicked." Orlinsky speaks in terms of a whole new era of biblical translation—only the third such in the world's history—

in which we must learn to give whole English phrases that render accurately the *sense* that the Hebrew authors wanted to convey, rather than a verbatim rephrasing of each and every word into English sentences that twist the meaning into something other than what those authors would have selected were they alive today.

The problem goes beyond language. On many occasions, we may suppose, the original passage in our prayers actually did mean to limit its attention to men, inasmuch as there are instances when the wording seems to go out of its way to include women. For example, the 1895 *Union Prayer Book*, Volume 2, p. 76, reads: "Be with all *men and women* who spend themselves for the good of mankind and bear the burdens of others; who break the bread to the hungry, clothe the naked, and take the friendless to their habitation. . . ." Thus, when its editors wanted to include women in their purview, they did so, in this case possibly because the context of the prayer is charitableness, a feature that characterized many women who served as volunteer workers in the 1890s. But the opposite is also true. Had they meant to include women elsewhere, they probably would have said so as they do here. Thus, when they speak on almost every page of "men" who will awaken to their religious obligation to transform society by bringing about justice and righteousness, they probably did not have women in mind. Women could not even vote yet in the United States. Though declared equals by the Reform Movement as early as 1845 (see *Gates of Understanding*, Volume I, pp. 25–26), they were hardly so, either in the synagogues where they belonged, generally by virtue of their husbands' affiliation, or in their prayerbooks where God was a "God of all *men*," people were "the children of *man*," and God's covenant was made with "fore*fathers*."

Thus, it became evident to those who composed our current liturgy that the language of earlier ages was cast to reflect social attitudes that we no longer hold. To retain the old language would be to maintain its underlying values. So, in *Gates of Prayer* we changed all masculine-exclusive language to include women as well as men.

By the time the committee met to discuss its next project, our new *Machzor*, the issue of masculine language was extended to the way we describe God. On the one hand, it seems distinctly unlikely that any serious person today still pictures God as a man. Surely, no one would think that when we call God "He" or speak of "Him" as a "King," we really mean that God is masculine! On the other hand, even if that is true, it does not answer the real objection. The whole point is that language conveys attitudes independent of our conscious intentions when we use it. When we say "God of our fathers," we do not nowadays mean literally "fathers but not mothers." But, the effect of continued use of "God of our fathers" is equivalent to our championing the view of an earlier time when authors did mean that. Similarly, it can be argued that regular masculine language for God promotes the distinct presumption that though all of us are created in God's image, some of us are more Godlike than others. Or, to turn to the prayer that prompted this lengthy discussion, *"Avinu Malkenu"* ("Our Father, our King")—by retaining the image of Father and King, one might infer that important decisions about life are made, or should be made, by fathers (but not mothers) and kings (not queens).

After all this discussion, it may come as a surprise to discover that it was decided to retain masculine language for God anyway. Some people held that neutral language virtually does away with the concrete imagery that the Days of Awe demand. Calling God "Our Parent, our Sovereign" here, for example, seemed far more remote, far less compelling, than the traditional "Father" and "King." Others noted that doing away with "He" and "Him" presented insurmountable problems in translation, which could not be overcome without completely altering the sense of ancient Hebrew passages whose integrity we respected. Would the committee charged with our liturgy vote that way today, if we had it to do again? I doubt it. One's consciousness of language's subtle effect on our thinking rises slowly. Nevertheless, it does rise. And today, I think, we would have voted the other way.

The paragraph introducing *"Avinu Malkenu"* (pp. 120–121) was saved from an earlier draft of this *Machzor*, submitted at a time when it seemed possible that we might eliminate masculine language for God. Rather than calling God "Father" or "Mother," "King" or "Queen," the Hebrew words *Avinu* and *Malkenu* were not to be translated at all, but transliterated, and this introduction would have indicated their meaning. Thus: "We call You *Avinu*. As a loving Parent, forgive our sins and failings, and reach for us as we reach for You. We call you *Malkenu*. As a wise Ruler, teach us to add our strength to Your love, that we may redeem this world and build Your Kingdom" (p. 121; in the original, the word "Kingdom" was "Realm").

"The Lord, the Lord God . . . " (p. 122)

See below, page 106.

Torah and Haftara Readings

Few Jews appreciate as they should the High Holy Day Torah and *Haftara* readings anymore. Though the portions are translated in our prayerbooks, we tend not to follow them. Yet the readings have been chosen with great care so as to present, in story form, the grand messages of the

Holy Days. Even ordinary Sabbaths sometimes take on symbolic magnitude because of a specific reading that marks those days: *Shabbat Shuva,* The Sabbath of Return, for example, which falls between Rosh Hashana and Yom Kippur and features the prophet Hosea's call to return to God in repentance. How much the more should the readings for the Days of Awe be appreciated for the light they shed on the message of the moment! We shall find more than one theme represented. The High Holy Days feature a great deal of condensed symbolism. That is, a single prayer or reading may point to more than one thing, and different readings may illustrate many lessons. But of them all, there is only one central message; the other themes are secondary sub-plots that have been attracted by the magnetic quality of these most holy of days. We can arrive at this central theme by looking at the traditional reading for the second day of Rosh Hashana: the Binding of Isaac (pp. 125–127), or, in Hebrew, the *Akeda,* a word meaning tying up or binding. (On the second day of Rosh Hashana, see above, pp. 25–28.)

As we have said, this is the traditional reading for the second, not the first day. And, in point of fact, consistent with their principle of celebrating only the first day, many Reform liturgies once did not read the *Akeda* at all, despite its popularity over the centuries. However, this decision to avoid reading about the binding of Isaac was based on more than calendrical principle. The real problem arose from the fact that Reform congregations initiated the translation of prayers into the vernacular. Thus, people were made suddenly (and painfully) aware of the peculiar tale that was now being read aloud to them. On the face of it, we have a shocking account of a father—Abraham, no less—who blindly accepts a command from God to sacrifice his son! The son, for his part, goes meekly along, like a lamb to slaughter. Abraham who contends God's decision to destroy Sodom chooses in this case not to argue with God. Rather, he steals out of the house early in the morning, without even consulting with Sarah, Isaac's mother. True, at the last moment, he is saved from committing the awful deed, when an angel intercedes with the welcome news that this is only a test of faith and that Abraham can sacrifice a ram caught in the thicket instead of his son.

But what kind of story is this to tell the assembled multitude on the High Holy Days? Is the blindly obedient father ready to kill his son the role model we wish to provide? And what judgment are we to pass on God for imposing so cruel a test? These considerations led many Reform congregations to select the first day's reading instead (Genesis 21, on which, see below, p. 94), or, in some cases, yet another passage entirely. Our *Gates of Repentance,* too, provides such an alternative reading, the Creation narrative from Genesis 1, since our New Year has traditionally

91

been seen as "*yom harat olam*," the day of the world's birth (see pp. 143, 147, and 150 of the *Shofar* Ritual for the liturgical citations).

Still, it is the *Akeda*, the frightening tale of Abraham binding Isaac on the altar, which has held its place despite all opposition. Certainly, the Rabbis who initiated it as the reading for Rosh Hashana understood the tale no less than did the Reform Jews who translated it. What could these Rabbis have seen in the story to justify its inclusion on Rosh Hashana?

To this question there are infinite answers. Every year, rabbis around the world give sermons elucidating new meanings in the story. So it is helpful to break down the question into three related parts. First, why was the story included in the Bible to start with? Second, what meanings have people seen in it, that it resonates deeply enough within us for us to insist on including it on the High Holy Days? Finally, regardless of what we may think today, why was it selected for Rosh Hashana by our forebears?

1. *Why was the* Akeda *story included in the Bible?* The usual answer to this question is that the ancient Israelites broke with their surrounding religious environment, where human sacrifice was still common. Thus, our story of Abraham and Isaac should be explained as a passionate rejection of human sacrifice. The whole point of the story becomes the fact that God does *not* want Abraham to kill his son. Instead, God provides a ram, an animal. This story, then, dramatizes the transition in the history of religion from human to animal sacrifice.

This answer to our first question may or may not be true. There is some evidence that, by the time our story was written, human sacrifice had already largely ceased, so that the Israelites would have had no need of a story reminding them not to adopt the sacrificial ways of their neighbors. But even if it is true, it still does not answer the second question. Even if, for the sake of argument, we assume that human sacrifice was still prevalent in the 10th or 11th century B.C.E., when this story was composed, it had surely come to an end by the fifth century B.C.E. when the Torah was redacted, and someone made the conscious decision not to exclude the tale of the *Akeda*. When we look for the deep, resonating meaning that the story might have evoked in people then and now, we can hardly be satisfied with saying that it is a political diatribe against ancient Canaanite tribes and their sacrificial rites.

2. *What meaning might people see in the* Akeda *story today?* Since we are not concerned with polemics against Canaanite sacrifice, we must seek other explanations for the story's mysterious appeal. We might, for example, adopt a psychological perspective and say that the story explores intergenerational relationships between parent and child. We have Abraham representing all those times when a loving parent is overcome by the

other pole of the love-hate relationship; when a father or mother feels of a child, who has gone just a bit too far, "I could have killed him!" Is Abraham's anger projected onto God, so that he intuits now a divine command to kill his son? Perhaps the moral of the tale is that, at times, intense love brings with it intense anger, but in the end, feelings themselves need not result in action. Isaac is spared, after all.

We need not hold that this is what the *Akeda* "means," in the sense of its having only one meaning. Nor do we deny the very real existence of God, if we say that Abraham projects his anger onto God. We note only that some stories contain deeper layers of meaning of which we may be only dimly aware. These are the stories that prove their staying power with us; they last the centuries; they may have no obvious moral merit and may, in fact, suggest at first glance a facet of human nature or a side to our heroes that we would rather forget. But, because of their depth of signification, it is precisely these tales that we read publicly in some ritualistic communal act. And surely, the *Akeda* is such a story, whether the interpretation offered here is right, partially right, or altogether wrong.

3. Regardless of any meaning that might satisfy us, *what originally prompted the Rabbis to add the* Akeda *to the liturgy?* Perhaps the possibility of political polemic against ancient Canaanite human sacrifice or even some other deep-seated meaning we assume the *Akeda* to have, explains the Rabbinic decision to include it on the second day of the New Year. But we cannot say for sure; we can only speculate. As we saw (above, pp. 25–28), our reading could only have been used outside Palestine, since until the Middle Ages only Diaspora Jews kept a second day. On the first day they would have read the normally prescribed first-day reading, which happens to be Genesis 21, the story of God's visiting Sarah and promising Isaac's birth. But at the end of the first day, the Torah would have been rolled to the end of Genesis 21, and the very next chapter, Genesis 22, is none other than the Binding of Isaac. So it is even possible that the Rabbis chose the *Akeda* just because that is the chapter to which the Torah was rolled on the second day; lacking all precedent, they simply read the story before them.

Once the story became common, other meanings were discovered within it, particularly since Isaac's near sacrifice was interpreted by neighboring Christians as a Christological foreshadowing of Jesus's crucifixion. For Jews, on the other hand, the ram could not have failed to evoke reflection on the ram's horn, or *shofar*. God's mercy in saving Isaac reminded people of divine graciousness that even sinners, in every age, would encounter. Unlike Christians, then, Jews would evoke God's saving grace by sounding the *shofar*, reminiscent of the paradigmatic delivery of Isaac.

But the truly central theme of Rosh Hashana is not to be found in the story of Isaac's binding. That story, from Genesis 22, was probably just tacked on to the important tale before it, Genesis 21. To get at the central theme of the holiday, then, we must turn to the narrative that the Rabbis prescribed for the first day of Rosh Hashana, Genesis 21.

Genesis 21 is the story of Sarah's conception of Isaac. It thus presents the familiar motif of a barren woman who is finally granted children. Sarah was so old that people laughed in disbelief when they heard of Isaac's birth. But even the impossible is possible for those to whom God makes a commitment, and just such a promise was made to Abraham when God told him that his children would cover the earth and prove a blessing to all humankind. So our tale begins: "God took note of Sarah as He had promised; the Lord did for Sarah as He had said." *Rosh Hashana's central theme is this: God takes note; God remembers.*

Taking note and remembering are not the same. One takes note of the present; one remembers the past. But Rosh Hashana posits a connection between past and present. What we did once has repercussions later, just as what we do now will unfold in all its fullness only in years to come. On Rosh Hashana, the past catches up to the present. God remembers.

This lesson is underscored regularly in the Rosh Hashana liturgy. We see it in the evening *Kiddush* for Rosh Hashana (*Gates of the House*, p. 52, or *Gates of Repentance*, p. 42.); in its equivalent, the middle blessing of the *Tefila* (*Gates of Repentance*, p. 35); and in the last blessing after the *Haftara* (p. 137). Rosh Hashana is defined in the last line of each of these prayers. It is preeminently not a day of judgment, or a day of awe, but "*Yom Hazikaron*," the Day of Remembrance (see above, pp. 19–20).

Although on the Days of Awe we think readily of God's remembering our sins, remembrance is not necessarily a negative concept. Human nature is composed of both good and evil. Despite our sins for which we seek forgiveness, we dare to pray that remembrance of us shall ascend to God on high (p. 34) so that the reward of continued life shall be ours. "Remember us unto life," we plead (p. 30); "Who is like our God," reads the Hebrew (p. 31), "who remembers all creatures for life?" These days are days of awe because on them God remembers.

The traditional *Haftarot* for both Rosh Hashana and Yom Kippur underscore this theme. We can look at two of them: I Samuel 1 (pp. 129–133), which is read on Rosh Hashana morning (the first day, if one keeps two days), and Jonah (pp. 457–463), which we read on Yom Kippur afternoon.

The message of Samuel is not at all clear, until one recognizes what the normal accompanying Torah reading is. Just as the Torah reading presents the birth of Isaac, so the *Haftara* reading depicts the parallel birth of Samuel. Here, it is Hannah who is barren and prays to God;

she, like Sarah, is remembered.

The Jonah story is a little more complex, though its message is unmistakably the same. We hear first how God instructs Jonah the prophet to go to the city of Nineveh and there to prophesy its destruction, which will most certainly come unless the Ninevites repent. Rather than fulfill his task, Jonah flees on a ship. So God brings about a storm that threatens to capsize the ship, unless Jonah is tossed overboard. Jonah recognizes his sin, consents to his fate at sea, is swallowed by a large fish, and is coughed up at Nineveh.

In the second half of the story, Jonah fulfills his mission, only to find to his chagrin that the Ninevites listen to him and repent. Naturally, God withholds punishment, but Jonah, who had found satisfaction in foreseeing doom, becomes despondent as his prediction fails to materialize. God has to remind him that the mission to prophesy was prompted by divine compassion, not wrath. "Should I not care about Nineveh, that great city in which there are more than one hundred and twenty thousand persons?"

With the story of Isaac's birth and the parallel *Haftara* regarding Samuel, God remembers the positive. Both Sarah and Hannah are sinless. They have a claim on God to fulfill the divine side of the covenant with the Jewish people. God remembers them. With Jonah, the accent is on the negative. First Jonah sins: he runs away from God. But he finds that God still takes note of him, and because he repents, he escapes even the fish's belly and is able to proceed with his task. The Ninevites, too, have sinned. But they, too, repent, and God has no need to punish them either. All this is explained to the grieving prophet who mistook God's message for wrath, when it was simply, "God takes note; God remembers."

Both Torah and *Haftara* readings portray the central message of the Days of Awe. We stand in covenant with our God who takes note of us and remembers us. As creatures who combine both good and evil impulses, we celebrate the memories of our goodness that rise to God, even as we seek pardon for our evil-doing, which is also recalled. But God who cared even for the evil Ninevites, also cares for us. God takes note; God remembers. May we be remembered for life!

In sum, *Gates of Repentance* provides a traditional reading, the *Akeda* (the Binding of Isaac), as part of the Torah ritual for Service I. But Genesis 1, the Creation narrative, is given as an alternative, in Service II. Congregations may utilize either selection regardless of which service they are using at the time. Originally, alternatives within each service were contemplated. An earlier manuscript draft offered also Genesis 21 (Isaac's birth) and even the thematically similar Genesis 18 (the visit of the angels to Abraham, announcing the fact that Isaac would be born, and the story of Sodom and Gomorrah). The former, as we saw, is traditional for the first day of Rosh Hashana, and the latter combines the traditional theme of God's remembering (and, therefore, visiting us) with the message that, as in Sodom, sins do not go unpunished, although God is both merciful and just in judging us. These two readings would have appeared as the alternatives in Service I, while Service II would have carried Genesis 22 (the *Akeda*) and Genesis 1 (Creation). In the end, because the book was too long, we did away with both of the first day's readings and apportioned the two remaining readings so that a different one is now featured in each of the two services.

Sounding of the Shofar

Traditionally, the *shofar* is blown on two occasions during the day: first, during the Torah ritual, and again, during the *Tefila* of the *Musaf* service. The latter is more central to the liturgical message of the day, in that it is itself subdivided into three separate series of blasts, each of which is devoted to a different Rosh Hashana theme. Before turning to the themes, however, we should note how our *Machzor* alters this essential structure.

A change is required because of the simple fact that Reform worship has no *Musaf* service (see above, pp. 8–9). So we have excerpted the primary *Shofar* Ritual that normally would occur there, and offered it in place of the secondary *shofar* blowing that would have been set in the Torah ritual.

The *Shofar* Ritual is highly structured, comparable to a beautiful painting, a finely-crafted play, or a symphony, in that its appreciation depends on our ability to recognize the artistic scheme that governs the relationship of the parts to the whole. What follows, therefore, is a description of the *Shofar* Ritual's structure, so that worshipers may fully recognize its drama as it unfolds. Since the *shofar* itself is primarily a listening experience, we shall compare it to a classical symphony.

Consider a piece of classical music—Beethoven's Ninth Symphony, or Brahms Symphony No. 1, for example. These are not only exceptional musical works considered in their entirety; they are also artistic combinations of smaller musical masterpieces—individual themes, perhaps, or particular movements—which can be enjoyed in their own right without consideration of their place in the symphony as a whole. Indeed, we regularly purchase records containing collections of diverse musical snippets, such as a single aria from an opera or the final movement of a symphony. Even purists who would never listen to the last movement alone (as a detective buff would not read only the final chapter of a book) would agree that one can successfully study just one movement or just one series of notes or just one element of harmony. Music is always enjoyable both in terms of its parts and, on a grander scale, in the way those parts fit together to make a pleasing whole.

The *shofar* sound alone is like one such element in a larger symphonic whole, the entire symphony being the service in which the *shofar* is embedded. We shall see, for example, that introducing each blast we have the chanted calls of *Teki-a, Shevarim,* and *Teru-a.* These serve to indicate the sound that will follow, but the calls without the sound are, in themselves, pleasing. We have different literary genres of prayers here also: biblical verses, blessings, and medieval poetry. And the service is arranged in a tripartite fashion reminiscent of a three-act opera, or a symphony (but in just three movements). Let us, then, look at the actual act of blowing the *shofar* not as an isolated element but as the climax of a liturgical symphony. We have all learned to appreciate that climax taken by itself, surely, just as even the most ignorant listener recognizes the theme at the beginning of Beethoven's Fifth, without having to hear the whole symphony. We are ready to take the next step and understand the structure of the symphony as a whole.

The *Shofar* Ritual can be found on pages 138–151. Consider page 138 to the middle of page 139 as a prelude to the three-part main piece. Now find the three titles, each defining the concern of one of the parts (they appear in Hebrew, English transliteration, and English translation): Sovereignty (p. 139), Remembrance (p. 143), and Revelation (p. 148).

Sovereignty and Remembrance are English translations of the respective Hebrew titles of Parts 1 and 2, though a more precise rendering in context would be "Sovereignty [biblical] verses," by which we mean a collection of biblical verses about the sovereignty of God, and "Remembrance [biblical] verses," or biblical verses about God's remembering. (We have already looked at these two major Rosh Hashana themes, above, pp. 19–20, 21–22, and 93–95; but for the sake of clarity, we shall describe them also below.) Revelation is a derived meaning of the Hebrew title for Part 3, which reads *Shofarot* (biblical verses regarding the *shofar,* in Hebrew). The connection between revelation and the *shofar* will be evident shortly.

So, considered conceptually, we have three movements to our symphony, dealing, respectively, with our doctrines of God as Sovereign; God as Rememberer; and God as Revealer of Torah. But each of these concepts is expressed through the medium of biblical citations, so the basic "stuff" of which our symphony is made, is a threefold series of scriptural sentences, each one illuminating one of the three themes. They are found on pages 140–141 (the Sovereignty verses), 145–146 (the Remembrance verses); and 148–149 (the Revelation, or *Shofar,* verses). Stylistically, all three themes are presented in parallel style, based on the traditional tripartite division of the Bible into *Torah, Nevi-im* (Prophets), and *Ketuvim* (Writ-

97

ings). Thus, there are four paragraphs for each theme: the first (Torah), beginning with the words "The Torah proclaims . . . "; then (*Ketuvim*), "The psalmist affirms . . . "; then (*Nevi-im*), "The prophet declares . . . "; and finally (Torah again), "As it is written. . . . " In this way, each series moves from *Torah* to Psalms (that is, the *Ketuvim*, or the Writings section of the Bible) and to the Prophets (the *Nevi-im*), the three sections into which the Bible is divided; at last, each one returns to a general concluding line cited from *Torah*, and beginning with "As it is written. . . . "

In each case, these semi-climactic biblical testimonials to God's presence are introduced and then concluded by classical Hebrew readings from the Rabbinic period. The introductions describe the theological affirmation that the following verses illustrate. The conclusions (beginning in each case with a direct address to God as "Our God") petition God to demonstrate once again the fact of divine sovereignty over all, divine remembrance, and revelation of the divine presence.

Like describing music in a music appreciation course, however, one must actually have the music (or at least the score) on hand to appreciate what one is doing. So, before proceeding any further, take out the script, *Gates of Repentance* (if you haven't already done so), and find the three introductions, the three sets of verses they introduce, and the three conclusions. You should be able to see three parallel structural units, each committed to a different aspect of Rosh Hashana theology. Each, we said, is a liturgical movement; combined, they constitute the liturgical symphony. The chart on page 99 demonstrates the structure.

Our symphony is both "program music," that is, music with a message, and pure musical composition, in which the medium itself is so pleasing that it constitutes an aesthetic joy in its own right, quite apart from any message it might convey. Until now we have emphasized the compositional, or structural, component; but the content is no less important. We now turn to the ritual's theological message.

First, we consider the Remembrance "movement." The importance of remembrance on the Days of Awe has been emphasized above (pp. 19–20 and 93–95). Remembrance derives its Jewish connotation from the fact that we believe ourselves mutually bound with God in a covenant stretching back through history. We can expect God to remember us, not simply because we are individual human beings who happen to live in the here and now, but because as members of the Jewish people, we have a claim on God as our covenanting partner. God made a covenant with Abraham and Sarah and their progeny forever; that covenant was renewed at Sinai, and continued ever after. For example, Hannah was barren, but as God remembered Sarah, so God remembered Hannah in her hour of need. God's remembrance of Jews goes hand in hand with the covenant in

Opening prelude (pp. 138-139)

In the seventh month . . .
Hear now the Shofar . . .
Awake, you sleepers . . .

The three symphonic movements

	Malchuyot Sovereignty (pp. 139-143)	*Zichronot* Remembrance (pp. 143-147)	*Shofarot* Revelation (pp. 148-151)
Introduction	We must praise the Lord of all . . .	You remember the work of creation . . .	In a cloud of glory You spoke in holy address . . .
	Let all who dwell on earth acknowledge . . . God . . .	This is the day of the world's beginning . . .	We heard the majesty of Your voice . . .
Thematic development through biblical verses	The Torah proclaims . . . (i.e., *Torah*)	The Torah proclaims . . .	The Torah proclaims . . .
	The psalmist affirms . . . (i.e., *Ketuvim*)	The psalmist affirms . . .	The psalmist affirms . . .
	The prophet declares . . . (i.e., *Nevi-im*)	The prophet declares . . .	The prophet declares . . .
	As it is written in the Torah . . . (i.e., *Torah* again)	As it is written in the Torah . . .	As it is written in the Torah . . .
Conclusion	Our God . . . rule in glory . . .	Our God . . . remember us with favor . . .	Our God . . . sound the great Shofar . . .
Shofar blessings (before the first blast only)	Blessed is the Lord . . . 1) [who] calls us to hear . . . the Shofar 2) . . . for enabling us to reach this season.		

THE SHOFAR IS SOUNDED

Thematic recapitulation	This is the day of the world's birth . . .	This is the day of the world's birth . . .	This is the day of the world's birth . . .
	O God Supreme, . . . we acclaim Your SOVEREIGNTY.	O God Supreme, . . . we invoke Your REMEMBRANCE.	O God Supreme, . . . we call to You with THE SOUND OF THE SHOFAR.

which God promises to remember us.

Now we understand the third, or *Shofar,* "movement." Though entitled "Revelation," the concluding paragraph switches the focus from revelation at Sinai to the anticipated "End of Days," when redemption will occur. These are two sides to the same coin: the beginning and the end, so to speak, of the covenant relationship. We covenanted with God at Sinai and marked that event by blowing the *shofar.* However, we covenanted not simply to exist, but to do God's will and, thus, bring ever nearer the perfect messianic age in which evil and suffering will be unknown. The purpose of the covenant will be fulfilled only when the messianic Time-to-Come actually arrives, and then, again, we shall blow the *shofar*. Thus, the *shofar* sound represents the covenant's inception and its fulfillment, both the beginning and the goal of Jewish history.

The Sovereignty "movement," too, is allied conceptually. Simply put, the world will be perfected at the End of Days because only God is the ultimate Ruler of the universe (see above, pp. 20–21).

The theological content of our symphony, then, takes us out of ordinary time and space to consider the ultimate origin and destiny of Jewish existence. Only God is our ultimate Ruler. With God we made a covenant, such that annually, on these High Holy Days, God remembers our deeds, while we, for our part, readjust our mutual covenantal relationship until we have made amends for our sins and are able to plead once again that we should be remembered for life. We recall not the ordinary events of yesterday, but the ineffable revelation at Sinai which made us what we are; not the mundane appointments for tomorrow, but the majestic End of Days.

Like any good musical composition, the liturgical symphony of the *shofar* presupposes enlightened liturgical participants who know these program notes. In sum, each of the three sections explores one of the three theological underpinnings of Rosh Hashana: God the Ruler, God the Rememberer, and God the Covenanter and Redeemer. We punctuate each tenet of faith with the sound of the *shofar*, which once heralded God's presence at Sinai and which will one day announce the End of Days as well.

So far, we have looked exclusively at the *Shofar* Ritual for Morning Service I. The alternative order for blowing the *shofar*, which we provide for Service II (pp. 208–217), follows the same traditional structure, but it presents its own unique features also. All along, we have emphasized the continuity of *Gates of Repentance* with the early Rabbinic principle of building our liturgy on a combination of a fixed structure (*keva*) and variable wording (*kavana*). (For a discussion of this principle, see above, pp. 11–12.) Thus, our two *Shofar* Rituals represent alternative, but equally acceptable, expressions of the same age-old *shofar* themes.

How, then, do the two *Shofar* Rituals differ from each other?

We have seen how the *shofar* "symphony" contains three parallel sets of *shofar* blasts, each set punctuating a statement of faith in God as Ruler, Rememberer, and Covenant Partner, and how these are developed thematically by the presentation of biblical verses testifying to their basis in Israel's historical roots. The Rabbis of the first two centuries C.E. debated how many such verses to include, until eventually it was decided that the number should be ten: three from each of the three sections of the Bible

(Torah, Prophets, and Writings), and a final tenth citation from the Torah, indicating its superior scriptural status.

In Service II, we have retained the traditional number, ten, but we do not use the same verses that are preferred in traditional books; we select our own instead. Also, we have balanced our traditionalism there by introducing the verses with a creative reading, and we have accompanied that reading with a novel interpretation of the traditional theme, which we have printed in capital letters below the traditional trilogy of *Malchuyot*, *Zichronot*, and *Shofarot*. Thus, the titles for the three "movements" are given as "CREATION" (p. 209), "MEANING IN TIME" (p. 212), and "REVELATION AND REDEMPTION" (p. 215). For our first introduction (p. 210) we provide "God of space and time . . . ," a reading drawn from the *Union Prayer Book*. The introduction to the second "movement," *Zichronot* (p. 212), is partly based on the 1973 Liberal British *Machzor* called *Gate of Repentance*, and partly new here. The two poetic paragraphs on page 213, beginning "We remember . . . ," constitute creative extensions to that introduction, and are composed by the editor of our *Machzor*, Chaim Stern. The creative introduction to *Shofarot*, the third and last section (p. 215), comes also from the *Union Prayer Book*.

In Service I, on the other hand, instead of utilizing three introductory verses from each section of the Bible, we use only one, indicating with a standard opening phrase whence it comes ("The Torah proclaims," "The psalmist affirms," or "The prophet declares"); then we conclude with an extra verse from the Torah, thus remaining true to the rationale behind the traditional practice, but avoiding excessive verbiage. (The preference for four verses only is attributed also to some of the rabbis in the second century, incidentally, so it is not new here.) We balance this "unorthodox" approach in Service I by introducing and concluding our four verses there with the traditional *Machzor's* readings. These traditional introductions are worthy of special note. Traditionally, they have usually been attributed to the school of a leading Babylonian rabbi of the third century, Rav (d. 247), who is credited with establishing the basis for that society which eventually produced the Babylonian Talmud. Scholars today tend to discredit that attribution, but the compositions in question are still believed to date from the second or third century. The introduction to *Malchuyot* (pp. 139–140) is none other than our familiar *"Aleinu"* which (as we saw above, pp. 42–46) was originally composed exclusively for inclusion here. It is chanted here according to a melody reserved for this rubric and known, appropriately, as "The Great *Aleinu*."

The prelude to both services contains a paragraph drawn from Maimonides: "Awake, you sleepers . . . " (pp. 139 and 209).

Only Service I concludes each of the three segments with the traditional concept, "This is the day of the world's birth . . . " (e.g., p. 150). This prayer was already included in Amram's ninth-century prayerbook (see p. 56 above) and, in its wording, reflects several citations from biblical and Rabbinic literature. The idea it presents is central to Rosh Hashana, so much so, that it deserves independent treatment.

"This is the day of the world's birth . . . "
(pp. 143, 147, and 150)

A recurrent idea found in the world's religions is what Mircea Eliade, the student of comparative religion, has called "The Myth of the Eternal Return." In contrast to secular time, which simply comes and goes, Eliade speaks of liturgical time which is cyclical. Liturgical time celebrates the great events of the cosmos, the most obvious one being Creation itself. Through annual holy days, religions present us over and over again with the opportunity to re-experience these cosmic events. In our case, Eliade holds, Judaism provides a Rosh Hashana in which more than the year is renewed; all of creation is regenerated, ourselves included. We break out of the shackles of profane time and relive the possibility of starting completely afresh.

This thought should not be altogether new to us. It is reminiscent of the *Tefila*'s petition that we be inscribed in the Book of Life for the year ahead (e.g., p. 105). Later, the liturgy for returning the Torah to the Ark will conclude with the wish, "Renew our days, as in the past" (p. 155). Now we have an explicit statement that Rosh Hashana is a recollection of that past. It is "the day of the world's birth."

Jewish sources first discuss the idea in a Talmudic debate on the significance of various New Years, similar to our modern fiscal year, calendar year, school year, and so on (see above, p. 19). In the course of the debate, two second-century rabbis introduce the thought that these purely calendrical realities have also mythic proportions, in that cosmic events are connected to them. In Tishri, the Hebrew month that contains both Rosh Hashana and Yom Kippur, says Rabbi Eliezer, the world was created.

Further tradition fleshed out the idea in concrete imagery applicable to the Days of Awe. We are told, for example, that God began creation *before* Rosh Hashana day, so that the creation of Adam and Eve would occur precisely on the first day of the first year. It is as if the universe existed for a while with no humans to inhabit it, but the counting of days did not begin until Adam and Eve. Without them, historical time was impossible, since there can be no history without humans to make it. Thus, exactly on the original New Year's day, God created man and woman, and only then could it be said that "the world was created."

But the essence of human beings is our free will, so our Midrash emphasizes the fact that on the very day we were created, we were set free to act, and, as a consequence, we sinned. Though holding no belief in original sin or the essentially sinful condition of humanity, Judaism is quite clear about the fact that all of us possess an evil inclination that leads us to error. God thus tried Adam and Eve for their first human crimes, and, miraculously, sent them forth from judgment as free people able to begin life again. "This," concluded God, "shall be a sign for all posterity. As you came into My presence for judgment on this day and went forth free, so will your children come into My presence for judgment on this day and go forth free." Quoting yet another of our prayers in the *Shofar* Service (p. 144), the Midrash summarizes: "This is the day of the world's beginning; . . . creation's first day." On Rosh Hashana we revert to the simple primeval state of Adam and Eve, reduced to the calculation of the good and bad we have wrought. But if we will it, we, too, may start again, as if the world itself were beginning anew.

Now, Eliade has claimed that all great religions provide a mythical celebration of new beginnings by utilizing the idea of "re-creation." He points to a great mass of evidence from religions that use sacred readings or drama to reproduce their myths of the world's origins. But we have seen that, traditionally, Judaism does not prescribe the Creation narrative for Rosh Hashana. Instead, the traditional reading for the first day is God's visit to Sarah, to inform her of Isaac's birth. And on Day Two, we read of the near-tragedy, the possibility that Isaac might himself not live to propagate his own children (see pp. 91–94 above). *For Judaism, then, the root metaphor for renewal is not re-creation but procreation!* As there is no history without humans to make it, so the cosmic event that Judaism calls to consciousness is the guarantee that human life will go on. Like Adam and Eve on the fated first day, we, each of us, can begin our lives again; but we do so knowing that our own mortality should not be taken as an indication that life is meaningless. Beyond each of our lives lie others. Isaac stands for the eternally necessary "next generation."

Perhaps most fascinating of all, then, is the first of the two Hebrew words, which we have translated as "the world's birth." It is *harat*, a derivative of the noun meaning "conception," not "birth"; the beginning of the process leading to life, not the end of it. A truer translation might be: "This is the day the world was conceived."

As an idea, conception surpasses birth, because it carries with it the dream of unsurpassed potential. Imagine planning an entire universe without having to worry about one already in existence. What pregnant woman has not dreamed of the some-day child in her womb? Ideas not yet tried can go anywhere. Whether of the world, of a child, or of an idea, conception implies the possibility of great expectations, untold promise, visions of greatness.

Accordingly, the Kabbalist Isaiah Horowitz (1565?–1630) links Rosh Hashana with the potential greatness inherent in God's conception of the universe. "Since we say, 'This is the day of the world's conception,' Kabbalistic commentators have explained that when Adam and Eve were created on this very day, it was the climax of creation, the coming of fruition of God's conception of the world, as if on that day the world in its entirety had been renewed."

Concluding Prayers

"Aleınu" (p. 156)

See above, pages 42–46.

Kaddish (p. 158)

See above, pages 47–50.

"All the World" (p. 160)

"All the World" has proved to be one of the most popular and lasting of Reform hymns. The English words are those of the translator, Israel Zangwill, who captures well the flavor of the Hebrew. But the Hebrew is not new. It goes back to an unknown date, place, and author and describes the ultimate vision of a messianic age.

Its style identifies it readily as a *piyut* (see above, p. 77). The author used an alphabetic acrostic. The poem is composed of several pious wishes, each beginning with a verb: *veye-etayu*, *viyvarechu*, *veyagidu*, and so on. If one strips the verbs of their prefixes mandated by the rules of Hebrew, one finds that the first letter of each of the verbs follows the Hebrew alphabet from start to finish. The selection of the peculiar *veye-etayu* as the first word, instead of the more usual *veyavo-u* (which means the same thing) is due to the fact that the root of the former word begins with an *Alef*, which the poet needed to begin his poem.

(See further discussion of "All the World" in connection with Yom Kippur, below, p. 144.)

Morning Service II (pp. 163–226)

On the differences, generally, between the various rubrics of the two morning services, see above, pages 53–54.

Preparatory Prayers (pp. 163–167)

Unlike Service I, Service II uses no traditional material here, and does not even divide this unit into the two traditional rubrics: Morning Blessings, and Poems of Praise (see above, pp. 53, 55–56, and 59). Instead, we have a series of contemporary poems, of which, perhaps, the last stanza on page 163 bears special mention. Until that point, to cite its author, Chaim Stern, "The passage is very much earthbound, and then it takes wing. The rhythm changes, and it becomes an incantation."

Reader's Kaddish (pp. 166–167)

See above, pages 47–50, for discussion of the *Kaddish* in general.

Here, a small Reader's *Kaddish* is used traditionally, to divide rubrics from each other.

"Shema" and Its Blessings (pp. 167–173)

See pages 29–40 above for fuller discussion.

For differences between the two Morning Services regarding this rubric, see pages 53–54 above.

We follow the traditional rubric themes of voicing our faith in God the Creator, the Revealer of Torah, and the Redeemer, and generally do so with the traditional blessings rather than with creative adaptations of the themes. Of special interest, however, is one exception: the insertion of a poem by Judah Halevi (1086–1141) in the first benediction (p. 168).

Halevi remains one of the outstanding geniuses in all of Jewish history. A Spaniard by birth, he reaped the fruit of the Golden Age under the Moslems, learning the best of Arabic and Hebrew culture. At an early age, he had already proved himself to be an outstanding poet, both religious and secular. Above all, Halevi was a man of the spirit. He argued passionately that ideal Jewish existence could be found only in Palestine, since an almost mystical relationship exists between the God of Israel, the people of Israel, the language of Israel (Hebrew), and the Land of Israel. He eventually left his native Spain, but died in Egypt before reaching the Holy Land. Later legend embellished the end of his life by picturing him arriving in Jerusalem, kissing its stones, and then—while reciting one of his famous elegies for Zion—being trampled to death by a passing Arab horseman

The six lines on page 168, beginning with "To You the stars of morning sing," show the poet as the deeply religious soul he was, a man who could sing of nature, of love, and of his people, while finding the hand of God everywhere.

COMMENTARY TO *GATES OF REPENTANCE*

Tefila (pp. 173–187)

For general discussion of the *Tefila*, see above, pages 18–23.

For differences between our treatment of the morning *Tefila* in this service and in Service I, see above, pages 12–14.

For the *"Unetaneh Tokef"* (pp. 175–179), see above, pages 75–78.

For the *"Uvechen"* insertion (pp. 181–182), see above, pages 20–21.

For the special insertions in the first and last two benedictions of the High Holy Day *Tefila*, see above, pages 21–22.

For the silent prayer that follows the *Tefila* (p. 187), see above, pages 82–84.

Service for the Reading of the Torah (pp. 188–207)

For the nature of this rubric in general, see above, pages 84–87.

For *"Avinu Malkenu"* (pp. 189–190), see above, pages 23–25; for the introductory paragraph to *"Avinu Malkenu"* (p. 189), see above, pages 87–90.

"The Lord, the Lord God . . ." (p. 191)

This is a traditional passage of special importance on the Days of Awe. The passage itself is biblical (Exodus 34:6) and consists of what are known as the thirteen attributes of God, which were revealed to Moses. The last one is, "God will surely not grant pardon" to sinners. The notion of "surely" is conveyed in the Hebrew by prefacing the negative "will not grant pardon" with a peculiar grammatical form called an infinitive absolute, which is itself not negative, but which serves in biblical style to strengthen the force of the negative verb that follows. The Rabbis were unwilling to believe that God would "surely not grant pardon," so for liturgical purposes, they simply stopped reading the passage at the end of the infinitive, and before the negative particle. They, thus, omitted the last half of the verbal phrase, and were left with the exact opposite of the Bible's intent! As it occurs in the liturgy, therefore, the last divine attribute is that God does grant pardon.

The divine attributes were considered to be particularly efficacious. According to a third-century Palestinian teacher, it is as if, while wrapped in a *talit* like the reader at worship, God told Moses each of the divine attributes ("The Lord, the Lord God is merciful and gracious . . .") as part of the order of prayer. God then added the injunction, "When Israel sins, let them carry out this service before Me and I will forgive them." For the Torah readings (pp. 193–207), see above, pages 90–96.

Sounding of the Shofar (pp. 208-217)

For the ritual of the sounding of the *shofar*, see above, pages 96-102.

Concluding Prayers

"Aleinu" (p. 222)

See above, pages 42-46.

Kaddish (pp. 223-224)

See above, pages 47-50.

"Ein Keloheinu" (p. 225)

This final hymn is of unknown origin, but was already known by the ninth century, when it was used to conclude daily services. By the 11th century, however, tradition limited it to Shabbat, for the following very interesting reason.

We have already seen that the traditional daily *Tefila* carries nineteen blessings, and that on Shabbat, the internal thirteen that express petitions are replaced with a single benediction proclaiming the sanctity of the day. Consequently, relative to the daily service, the Shabbat liturgy was exactly twelve benedictions short.

Before concluding this lesson on medieval rabbinic mathematics, we require a closer look at the verses in *"Ein Keloheinu."* There are five of them, each containing four lines. Stanzas are differentiated from one another by a variable first word, which recurs in each of the four lines: the first being *Ein* ("There is none like . . ."), the second being *Mi* ("Who is like . . ."), etc. But the stanzas, as we have them, seem to be out of order. Our poem begins by asserting that, "There is none like our God . . . our Lord . . . our King . . . our Savior," and only then asks, "Who is like our God . . . our Lord," etc. Surely, the logical order would be the very reverse. The poet must originally have intended to ask the rhetorical question, "Who is like God?", to which the only reply is, "There is none like God." The next three verses follow: since there is none like God, we assert our intent of giving thanks to God (verse 3), which we do immediately (in verses 4 and 5), by citing the beginning of the standard blessing formula *"Baruch . . ."* as the variable word in verse 4; and then the second word in the formula, *ata*, as the introduction to verse 5. That, in fact, is the order of the poem in the ninth-century prayerbook, where it is first found. Thus, in a very simple way, our poem goes from question to answer, to consequence that follows, and to the carrying out of that consequence—praising God.

For medievals in Western Europe, however, what counted most was not the poet's logic, but the fact that the variable words marking the first three stanzas can be rearranged to make an acrostic. If the first two verses are interchanged, we have the letter *Alef* from *Ein*, *Mem* from *Mi*, and *Nun* from *Nodeh*, which, together in this order, spell *Amen*. It happens also that the word *Amen* is spelled by a total of three letters, each of which occurs four times (since a stanza's variable word is repeated at the beginning of each of its four lines). Three times four is twelve, the exact number of blessings we are lacking; and saying *Amen* is technically all a worshiper has to do in the *Tefila*, because the Reader can be counted on to say each blessing out loud. To the medieval mind, rearranging the verses is tantamount to saying twelve extra blessings, thus making up for their loss in the Shabbat service.

Yom Kippur

General Comments

Yom Kippur is a cumulative experience. Known biblically as the day on which one should afflict oneself, thus atoning for sin, it emerged early as the fast *par excellence* of Judaism. Rosh Hashana, by contrast, was known as a High Holy Day only much later in history, swept along, possibly, in the wake of Yom Kippur, for which it was seen increasingly as preparatory.

The experience of Yom Kippur begins with penitential poems called *Selichot* (see pp. 123–124 below) even before Rosh Hashana and continues for the next ten days after it; these are known as *Aseret Yemei Teshuva*, the Ten Days of Repentance. Liturgically, one is reminded of the task of repentance as part of the liturgy of the Sabbath that falls within these ten days. Known as the Sabbath of Return [to God] (*Shabbat Shuva*), this Shabbat features a *Haftara* taken, in large part, from the end of the book of the prophet Hosea, "Return, O Israel, to the Lord your God, for you have stumbled in your iniquity. . . ."

By the time the day before Yom Kippur dawns, people engage seriously in preparing themselves spiritually for the inner ordeal Yom Kippur represents. It is not easy to come to terms with the singular occasion in which one is reminded that evil is a reality, and that each of us is responsible for some of it; without confession and a serious effort to change our lives, we shall some day die the death of fools, deluded by the seeming magnitude of accomplishments that fade into nothingness in the face of our greater failings; and, since we do not know when death will come, if we are to turn at all, we must do so now.

No wonder tradition is replete with customs preparing us for Yom Kippur, beginning even before Rosh Hashana—with midnight *Selichot* services, for example, generally held the Saturday night before Rosh Hashana—and culminating in the twenty-four hours immediately prior to the day of the Great Fast. The most interesting act of preparation, perhaps, is the practice of making our rounds, to apologize to those we have wronged in the year past, since "for transgressions against God, the Day of Atonement atones; but for the transgressions of one human being against another, the Day of Atonement does not atone until we have made peace with one another" (p. 251, quoting Mishna, Yoma 8.9). Our tradition is unequivocal: all the fasting in the world is useless, unless we seek out the people we have hurt to ask their forgiveness directly.

A story told by Judah Steinberg (1863–1908) illustrates the mood of the day. Steinberg had been born into a traditionalist Hasidic milieu in Eastern Europe, but soon emerged as a self-taught man of Western culture, at home in mathematics, Russian, and science. For a while he earned his living as a school teacher, but later turned to newspaper reporting for a Yiddish paper in Odessa, and to writing. Unlike many who had abandoned their strongly Hasidic childhood, Steinberg saw value in simple piety and retained his faith in folk traditions rooted in genuine religiosity.

Steinberg describes the mood of the wealthy man, Avraham Yossi, one of the town's leading citizens, whose business consisted of running the banking system, such as it was, in the Jewish community. In short, he made loans to people, and spent his days collecting debts. He was so wealthy, however, that, by and large, others did his work for him, so that he rarely found it necessary to arise from bed before nine in the morning, a full three hours after hard-working individuals normally got up to their labors.

But the day before Yom Kippur, he awoke before the sun rose. Even during the night before, he had looked ahead to the task of Yom Kippur day, reciting long penitential poems (*Selichot*) in the synagogue, and engaging in a ceremony going back to the Middle Ages, *Kaparot*, i.e., the act of ritual transference of one's sins to a chicken. He had slaughtered a chicken, passed it in circles over his head, and uttered a time-worn formula, beginning, "This instead of me. . . . May this chicken go to its death, while I enter a long and good life of peace." But with it all, day was just dawning, and Avraham Yossi's work of preparation was only beginning. The next day was Yom Kippur itself, on which nothing financial could be accomplished, and today, too, would be a lost cause from the perspective of business, because even the day before Yom Kippur was treated as if it were at least partially holy.

Avraham Yossi observes that the morning must be spent making amends among the many people one has injured during the year, this being no inconsiderable number, when one considers all the times one has even inadvertently slandered, passed on (or even listened to) false rumors or gossip, and the like. The task of apologizing alone takes half the day, and by early afternoon, it is time to prepare for the fast itself: physically, certainly, as one harnesses one's strength and carries out the necessary preparations for the evening's dinner; but spiritually too, for as Avraham Yossi tells us, "Taking stock of the days of the year that have passed, [is] surely no light matter in your eyes. How many days in the year, and for how many hours each day, does one drag sins, willingly and unwillingly, at one's heels? Thus, in that hour when you prepare yourself to greet the great and awesome day, Yom Kippur, half of it is already considered as if it were the holy day itself."

The Yom Kippur liturgy bears this sense of continuity with the days leading up to it. To begin with, traditional services begin even before dark, as if one cannot wait to start the actual worship of the great fast day. On a more general level, most of the prayers are not new, but have already been said on Rosh Hashana. This is the climax, as Rosh Hashana was the beginning.

But even when the words are the same, the internal echo in the consciousness of those who say them is not. There is no way to describe adequately the intensity of Yom Kippur. Jews have come early in the evening to be immediately struck by the haunting *"Kol Nidrei,"* the description of which eludes the grasp of language. The next day, one sits ceaselessly in the synagogue awaiting the final blast of the *shofar* to end the concluding service. When it comes, one senses release from burdens one never would have thought existed. Those who walk casually in and out of services on Yom Kippur rob themselves of a profound spiritual awakening. Only the cumulative intensity of total immersion in the whole day's worship transports the human soul to the threshold at which one dares to sense anew that life begins again today, because, despite all failings and suffering, life is good, God is real, and we, creatures of a universe we little comprehend, walk on with new-found courage and hope, through paths that offer promise beyond our wildest visions.

Meditations (pp. 229–245)

The practice of offering meditations for individuals to read as private preparation for prayer is old. For example, the introduction to each *Tefila* (printed by us in smaller Hebrew type with varying translations and paraphrases; cf. pp. 30 and 260) is such a meditation, attributed to Rabbi Yochanan, a third-century Palestinian authority. Similar thoughts on prayer are assigned to other worthies throughout Jewish history. Some of these enter the prayerbook as prayers in their own right, while others exist as marginal comments willed to us by eye-witnesses impressed with the meditative power of something seen or heard.

111

By the 16th century, however, these meditations became more than secondary preparations for the real prayers they precede. Instead, they emerged in Kabbalistic circles as keys without which the secrets of the liturgy would remain locked. Almost with mechanistic certainty, the universe was imaged as existing in an unredeemed state of good mixed with evil. Mystical doctrine insisted that beneath the manifest message of a prayer lay a deeper purpose related to that prayer's unique role in fighting the battle of good against evil. Ultimately, one prayed not for the obvious promises that prayers contained, but for the latent benefit that would accrue to the universe as the prayer brought about final *Tikun Olam*, "Reparation of the Universe" (see above, p. 39).

But Reparation depended on a prior will to say the prayer for the proper end. Mystical adepts were cautioned not to be lulled into thinking that prayers meant only what they said on the surface. So Kabbalistic prayerbooks were equipped with meditations known as *kavanot* (singular—*kavana*) which stated the secret reason for the prayer about to be said. Gradually, the inner complexities that distinguished the *kavana* of one prayer from another were lost, and instead, it became usual to say a generalized *kavana*, one that had first appeared in 1662, and could be applied with equal justification to all prayers. It reminded the worshiper that the state of the unredeemed universe was tantamount to a rupture in the very unity of God, such that all prayer was "for the sake of the unification" of the divine. Some took this *kavana* seriously enough to hold that it was better not to pray at all, than to pray without it. This bold doctrine became a subject of much controversy, especially after the debacle of Sabbetai Zevi's false messianic claims that were similarly rooted in the Kabbalah; and in the 18th century, Rabbi Ezekiel Landau of Prague (1713-1793) demonstrated the intensity of rabbinic reaction by going so far as to deny absolutely the validity of such mystical preparatory meditation.

Nevertheless, meditations continued, either in the mystical sense still followed by the Hasidic communities, or in what would appear at first glance to be the exact antithesis of Hasidism: Reform Judaism. As we have seen, the Reform concept of the universe differed little from that of the mystics. Only the grand metaphor varied. Both groups of worshipers took the position that the world was unredeemed, but Reform Jews spoke of their Mission (see above, e.g., pp. 39-40 and 42-43) to redeem it. Reform Jews, too, believed that prayer was valid not for its own sake alone, but also because it would hasten the messianic End of Days by adding to the sum total of good in the world, frequently by making a better person of the one who prayed. So Hasidic mystics and Reform rationalists were actually united in their commitment to labor on behalf of a world whose unity was shattered, and both held up prayer as the ideal act designed to imbue the universe with its primeval harmony once again.

Of course, Reform rabbis could not accept the mystical mythos reflected in the imagery of the generalized *kavana*. Nor would they go so far as to hold that without the right intention, prayer was not valid. But they did show a fondness for prefacing their prayerbooks with citations on the value of prayer and on its direct efficacy in building an ethical world. The original *Union Prayer Book* of 1894, for example, tells us (p. 8): "Prayer is the purest service that the heart can offer. . . . 'Thou shalt love thy neighbor as thyself,' this is the chief command of the Torah."

Our meditations in *Gates of Repentance* are numerous. Their major distinctive feature is the vast gamut of tradition from which they are drawn. The liturgy of liberal Jewry stands out in its will to take hold of every strand of Jewish wisdom through the ages and not to rest content with the Bible or the Talmud alone; not to choose only from antiquity, nor to depend solely on modern insights.

So, on pages 229–245 (and on pp. 3–14, for Rosh Hashana), we continue the tradition of citing meditations on prayer. We turn to them at any time on this long day of prayer, before any service, not just the evening one.

The Talit

We saw above (pp. 56–62) that the wearing of a *talit* is now optional in Reform congregations. The blessing for donning it is given at the beginning of each Morning Service (p. 79, for Rosh Hashana, and p. 291, for Yom Kippur). Yom Kippur eve is unique, however, in that it is the sole Evening Service at which the *talit* may be worn. Many reasons have been advanced for this custom, one being the Talmudic tale which relates that God appeared wrapped in a *talit* and told Israel to do the same when they wished to have their sins forgiven (see above, p. 106). Others note the similarity between the white *talit* and the shrouds in which the dead are traditionally buried. On this day, we stand face to face with our mortality: "On Rosh Hashana it is written, on Yom Kippur it is sealed . . . who shall live and who shall die" (from the "*Unetaneh Tokef*," pp. 108. 177–178, and 313; on which see above, pp. 75–78).

Evening Service

Preparatory Prayers

As with every other service, here, too, we find a rubric designed to prepare us for communal prayer. This one differs from others, however, in that its central text is the magnificent *"Kol Nidrei."*

"Kol Nidrei" (p. 252)

The *"Kol Nidrei"* is popularly associated with the context of 15th-century Spain, the home of a rapidly expanding Roman Catholic Church, which had instituted the Spanish Inquisition in order to enforce its will on deviant Christians. Under the terms of the Inquisition, any Christian violating his or her religious precepts was liable for severe punishment.

By the beginning of that century, many upper-class Jews had converted to Christianity. Some had done so because their economic or social life was made more convenient that way; others feared that the Inquisition's mandate might turn its attention to Jews, too, because they were a conspicuous minority within an otherwise homogeneous Christian society. But conversion, though technically simple, was in fact extremely difficult. Converts to Christianity were not accepted very readily within the social circles in which born Christians moved. Disparagingly labeled "New Christians," these apostates obtained none of the benefits they had expected, so that many of them longed to revert to the Judaism that had been their birthright.

But, Jews who sought to return to Judaism were categorized by the Church as if they were born Christians reneging on their faith. They were "Judaizers," whom the Inquisition was empowered to arrest, torture, and put to death, if necessary, in its effort to purify the faith. To return openly to Judaism was, therefore, out of the question. Thus, 15th-century Spain was the home of thousands of one-time Jews, newly converted to Christianity, but nonetheless secretly still clinging to their Jewish ancestral faith. These people were known as *Marranos*.

The *"Kol Nidrei"* enters our tale because it is a legal formula in which worshipers declare that they should not be held liable for oaths made under such unusual circumstances as anger or duress. There are two versions of this "prayer": one renounces such oaths as were made between last Yom Kippur and this one; the other (which is in our prayerbooks) refers to promises made between this Yom Kippur and the next. But, both versions reflect the medieval Jew's serious belief that any vow, even those taken without any intention of fulfillment (such as one's furious oath, "I swear I'll never speak to you again!"), must be carried out, because a pledge, even rashly made, is sacred. *"Kol Nidrei"* renders these oaths null and void, so that on Yom Kippur, Jews can safely turn to more serious matters of concern, making atonement for real sins, without allowing their impulsive vows to impede them as they try to repent, achieve pardon, and make a good beginning in the new year.

Popular opinion connects this formula for nullifying oaths made under duress to the existence of guilt-ridden *Marranos* who knew they had sworn loyalty to the Christian Church. They are said to have met secretly every Yom Kippur—in basement, makeshift synagogues perhaps—where they stealthily celebrated their particularly poignant Yom Kippur ritual. Theirs was the ultimate sin of denying the God of their people, and capitulating to the threats of earthly tyrants. How could God countenance such disloyalty on the holiest of days? So these *Marranos* are said to have created *"Kol Nidrei"* to atone for their pretended conversion. The *"Kol Nidrei"* formula rendered their formal acceptance of Christianity null and void. So, at least, goes the tale.

To the best of our knowledge, however, this tale is only partially true. Though there are reports of *Marranos* who included their rash pledge of allegiance to the Church within the broad category of vows to which the *"Kol Nidrei"* referred, *Marranos* did not compose our prayer; nor did they popularize it.

We do not know exactly when, where, or why the *"Kol Nidrei"* formula began. It is usually said to have originated in the Land of Israel some time after the Talmudic period, that is, after the sixth or seventh century C.E. On the other hand, its Aramaic wording closely resembles magical formulas in use in Babylonia, so it may have originated there. In either case, even though we find a possible reference to it in the eighth century, the first unmistakable citation of *"Kol Nidrei"* occurs 100 years later, when Rav Amram, the author of our first known comprehensive prayerbook (see above, p. 56) says that he has heard of it from his predecessor in office. Far from recommending the *"Kol Nidrei,"* this rabbi actually condemns it as a nonsensical custom that should be avoided. Despite his censure, however, the recitation of *"Kol Nidrei"* persisted. Some fifty years later, another authority, named Saadia, also attests to the existence of *"Kol Nidrei,"* but he concedes to the popular will by allowing it to be said in certain specified cases, namely, when an entire congregation has unwittingly erred in making a vow and wishes, as a group, to have its rash act nullified. Since such a situation probably would never occur, our author may well have intended to legislate the *"Kol Nidrei"* out of actual existence. But he, likewise, failed.

Throughout the following centuries, the *"Kol Nidrei"* was said with increasing fervor and was even provided with an expanded introduction (which we still use, "In the sight of God . . . ," p. 251) by a German authority, Rabbi Meir of Rothenburg (d. 1293). Gradually, it became linked with the haunting melody with which Ashkenazic, though not Sefardic, Jews always associate it. More than anything else, it is that tune to which the *"Kol Nidrei"* owes its present appeal.

Generally, liturgical melodies do not go back as far as we like to suppose. Because we love our familiar tunes so dearly, we mistakenly assume that the music, no less than the words, is hallowed by age. We go so far as to label our favorite melodies "Jewish," as if "authentic" Jewish synagogue tunes are those arising in some mystical way from the depths of the Jewish psyche. Certainly, there are old Jewish musical modes—most notably, aspects of chanting—which can often be traced to antiquity. But with very few exceptions, no synagogue music predates the 11th century, and our more familiar melodies are often rooted in non-Jewish European folk tunes only a century or two old.

On the other hand, we are able to extrapolate remnants of a general stratum of synagogue prayer melody going back to German Jewry of the 12th-15th centuries. They are called *"miSinai"* tunes, that is, those that are imagined, as it were, to have come "from Sinai," like the Torah itself. *"Kol Nidrei"* is such a tune. Though the actual musical settings we hear nowadays in our temples do not go back that far, they do display themes characteristic of *"miSinai"* melodies.

In the 17th century, the Cantorate (the origins of which we examined earlier, pp. 14-15) was developing into a professional class, so that travelling cantors carried the *"Kol Nidrei"* melody into countless Ashkenazic synagogues throughout Northern Europe. By the 19th century, the *"Kol Nidrei* Service" was inextricably bound together with its old Aramaic legal formula—which no one except scholars even understood any more—and with the haunting melody to which it was sung.

Thus scholarly investigation has emended the popular account of *"Kol Nidrei."* The prayer was obviously composed long before either the Spanish Inquisition or the *Marranos*, and it was already so popular in the ninth and tenth centuries that attempts by the most respected rabbinical authorities to remove it, were systematically ignored. The popular *"Kol Nidrei"* must have been carried to Spain, where some *Marranos* may have taken advantage of its theme of annulment of vows, so as to effect dispensation for their conversion to Christianity. But, in a totally unrelated development, *"Kol Nidrei"* had been carried also to Germany, where Jews who knew nothing of the Inquisition and who, in fact, antedated that institution's appearance in Spain by hundreds of years, developed a fondness for the prayer. They began setting it to the earliest known Ashkenazic liturgical music. One of their most prestigious leaders, Rabbi Meir of Rothenburg, raised the *"Kol Nidrei"* to a new and higher level of communal consciousness by composing a dramatic introduction for it. So, despite activity regarding *"Kol Nidrei"* among the Spanish *Marranos*, it is *Kol Nidrei*'s musical setting, typical of Germany, to which we of the Ashkenazic community are heirs.

Reform rabbis of the 19th century, however, were Western-European, university-trained scholars. They understood the *"Kol Nidrei"* formula and were embarrassed by it. High on their agenda, after all, was the attainment of civil rights for Jews who hitherto had been cloistered in ghettos, and the ground for their claim to equality in modern society was the assumption that Judaism, no less than Christianity, preached only the loftiest of values. They could hardly countenance a prayer that cancels promises Jews make, even though they knew that, technically speaking, the promises nullified in the *"Kol Nidrei"* were really not promises at all, but only rash vows thoughtlessly uttered in anger or jest. To make matters even more difficult, Reform Jews prayed from prayerbooks containing faithful translations of the original Hebrew, so Reform rabbis could not simply gloss over the *"Kol Nidrei,"* hoping no one would notice what it said. Above all, however, it should be noted that the *"Kol Nidrei"* issue was not simply an academic matter. Beyond embarrassment, moral discomfort, and theoretical politics lay the reality of the *more Judaico,* the Jews' oath. It was this oath which occupied the speakers' remarks when the rabbis met in the 1844 Brunswick Conference to discuss religious reform. According to the German law of the *more Judaico,* any Jew who appeared in court could be asked by the judge to proceed to the synagogue and there, in the company of ten Jews over the age of 13 and the judge himself, to don *talit* and *tefilin,* and to hold aloft the Torah while solemnly testifying before the rabbi that the witness's oath of the courtroom would not be considered annulled by the *"Kol Nidrei."* Little wonder, then, that the rabbis in Brunswick declared the *"Kol Nidrei"* unessential and promised to do their best to omit it in the future. Little wonder, also, that by 1817, the Berlin congregation had already begun what would become a general Reform practice of omitting the *"Kol Nidrei"* from its prayerbooks.

What the Reform rabbis did not count on is the power of music and the will of the average congregants, who cared little about the theological or moral consequence of the *Kol Nidrei*'s words relative to their fondness for the traditional melody, which obviously spoke very deeply to them of the mood and message of Yom Kippur. Despite rabbinical protestations, cantors continued to sing the *"Kol Nidrei,"* even when it did not appear in the books. The rabbis tried to substitute alternative lyrics, such as psalms, to which the tune could be fitted, but cantors remained faithful to the old familiar words rather than take a chance that by changing the lyrics they might render the people's favorite chant haltingly. So, officially, the *"Kol Nidrei"* disappeared from most Reform liturgies, while, unofficially, it remained.

As recently as the 1940s, the *"Kol Nidrei"* issue raged furiously in the United States and Canada. The committee charged with reworking the

1922 *Union Prayer Book* (Revised Edition) was divided on whether to include the Aramaic text. The first printing of the newly revised prayerbook contained it. One member of the committee charged another with disregarding the committee's decision to omit *"Kol Nidrei."* The latter denied the charge, asserting that the committee had agreed on its inclusion. In the end, the entire first printing, which contained *"Kol Nidrei,"* was withdrawn from the market, and in the second printing, the prayer was deleted. Rather than go to the expense of printing the entire book anew, however, only the page that had included *"Kol Nidrei"* was altered. Readers who recall the old (Newly Revised) *Union Prayer Book* will remember that the Yom Kippur Eve service contains a page with a double-spaced prayer asking that our promises may be found acceptable to God. Below, there appear the words *"Kol Nidrei,"* and instructions in tiny italics, "The *Kol Nidrei* chant." That was the compromise. In the extra blank space only partially used up by the double spacing, there once appeared the *"Kol Nidrei"*!

In *Gates of Repentance*, *"Kol Nidrei"* has been restored (p. 252), with, however, an altered English "free translation" which informs us that only vows to God, not to people, are nullified; and then, only "should we, after honest effort, find ourselves unable to fulfill them." No one can now mistake the message of the prayer as evidence of Jewish irresponsibility in the face of promises.

"Kol Nidrei" accumulated such psychic force through the ages that it soon lost its quality of being mere preparation for later liturgical staples, and demanded, instead, its own preparatory material, even beyond the formula composed by Meir of Rothenburg. The Kabbalistic author Isaiah Horowitz (1565?–1630), for example, tells us that he used to prepare for *"Kol Nidrei"* privately, by saying: "Woe unto me. What have I done? I have rebelled against the Sovereign of Sovereigns and against God's holy Torah. How have I marred my soul by exchanging an eternal world for a transitory one?" Our modern equivalent is found on pages 249–250, "In the beginning. . . ." Stylistically, it moves from past to present, in the juxtaposition of the instructions "Say then," a conclusion drawn from our past, and "Say now," the identical demand seen arising out of the present moment (p. 250).

"In the beginning . . . ," it should be noted, demonstrates well the changing consciousness regarding sexist language (see above, pp. 87–90). In the original poem, the third line ended with the word "man"; we have added "and woman." The pronoun "he" in line 4 was changed to "they." "The vision was seen by the founders of our people . . ." (middle of the page) originally read "fathers," not "founders."

For the Reader's prayer before the open Ark (p. 247), see discussion of *"Hineni,"* above, pages 14–16.

"Shema" and Its Blessings *(pp. 253–260)*

We follow the normal threefold statement of Jewish belief regarding God, along with the traditional fourth blessing said only in the evenings (see above, pp. 29–40). Our English versions are largely taken directly from the *Union Prayer Book* and paraphrase, rather than translate, the Hebrew texts.

The Reader's *Kaddish* concludes this rubric, preceded by Leviticus 16:30 ("For on this day . . ."), the biblical basis for Yom Kippur, as well as the most direct statement of the day's theme and purpose.

The Tefila (pp. 260–268)

Here too, we follow the traditional sevenfold series of themes (see above, p. 19), with, however, paraphrases of the Hebrew texts.

For the special *"Uvechen"* prayer (pp. 262–264), see above, pages 20–21.

For the insertions in the first and last two benedictions, regarding the imagery of being inscribed in the Book of Life, see above, pages 21–22.

For the significance of our reference to Zion, page 266, see above, pages 22–23.

For the silent meditation (p. 268), see above, pages 82–84.

Confession and Prayers for Forgiveness (Selichot) (pp. 269–281)

Confession (pp. 269–272)

No element is more indigenous to the Yom Kippur services than the Confession. Religions handle the problem of individual sin differently, of course, but Judaism has generally eschewed the kind of personal confession typical of, say, Catholicism, in favor of the communal recitation of a fixed litany of errors at specified times in the year. To be sure, personal confession on one's deathbed has been customary through the ages, and the Rabbis are unanimous on the point that even on Yom Kippur, liturgical confession in public does not obviate our having to seek forgiveness directly and personally from the people we have wronged. Nor does confession permit us to repeat our old, erring ways, even if we do intend to ask forgiveness again next year. So, with all these caveats, one of the highlights of the Yom Kippur services is the repeated communal Confession of specified sins, most of which the individuals present have not themselves committed.

Let us, then, consider the traditional Confession prayers that have come down to us. There are two of them: the Long Confession and the Short Confession (called respectively in Hebrew, the *Vidui Rabba* and the *Vidui Zuta*). In their present form, both go back to, at least, the ninth century.

They are said together (the Short followed by the Long) at every Yom Kippur service, with the exception of the Concluding *Ne-ila* Service, when only the Short Confession is recited. Readers familiar with traditional Hebrew services may recall them by their more common Hebrew names derived from their introductory words: the Short as *"Ashamnu,"* and the Long as *"Al Chet."* They are said, traditionally, while standing; many traditional Jews beat their breasts at each line, softly punctuating the rhythmic litany, every blow intended as a heartfelt atonement for another sin in the liturgical catalogue.

Gates of Repentance contains both Confessions. (That was not always the case in Reform liturgy, which often considered two Confessions redundant.) But they are abridged, and the English equivalents vary from service to service, especially in the Short Confession, the *"Ashamnu."* These two facts, the inclusion of traditional material and, simultaneously, the freedom we feel to enhance traditional texts by creatively adding to or subtracting from them, define the position of Reform Judaism today. In the past, Reform Jews were often as dogmatic about taking material out—like the *"Kol Nidrei"* (pp. 114–118 above), and particularistic references in the *"Aleinu"* (pp. 42–46 above)—as Orthodox Jews were about leaving everything in (recall the Chatam Sofer's insistence that nothing be altered, and his determined inclusion of the benediction, " . . . who has not made me a woman"; cf. pp. 64–66 above). Reform Judaism today reemphasizes tradition. We assume that traditionally received texts have a life of their own which may not be lightly cast aside. Yet tradition survives only insofar as we, the living Jewish community of today, appropriate it as our own.

How, then, have we dealt innovatively with the Confessions? The most obvious feature is the novel English which appears in each service. Let us look at three examples.

First, we must locate the Confessions in *Gates of Repentance*. The Short Confession appears on page 269; the Long, on page 271. A glance at the former reveals the fact that the first Hebrew letters of the words are arranged as an acrostic, that is, the words begin with each letter of the Hebrew alphabet, in order: *Alef, Beit, Gimel,* and so on. This was a favored form of poetry in the Byzantine period, when synagogue *piyutim,* it will be recalled, began (see above, p. 77; and for discussion of another acrostic, p. 104).

Now, if we turn to the English translation · below the last Hebrew paragraph on page 269, we find that although the first two lines offer little of note, the list of sins that follows has been composed so as to constitute an English acrostic, the equivalent, stylistically speaking, of the Hebrew prayer it is intended to replicate.

People often demand that a prayer's English content be a verbatim translation of the Hebrew original, so that they may know what the Hebrew is saying. The editors of *Gates of Prayer*, for example, were charged with failing to differentiate between literal translations of Hebrew prayers and free paraphrases. (This situation was remedied in *Gates of Repentance*, where all English paragraphs that do not adhere literally to the Hebrew original are prefaced by a small circle. Our prayer here is an example.) We see, therefore, that people treat English prayers as if they ought to be exact renderings of the Hebrew, thereby implying that the original authors of our prayers must have selected their words because of their meaning, and we should not presume to alter that meaning without saying so.

But, our Short Confession, the *"Ashamnu,"* indicates that the precise meaning of the Hebrew was not always the poet's primary concern. Surely, the author wished only to list a series of sins, with less regard for what they were than for the letter with which they started! Content, then, was secondary to style. The important thing was for a confession to occur, for worshipers to struggle in a communal fashion with the human penchant for error.

We are thus led to a solution to a dilemma often posed regarding the Confession. How, people want to know, should we expect them to admit that they have committed sins of which they may not be guilty? Would it not be better for each worshiper to confess his or her own errors privately, in a moment of silent prayer perhaps? Admittedly, silent prayer and the confession of sin thereby is a gallant thing, traditional in Judaism since Talmudic times, and is included explicitly in our prayerbook here; but public confession, too, has its place, and the content of the public recitation was never intended as a specification of sins each of us actually committed. This is clear from the fact that our public Confession contains a list of sins at which the poet arrived arbitrarily through a desire to follow the Hebrew alphabet. The purpose of public confession is to facilitate the process whereby the community as a whole stands together in common recognition that all people fail at times to live up to their highest possibilities. Recognizing that fact, we may be quicker to forgive others, better able to resist becoming obsessively involved with our own wrongdoing, and committed all the more strongly to work with others to eradicate the human pain and suffering which human beings have wrought. The very *act* of public contrition may be as necessary as its content.

We, therefore, need not convince ourselves that we are personally guilty of every sin catalogued. Like its Hebrew counterpart, the list on page 269 was selected, above all, because of stylistic considerations, its purpose being to facilitate the very act of confession on Yom Kippur Eve. We preferred listing sins that spoke to the modern condition, naturally, and so, omitted some of the sins contained in the Hebrew original. For example, "bigotry" (a word from our poem) is a modern concept that would not have occurred to the author of the Hebrew, while "rebelliousness" (a translation of one of that author's Hebrew words) sounds strange in our time and is, therefore, not used here for the "R" word.

How was this attempt at reproducing an ancient art form in a modern style greeted? It has received mixed reviews. When the first draft of the prayerbook was completed, it was circulated to every member in the Central Conference of American Rabbis. A large majority approved, but several demurrers voiced their opinions: some urged us to replicate in English the exact Hebrew meaning; others argued that we should abandon the acrostic style completely, because it seemed artificial or pretentious. The result was a compromise. The full acrostic appears in the Confession here, but not in other Confessions elsewhere in the book. In fact, even this is not a full acrostic. Certain letters are missing, and my earlier notes indicate that for the missing "H," "T," and "U," we once had "haughty," "tyrannical," and "unforgiving." The editor removed them for stylistic reasons. He wanted to facilitate congregational recitation by preserving a certain linguistic rhythm, which would have been interrupted by their inclusion.

We turn now to the Short Confession on page 327, which displays the beginning of an acrostic, followed by a conclusion with a double entendre: the last line reads, "Our sins are an alphabet of woe."

A third Confession, however (pp. 438–439), emphasizes content rather than style, specific sins rather than the fact of sin. We shall examine this entire section of the service (the *Avoda*) in greater detail later (pp. 138–144), but for now we need note only that the context in which this Confession falls is a recollection of the Holocaust and the fact of human perversity to which the death camps attest. In that context, both a silent meditation, in which we examine our own ways, and a public affirmation of failure are in order. So we have both, the public list this time being chosen with a deliberate eye to content. Read the list. Read it out loud as if engaged in public affirmation of human failure—this is exactly what a liturgical confession is in Judaism. Read it with your congregation at prayer after you have spent most of Yom Kippur day fasting. Is there even one person who can rise thereafter and assert that this world is not still sated with woe or that we are guiltless in maintaining it that way?

We have seen, then, that Judaism favors both personal and public confession, and that the public one can be both long and short. In looking at the latter, we discovered that in liturgy, form is sometimes more important than content, since form may facilitate a liturgical act—in this case, the communal expression of universal sinfulness—and a consequent commitment to altering the world's sorry state. We were led to consider how an old form (in this case, the acrostic) could be maintained, but with new content. And, unlike traditional services in which the same content is necessarily repeated at each Confession, we saw how Reform Judaism has used its license to alter the Confession slightly, in order to achieve a different effect at each point in the day's worship.

In traditional services, the Confession is said first by individuals at the end of their silent recitation of the *Tefila*, and then repeated by the Reader in the middle of that prayer's public repetition. During the *Tefila*, tradition understood the Reader as being the actual legal agent of the congregation (i.e., the *Sheliach Tsibur*, see above, page 15); so, where possible, the second order of Confession, the public one, was deliberately included in the middle of the Reader's repetition of the *Tefila* text, where the Reader's legal standing would be in no doubt. (The exception to this rule is the Confession in the Evening Service, since that *Tefila*, originally seen as optional—see above, pages 79–80—was not repeated aloud at all, and therefore it is impossible to insert the Confession in it.) Reform worship has dispensed with the practice of repeating the *Tefila*, so we have but one order of Confession, that one being placed after the *Tefila*, where the individual Confession would normally occur.

Prayers for Forgiveness (Selichot) (pp. 273–281)

"Ya-aleh" ("Unto You . . . ") (pp. 274–275)

Many readers of this commentary may well recall how, as children, they sat all day in a traditional synagogue, watching the pages being turned as apparently endless prayers were intoned by the cantor. Many of those "pages without end" contain *Selichot*, or Prayers for Forgiveness, of which our selection is both modest and varied, utilizing material both new and old (pp. 273–281).

Selichot (singular: *Selicha*) are a kind of *piyut* (or liturgical poem inserted in the standard liturgy, on which, see p. 77 above), the subject matter of which is forgiveness.

In many ways, "*Ya-aleh*" is a typical *Selicha*, and can serve as our model. Its anonymous author modeled it on Leviticus 23:32, which likens Yom Kippur to the Sabbath, *Shabbat Shabbaton*, and instructs, "You shall keep your Shabbat from nightfall to nightfall." Each stanza, thus, consists of three requests, each one a separate line: (1) that our prayers "arise" to God "at nightfall"; (2) that they "come" before God "in the morning" of the next day; and (3) that they "appear" to God "at nightfall" tomorrow night. What makes the poem interesting is the variety of synonyms it uses for prayer. The poet never uses the same word twice. Each occurrence features a different noun: "petition," "outcry," "voice," and so on. Moreover, the nouns are not chosen at random, but follow the Hebrew alphabet backwards, thus constituting a reverse alphabetic acrostic.

Because these poems were remembered frequently by the mnemonic device of recalling the letter next expected, different versions sometimes arose in which oral tradition substituted one word with another that fit equally well because it began with the same initial. In our case, the letter *Ayin* begins the word *atiratenu* (in some texts) and *inuyenu* (in others). We have chosen to reproduce the former reading, because it means "entreaty" as opposed to the latter version meaning "self-affliction."

"We are Your people . . . " (p. 279)

This traditional conclusion to the Confession and Prayers for Forgiveness is based on a midrash to Song of Songs 2:16, where the biblical phrase, "My beloved is mine and I am his," is expanded to include other models of relationship between God and Israel: parent–child, shepherd–flock, and so on, most of which are replicated in our poem. What the poem does not make clear is the magnificent conclusion to this midrash. Its whole point is the reciprocal nature of the covenant that binds God and Israel. "Whenever I require anything," says Israel, "I seek it from God." But the reverse is true, too: "Whenever God requires something, God seeks it from me." In our case, *we* require forgiveness, and hereby seek it from God with our Prayers for Forgiveness, which this poem concludes. But equally true is the fact that *God* instructs us to repent, since it is also *God*'s wish that we begin anew on this day of the soul's cleansing.

"Avinu Malkenu" (pp. 280–281)

For *"Avinu Malkenu,"* see above, pages 23–25.

This *"Avinu Malkenu"* differs from the others in *Gates of Repentance* in that it is longer. In this version, we include extra stanzas drawn from the traditional selection.

Concluding Prayers (pp. 282–287)

For *"Aleinu"* (pp. 282–283), see above, pages 42–46. For *Kaddish* (pp. 284–285), see above, pages 47–50.

"Yigdal" (pp. 286–287)

One often hears how Judaism differs from Christianity in that Judaism is a religion of action rather than belief, or, as the colloquial expression has it: "deed, not creed." There is some truth to this generalization, in that Christianity has tended to be defined by its adherents according to belief systems, the denial of which constitutes heresy. Our "heretics," however, have usually been adjudged guilty of contravening *mitzvot*, actions. For example, Polish *Mitnagedim* found fault with the way their Hasidic opponents prayed (they used a combination of Ashkenazic and Sefardic traditions, based on 16th-century mystical doctrines) and with the "fact" that they ate non-Kosher meat because their slaughtering knife was improperly honed. Similarly, in 1838, when the pioneering Reform rabbi, Abraham Geiger, was invited to occupy the community synagogue of Breslau, his Orthodox opponents were quick to accuse him, not of denying false doctrine, but of profaning the Shabbat. To be sure, disputed religious behavior is always emblematic of presuppositions of faith. But the fact remains that religious argument in Judaism has revolved about the way people behave, not the things they say they believe.

On the other hand, we have our creeds. The Mishna, for example, denies a share in the World-to-Come to "those who say that the resurrection of the dead is not prescribed in Torah, or that Torah is not from heaven." We saw also that the *"Shema"* and its blessings constitute a statement of belief in which Jews assert the existence of one sole God who created the universe, revealed Torah to Israel, and redeemed us from Egyptian bondage (see above, pp. 29–40). So doctrine is not unimportant to Judaism.

Formulating the essential features of Jewish belief was a favored philosophical activity in the Middle Ages. Several systems were devised, but none achieved the success or the notoriety of the Thirteen Principles of Faith proposed by our most illustrious philosophical genius, Moses Maimonides, known also as Rabbenu Mosheh ben Maimon, or (more usually) by the acronym formed by the Hebrew initials for that name, RaMBaM (1135–1204). We have appropriately referred to his opinions many times in these pages, but nowhere is his influence more evident than in the realm of Jewish belief.

Maimonides's Thirteen Principles became so popular by the 14th century that they were adapted for prayer in many synagogues. *"Yigdal"* is one such adaptation, ascribed to Daniel ben Judah of Rome. For reasons that we shall presently come to, Daniel composed the *"Yigdal"* for his philosophically oriented friends in Rome, in the 14th century. It did not become a staple in our services until two centuries later, however, when Polish prayerbooks were printed with the *"Yigdal"* in them.

Most interesting, perhaps, is the fact that, unlike most creeds, the *"Yigdal"* is not usually spoken. Jakob Petuchowski aptly calls it a creed that is sung. And it is not sung only by Jews! We find it also as an Anglican and Protestant hymn. Thomas Oliver, a Wesleyan minister, heard the singing of *"Yigdal"* in a London synagogue and liked it so much that he translated it from the Hebrew, as he put it, "giving it as far as I could a Christian character."

The Thirteen Principles which Maimonides formulated are: (1) God's existence; (2) God's unity; (3) God's incorporeality; (4) God's absolute existence as the sole entity upon which all else depends, but which is not itself dependent on anything; (5) the principle that God alone should be worshiped; (6) the validity of prophecy; (7) the superiority of Moses over other prophets; (8) Torah's divine and, thus, perfect origin; (9) the principle that Moses's Torah can never be abrogated; (10) God's omniscience; (11) divine retribution; (12) the coming of the Messiah; (13) the resurrection of the dead.

Maimonides's version of Jewish belief won acceptance liturgically, both in its *"Yigdal"* formulation and in a more prosaic statement that was placed as an optional reading at the end of the daily service. But the victory was not easily achieved. For some time, the Jewish world was divided on the merits of Maimonides's philosophy. These Maimonidean Controversies (as they are known) embroiled Jewish minds all over Europe, to the extent that some communities felt impelled to declare in some tangible way their acceptance or rejection of the master's teachings. That explains Daniel ben Judah's decision to compose *"Yigdal."* Our poet's creation reflected his proud definition of self as a Maimonidean partisan. The appearance of *"Yigdal"* 200 years later in Poland was equally motivated by controversy, since the 16th century witnessed a revival of philosophical speculation among some members of the scholarly elite of the Yeshivot, and a comparable rejection, by others, of Maimonides's views.

For Reform Jews, Maimonides loomed as a heroic personality insofar as he successfully wed tradition to the modernity of his own day, thus epitomizing the very example of synthesis for which 19th-century Reformers strove. Hence, the *"Yigdal"* became a preferred hymn for Reform, and is appropriately included here, with, however, one emendation that deletes the reference to a personal messiah, and another which replaces the affirmation of bodily resurrection with a phrase acknowledging the eternality of the spirit. Obviously, despite Reform Judaism's general adulation of Maimonides, its theology has not been able to accept all of his principles. (See also discussion on the 13th principle, "Resurrection of the Dead," below, pp. 136–138.)

Its usual melody is known as the Leoni *"Yigdal"* named after Cantor Meyer Leon, the very *Chazan* whom Thomas Oliver heard before writing and publishing his Christian equivalent in 1770.

Morning Service

Preparatory Prayers (pp. 291–304)

On the preparatory morning liturgy, divided into Morning Blessings (*Birchot Hashachar*) and Poems of Praise (*Pesukei Dezimra*), see above, pages 54–56 and 69–70.

Here, as in Rosh Hashana Service I, we include the usual morning traditional readings for this rubric, supplemented by translations of some poetry that is traditionally added on Yom Kippur, or that has only recently been composed for the occasion.

"*Shachar Avakeshcha*" ("Early will I seek You . . . ," pp. 292–293) was composed by the 11th-century Spanish poet, Solomon ibn Gabirol (whom we encountered above—pp. 51–52—as the author to whom "*Adon Olam*" is traditionally ascribed). "O Lord, where shall I find You?" (p. 297) is another poem by Judah Halevi (on whom see above, p. 105).

On the *talit* (p. 291), see above, pages 56–62.

On *Birkat Hashir* ("Our Immeasurable Debt to God," pp. 300–303) and on the significance of the words *hamelech*, "O KING" (p. 302), see above, page 74.

On the Reader's *Kaddish* as a dividing mark between rubrics (pp. 303–304), see above, pages 49–50.

"Shema" and Its Blessings (pp. 304–308)

Here, as with Rosh Hashana Morning Service I, we include free English interpretations of the usual threefold statement of Jewish belief (on which see above, pp. 29–40).

Tefila (pp. 308–323)

By and large, we use creative interpretative English throughout this rubric as well, with the exception of the "*Unetaneh Tokef*" (pp. 311–315), the *Kedusha* (Sanctification) (pp. 315–316), and the "*Uvechen*" insertion (pp. 316–318).

For a full discussion of the *Tefila*, see above, pages 18–23.

For the "*Unetaneh Tokef*" (pp. 311–315), see above, pages 75–78.

For the "*Uvechen*" (pp. 316–317), see above, pages 20–21.

For the High Holy Day insertions in the first and last two benedictions, with the metaphor of being inscribed in the Book of Life, see above, page 21.

For the Priestly Benediction ("Peace," pp. 321–322), see above, pages 79–82.

For the Meditation with which the *Tefila* concludes (p. 323), see above, pages 82–84.

Confession and Prayers for Forgiveness (pp. 324–337)

For fuller discussion of these rubrics, see above, pages 119–124.

The Silent Confession on pp. 325–326 appears in slightly smaller typeface, but for no liturgical or theological reason. Originally, all meditations were to have been printed this way, and when that original decision was rescinded, there was no way to change these two pages without drastically altering the pages following it. Thus, they were allowed to stay as they were.

This is an appropriate time to credit Rabbi John D. Rayner for his major contribution to our liturgy. Rabbi Rayner and Rabbi Chaim Stern together edited the British volume *Gate of Repentance* in use by the Union of Liberal and Progressive Synagogues in England since 1973. Much of our *Machzor* goes back to material composed or edited by Rabbi Rayner. The original version of this sizable meditation, for example, is his.

For "Who among us is righteous . . . " (p. 327), see page 120. In general, it should be noted that we have a partial acrostic in the English, to match the Hebrew of this Short Confession.

The following Long Confession (pp. 327–331) divides the sins under discussion into thematic categories, rather than following the traditional alphabetic order. Also, unlike the traditional version, the categories are clearly labeled here, and each category is introduced with a modern note: "We sin against You when we sin against ourselves" (pp. 327, 328, and 329).

"Merely to have survived . . . " (pp. 331–332) is a very striking reading by Anthony Hecht, published in 1968. Judaism instructs us that the survival of the Jewish people is itself a *mitzva*, so that survival for survival's sake would seem to be mandated by Jewish law. On the other hand, we have seen how Jews have variously interpreted this *mitzva* as implying a further purpose to Jewish survival, whether the mystical striving for *Tikun Olam* (Reparation of the World) or the Reform Movement's insistence on the Jewish Mission (on which see above, pp. 39–40, 42–43, and 81–82). Certainly in our own time, when the Jewish people has nearly been eradicated, the value of Jewish survival should not be denied. Our reading does not question the inherent validity of Jewish existence, but it does ask this probing question which Yom Kippur forces upon us: Granted our survival, what have we done with it? As Anthony Hecht puts it, "Merely to have survived is not an index of excellence."

For "We are Your people . . . " (p. 337), the traditional conclusion for this rubric, see above, page 124.

Service for the Reading of the Torah (pp. 338–357)

For the general nature of this rubric, see above, pages 84–87.

For "The Lord, the Lord God . . . " (The Thirteen Attributes of God, p. 338), see above, page 106.

For "*Avinu Malkenu,*" pp. 339–340, see above, pages 23–25.

For the Torah and *Haftara* readings, see discussion above, pages 90–91. The Rosh Hashana readings offered alternatives, but here we follow Reform precedent, at least since the original 1894 *Union Prayer Book.* The traditional reading in this place is Leviticus 16, where Aaron and his priestly progeny receive their instructions for performing the cultic minutiae for Yom Kippur. We have already seen how we Reform Jews denied the traditional belief in the eventual restoration of the cult, how we ended distinctions of class based on presumed priestly progeniture, and how Rabbi David Einhorn generalized the priestly charge to include all Jews who, together, were to practice the self-sacrifice necessary to achieve that totally just society of which our Jewish Mission speaks (see above, pp. 39–40, 42–43, and 81–82). As expected, therefore, Reform Jews have had difficulty identifying with this traditional passage.

In its place, we have elected to read a passage from Deuteronomy (29:9–14 and 30:11–20), stressing the doctrine of personal responsibility. We saw above (pp. 33–34) that the Rabbis denied the validity of miracles for their day. God, they believed, had supplanted miracle workers with the gift of Torah and had charged us with the difficult but necessary task of making decisions based on our study of the Torah. They, therefore, told a tale of a halachic debate in which miracles had properly been declared irrelevant in the decision-making process. The source of knowledge lies within the grasp of human experience, they held, and to support their position, they quoted our Yom Kippur reading: "It [the Torah] is not in heaven. . . . No, it is very near to you, in your mouth and in your heart, and you can do it" (pp. 343–345). This assertion, that each person's duty to walk in God's way cannot be delegated to others, is then followed by the ringing charge, "I have set before you life or death, blessing or curse; choose life, therefore, that you and your descendants may live" (p. 345).

The challenge to respond to this day of fasting by choosing life for ourselves and for others, is reiterated in the *Haftara* from Isaiah 58 (pp. 347–349). Isaiah prophesied at the end of the eighth century B.C.E., predicting the Assyrian invasion and destruction of the Northern Kingdom

129

of Israel (in 722/721 B.C.E.). As a champion of social justice, Isaiah condemned the Israelite ruling classes for perverting God's moral law even as they went through the motions of punctiliously observing Jewish ritual. It followed, for him, that the covenant was abrogated; God would use the Assyrian enemy as the divine rod of punishment.

Our passage, Isaiah 58, however, is generally said by Bible scholars not to have been written by Isaiah. Rather, it is an anonymous outcry appended to Isaiah's genuine prophecies, perhaps because of its similarity in content. Here, the prophet rails against the outward fastidious concern for fasting, which is unaccompanied by equally genuine zeal for human welfare. "Is this the fast I look for? A day of self-affliction? . . . Is not *this* the fast I look for: to unlock the shackles of injustice, to undo the fetters of bondage, to let the oppressed go free, and to break every cruel chain? Is it not to share your bread with the hungry, and to bring the homeless poor into your house? When you see the naked, to clothe them, and never to hide yourself from your own kin?" (pp. 347–349).

A clearer call to compassion in contrast to mere outward piety is not to be found. Traditional Judaism easily adopted this passage as its reading, seeing in it the value of true fasting, as opposed to symbolic gesture. The insistence on an ethical accompaniment to ritual, after all, did not have to await Judaism's reform in the 19th century. It was there all the time. But the passage spoke particularly eloquently to Reform Jews who had defined Judaism as *ethical* monotheism. Therefore, they readily adopted, and adapted, this *Haftara* by omitting part of the previous chapter (57), which had constituted the first half of the traditional reading, in order to emphasize the ethical message of the second half.

For the prayers on pages 354–355, see above, page 86.

Additional Prayers (pp. 361–391)

We have completed our survey of Yom Kippur's Evening and Morning Services (*Arvit* and *Shacharit*). In a traditional order of worship, we would still have before us the Additional Service (*Musaf*) typical of all holidays; the usual Afternoon Service (*Mincha*), thus completing the triad of services held on any day of the year; and the Concluding Service (*Ne-ila*) unique to the particularly awesome Day of Atonement. (For an outline of the various services, see above, pp. 7–10.)

Furthermore, in that same traditional order of worship, these services would appear largely identical to each other. They were generally seen as taking the place of sacrifice in the ancient Temple cult, and, thus, were constructed out of the same basic building block, the *Tefila* (the prayer the Rabbis likened to the "offering of our lips" rather than of our animals or our produce). If it was evening or morning, the *"Shema"* and its blessings were added. Preparatory and concluding liturgy bracketed the whole. And special *piyutim*, poems that expressed the character of the specific day in question, were inserted. The resulting *Machzor*, therefore, easily lent itself to the impression that with each successive service, one was repeating the same verbiage yet one more time, without any reasonable excuse for doing so.

Editors of modern liberal prayerbooks, thus, have faced this challenge: they have had to construct liturgies for worshipers who no longer view the sacrificial cult as the dominant model for prayer. One question that arises for them is what to do with the remaining services for Yom Kippur. Granted the necessary integrity with which one views the repetitive inclusion of the *Tefila* in each service (along with its normal insertions, such as the Confessions) and granted, also, the insightful recognition that a certain amount of cumulative litany-like repetitiveness provides a desired psychological state in the worshiper; but, how does one prepare a *Machzor* that will not simply bore people?

The most difficult stumbling block in this regard has been the traditional *Musaf*, or Additional Service, intended to correspond to the Additional Sacrifice featured on holy days in Temple times.

As we saw (above, p. 9), we Reform Jews have quarreled ideologically with this sacrificial basis for *Musaf*, and so, we could have avoided its redundant recapitulation of the *Tefila* simply by omitting it. But on Yom Kippur, it is appropriate to sit in prayer all day; we require not shorter, but meaningful prayer material to fill the hours until the final *shofar* blast announces the end of the fast. If the old *Machzor* had been exasperatingly repetitive in its apparently endless Hebrew prose, at least it contained enough liturgy to last the day. Hence, editors of liberal liturgy who excise *piyutim* and entire sections dealing with objectionable themes such as a return of the sacrificial cult have had to provide alternative worship material to supplement the usual rubrics. What we offer here (pp. 361–391), then, is by no means intended as a *Musaf* service; rather, these are Additional Prayers for use as time and intention allow during the afternoon of Yom Kippur.

The "Additional Prayers" section differs from the other "Services," in that it is arranged not by traditional rules—relevant rubrics inherited from the past—but by topic. As we have seen in this commentary, our traditional liturgy does not exhaust a particular theme and then move on to another one. Despite the fact that certain rubrics prefer certain ideas, other ideas are often mixed in, and any given theme may be encountered over and over again. The enormous extent of highly differentiated topics that we take for granted was not available to the Rabbis of the second

131

century, who rarely thought in terms of such discrete categories of human experience as happiness, loneliness, anger, and so on. They were much more likely to think in terms of what we called idea-complexes, in which they combined easily what might seem to us widely diverse notions: the nature of human beings and the nature of God, for example; or justice and mercy; or all the divine attributes together, rather than any single quality on which moderns are capable of reading or writing entire books.

But it is differentiation of subject matter that governs modern minds. "What is the book about?" we ask, or "What is the rabbi's sermon topic?". Authors write introductions explaining how their work differs topically from others, and they label chapters according to the logical subcategorization of their subjects. So, as modern liturgy is freed from the structural constraints of rubrics designed centuries ago, it is frequently reorganized according to topic.

A glance through the Additional Prayers offered in *Gates of Repentance* indicates this attempt to conceptualize the subcategories that together make up Yom Kippur. We find:

Prayer (pp. 363–365),

Human Nature (pp. 365–368),

Responsibility (pp. 368–370),

The Evil Inclination (pp. 370–371),

Turning (pp. 372–377),

Forgiveness (pp. 377–383),

Seeking and Finding (pp. 383–388), and

Life and Death (pp. 388–391).

None of these topics is so modern that tradition does not know of it. But traditional prayers spoke easily of all these things together, while we ask worshipers to spend part of this Great Day of Awe considering the implications of each one separately.

Internalizing the message of Yom Kippur through a thoughtful consideration of these, its sub-headings, is no easy task. In their rush for modernity, Western minds have relegated many of these concepts to what they view as a trash-heap of outmoded religious ideological baggage. They may use some of the same vocabulary, to be sure, but if so, they have filled the word with new content, usually drawn from more familiar universes of meaning, typically psychology. Judaism still insists that Yom Kippur's message is not reducible to psychology—or to sociology, or politics, or any other modern discipline with which we feel comfortable. We ask that worshipers think about these Additional Prayers in terms of their age-old religious meaning, not their modern definitions.

What does the fact that we begin our quest for meaning by considering "Prayer" (pp. 363–365) imply regarding the Jewish view of life? How does the Jewish definition of "Human Nature" (pp. 365–368) differ from systems contained in a university curriculum, or from the mechanistic model of Marx or Freud, for example? Are we mere atoms, set into motion by accidental processes? Are we battlegrounds between instinctive drives and the harness of conscience? Are we changeable? And, if so, how?

To whom do we owe "Responsibility" (pp. 368–370)—to ourselves, to family, to the Jewish people, to humanity, to God? What does it mean to have to admit not only that there is such a thing as evil in the world, but that we are capable of causing it ("The Evil Inclination," pp. 370–371)? In the end, we speak in ancient echoes of "Turning" to God (pp. 372–377) and sensing "Forgiveness" (pp. 377–383). We affirm the reality, and the difficulty, of the religious quest itself ("Seeking and Finding," pp. 383–388). As the "*Unetaneh Tokef*" already taught us (pp. 75–78 above), we insist that we shall have failed dismally this day if we do not come to terms with one fact above all: we are human beings whose mortal lives will some day end. What shall be said of our lives when they are over ("Life and Death," pp. 388–391)?

The modern material in the service speaks clearly to ears familiar with contemporary imagery and style. But juxtaposed to the new readings is a selection of traditional passages, some of it material that was originally to have been placed elsewhere in the Yom Kippur *Machzor*, but was omitted in its standard place in the course of our editorial deliberations on this book. Topically speaking, these traditional readings fit here because they illuminate a religious message for contemporary life.

The two Hebrew passages at the bottom of page 366, for example, are attributed to two rabbis of the first and second centuries (Hillel and Akiba). They are followed immediately by an English reading ("Then Isaac asked . . . ") composed by Edmond Fleg (1874–1963), who based his work on an ancient midrash. The interpretation of "You are my witnesses," which concludes the three entries (p. 367), is attributed to Shimon bar Yochai, another second-century sage, whom medieval Jews associated with Jewish mysticism.

The author of the middle piece, Edmond Fleg, deserves more than passing mention, because he illustrates well the dilemma posed by Judaism to many Jewish European intellectuals at the turn of the century. Our investigation into the High Holy Day prayers favored by the Reform Movement has necessarily biased our historical survey, in that we have dwelt on the "success stories" of those Jews who remained loyal to their heritage and devoted their lives to translating its message for the new age. Many other Jews succumbed completely to the allure of modernity, proving themselves more than anxious to flock to the banner of other ideologies, particularly Socialism, or failing that, to adopt the self-proclaimed status of universal lovers of culture, science, and the arts. Fleg might well have gone this last route but for a rude awakening provided by the infamous Dreyfus Affair (1894–1906). Until that time, he had lived comfortably in Paris as a successful playwright and theater critic, with little or no regard for his Jewish background. From 1894 to 1906, however, French liberals were shaken by the obviously trumped up charges of treason levelled against Alfred Dreyfus, a lone Jew in the professional French military establishment. Dreyfus was eventually cleared, but only after initial conviction and imprisonment, accompanied by mob hysteria and massive anti-Semitic demonstrations on the streets. Theodor Herzl, then an acculturated correspondent for the Viennese press, covered the Dreyfus Affair, from which he emerged as the proponent of political Zionism. He had become convinced that if descendants of the French revolution, the bastion of human liberty, could display such virulent hatred of Jews, surely Jews were safe nowhere in the world outside of their own sovereign state.

Fleg was equally aghast at the collapse of liberalism implicit in the Dreyfus Affair and was positively influenced by Herzl's miraculous success at establishing a Zionist organization with its own annual congress, meeting first in 1897. Awakened to his Jewish identity, Fleg now applied his considerable intellectual gifts to a rediscovery of the Judaism he had so long ignored. Of his many works on Judaism that followed, he is most popularly known for the conclusion to a little book called *Why I Am a Jew*, which he dedicated "TO MY GRANDSON who is not yet born." (It can be found in the Reform Movement's *Passover Haggadah*, p. 38, and in the supplementary readings to *Gates of Prayer*, p. 705). Our passage here demonstrates Fleg's newly found love for the Midrash which he encountered as an adult, probably in French translation, and which he used for a series of literary works based on the biographical lore surrounding biblical heroes.

Two traditional *piyutim* are included in this section of our *Machzor*. The first is *"Omnam Ken"* ("Yes, it is true . . .," pp. 376–377), which is of historical interest. This rather straightforward outcry for God's pardon is traditionally attributed to Yom Tov ben Isaac of Joigny, who died in a massacre in York, England, on March 16, 1190. The announcement, in 1187, of the third Crusade had been accompanied by violent anti-Jewish activity—first, by the masses who were overwhelmed by misguided religious zeal, and then by the nobility who owed considerable money to Jewish lenders and welcomed the opportunity to retire their debts by force. When rioting reached York, the Sheriff admitted the Jews to the castle for their protection, but in the end, the Jewish community recognized how hopeless was the task of holding out against the mob, and elected instead to commit mass suicide. It is not absolutely certain that Yom Tov is the author, but, in some manuscripts of the poem, his name occurs as part of the acrostic in the last line.

"Ki Hine Kachomer" ("As clay in the hand of the potter ... ," pp. 381–382) comes from an anonymous poet, probably from about the 12th century. It is the subject of pious commentary in a book called *Arugat Habosem*, penned in 1234 by Abraham ben Azriel. Abraham was the disciple of the medieval pietists known as the *Chasidei Ashkenaz*, who constituted the Jewish equivalent of militant Christian monasticism in their zeal to preach—and to enforce—morality among the rising burgher class. Particularly central in their approach to Judaism was the doctrine of repentance; so much so, that they recommended penitential exercises amounting sometimes to extreme self-abnegation.

The imagery of this poem depicts human beings as the work of God's hands, while God is the craftmaster who fashions them. God is the potter, we are the clay; God is the mason, we are the stone; and so on. Abraham ben Azriel's commentary adds the following insight: " 'As clay in the hand of the potter': all artisans feel compassionately toward their artwork which they would not want to destroy. ... An artist, for example, constantly adds to the beauty of the art, and would never do anything to break it." So our poem affirms more than the fact that God created us; more even than our dependence on our Maker. According to our medieval commentator, it tells us something of the relationship established by God in the very act of creation. We are to be pardoned on this day because our lives are potential works of divine art, striving for beauty that is Godlike.

Afternoon Service (pp. 394–474)

Overview

The Afternoon Service (*Mincha*) reverts, in part, to the normal liturgical structure, familiar by now to readers of this commentary. It consists of preparatory prayers; a *Tefila*, this time with a Confession within it; and one of the usual concluding prayers, the *"Aleinu."*

On the other hand, two items are very different: (1) The traditional *Machzor* includes in the *Musaf* service a lengthy epic poem called the *Avoda*. We have no *Musaf*, but we do have a modern *Avoda*, which we place here, in the Afternoon Service (pp. 410–449). Most people view this *Avoda* as the highlight of the entire Yom Kippur liturgy. (2) Unlike other Afternoon Services, the *Mincha* for Yom Kippur includes both Torah and *Haftara* readings, and we follow tradition in this regard (pp. 450–467), though we shall see that the Torah reading differs from that encountered in Orthodox synagogues.

Preparatory Prayers (pp. 394–398)

Only minimal preparation should be required of congregants who, by now, have been sitting much of the day in prayer, and who have just concluded the "Additional Prayers" section with its lengthy meditations. But we include three poetic works, juxtaposing a modern reading based on the thoughts of Leo Baeck (pp. 394–395) and two medieval poems: the first by Judah Halevi ("A Servant Unto Thee," pp. 395–396) and the second ("All This Day," pp. 396–398) by a relatively unknown 13th-century poet, Mordecai ben Shabbetai, who hailed from Greece and Italy. (On Judah Halevi, see above, p. 105; on Leo Baeck, see above, p. 40, and below, p. 163.)

The Tefila (pp. 398–408)

On the *Tefila*, generally, see above, pages 18–23.

On the insertions in the first and last two benedictions, which utilize the imagery of being inscribed in the Book of Life, see above, page 21. We do not include all four of them here.

The conclusion to the second benediction (middle, p. 400) is striking; it replicates the traditional thanksgiving to God for resurrecting the dead. When the Rabbis refashioned Judaism at the turn of the Common Era, it was this belief in God's power to resurrect the dead which they took to be the central promise to all good men and women, so they canonized it liturgically within the second benediction of the *Tefila*, the one that speaks of God's might. They held that to deny resurrection was to deny the core of Judaism. In the Middle Ages, this tenet constituted one of Maimonides's Thirteen Principles, though Maimonides's detractors accused him of not really believing it, and at one point, the philosopher penned a letter to suffering Jews in the community of Yemen, in which he underlined his acceptance of the doctrine. (See above, p. 126.)

In modern times, it has been Reform Jews who have had difficulty with the age-old promise of bodily resurrection. As Eugene Borowitz summarizes the dilemma, the problem with affirming bodily resurrection is that, "while [moderns] may not believe that science knows all about reality, they cannot easily ignore the scientific views of life, and thus of death." But 19th-century philosophy was as certain of the eternality of spirit as science was about the finality of bodily decay. So the idea of life after death could be maintained for our spiritual essence, our souls. In

1869, a Reform rabbinic conference in Philadelphia voted officially on the doctrine and concluded: "The belief in the bodily resurrection has no religious foundation, and the doctrine of immortality refers to the after-existence of the soul alone."

Now, more than 100 years later, we are more cautious in our description. The 1976 *Centenary Perspective* declares: "Amid the mystery that we call life, we affirm that human beings, created in God's image, share in God's eternality, despite the mystery we call death." Borowitz explains: "We cannot say very clearly what we believe, but we do not propose to abandon our faith that the God who gave us life will yet give us life after death."

The problem for prayerbook editors is how to express such an inexpressible concept in their prayers—more precisely, whether to retain the traditional Hebrew phrase which means "who revives the dead"; if so, whether to translate the phrase literally; if not, what Hebrew reading to put in its place, and then, what English to compose as the equivalent of the newly selected Hebrew.

Inasmuch as bodily resurrection has almost universally been denied in modern circles, one would have expected even the early Reform prayerbooks to delete all references to it. Remarkably, they did not do so. Jakob Petuchowski reports that though most of the more than 100 European liberal prayerbooks he surveyed changed the concept of resurrection to immortality in their German translations, not one altered the traditional Hebrew words. Here in America, Isaac Mayer Wise, too, retained the phrase. But the more radical David Einhorn (see above, p. 81) was not willing to do so. He, and the *Union Prayer Book* after him, borrowed a traditional phrase from another context: " . . . *note-a betochenu chayei olam*," which they translated literally as " . . . who has implanted within us immortal life." (For comparisons of the influence of Wise and Einhorn on Reform liturgy, see *Gates of Understanding,* Volume I, p. 23.)

When the committee on *Gates of Prayer* first met in the early 1970s, they faced the issue of deciding how Reform Jews today wish to express this age-old cardinal Jewish tenet of life eternal. Their answer (following older precedent) was to say ". . . *mechayeh hakol*," literally, " . . . who revives [or, gives life to] everything." Their preferred English equivalent became, " . . . the Sourc of life" (see *Gates of Understanding,* Volume I, p. 189, note 61, for details). For *Gates of Repentance,* the same editorial decision was generally retained, but not here. The English version of this benediction is a free paraphrase of the traditional theme, in which we emphasize the gift of life: purposeful life, in which we praise God, "whose cleansing rains let parched men and women flower toward the sun." Somehow, the usual "*mechayeh hakol*" seemed pale, too symbolically barren for the grandeur of our English blessing. So we returned to our

German Reform roots and allowed the original Hebrew to stand, with the understanding that it is open to many interpretations.

The paragraph in the middle of p. 401 is yet another *piyut* (see above, p. 77). It is attributed to the most famous *paytan* of all, a veritable genius with the Hebrew language, Eliezer Kalir. Scholars are not sure exactly when Kalir lived, but they usually place him in Palestine in the late sixth and early seventh centuries. If one removes the initial *Lamed* which begins both the first and the second half of each line (except the introductory line) an alphabetic acrostic is revealed, each and every word in the acrostic being another name for God. God is pictured here as a judge. The first half of each line ends with *"yom din,"* "day of judgment"; the last half concludes *"badin,"* "in justice." Thus, Kalir goes through the alphabet saying in as many ways as the Hebrew letters will allow him that on Rosh Hashana (the "Day of Judgment"), God judges ("in justice").

For the Confession (pp. 403–405), see above, pages 119–123.

The *Tefila* here contains some of the most remarkably lyrical interpretations of the traditional themes. They should not go unnoticed.

For the Silent Prayer (p. 408), see above, pages 82–84. We offer here two novel, final thoughts with which to conclude the *Tefila*. The one in the middle of the page is common to all our services, but the surrounding selections are not. The reflection at the top of the page is attributed to a Palestinian Rabbi of the second century. The last offering is said to have been the blessing with which priests who had just finished their turn of duty in the Temple greeted their replacement.

"Aleinu" (p. 409)

For *"Aleinu,"* see above, pages 42–46.

Avoda (From Creation to Redemption) (pp. 410–449)

The *Avoda* is a rubric devised exclusively for Yom Kippur. Most people agree that the *Avoda* in *Gates of Repentance* is the highlight of the day's liturgy, an opportunity for the spiritual climax that worship on the Days of Awe should offer. Accordingly, it deserves our detailed consideration.

The *Avoda* presents us with a liturgical recollection of Jewish history. Reciting it should be likened to the process of displaying an album of photographs taken during a visit to Israel.

Most Jews try to go to Israel at least once in their lifetime. These trips partake of the nature of what people used to call pilgrimages, sacred journeys from which they returned with equally sacred objects called relics. These relics were proudly displayed as both evidence and reminder of the sacred journey itself.

We still make those journeys, which are still pilgrimages; we still bring back relics. Real, three-dimensional pieces of Crusader forts or biblical cities are not available now, but two-dimensional photographs of them are. So before packing our bags we are advised by previous pilgrims, "Take lots of film!" We do. Yet, to our surprise, we never take enough. We buy more. And we use that, too. By the time we get home, we discover we have a problem: what do we do with all those pictures?

The problem is solved through photo albums that force us to limit the pictures to a manageable number. Slowly and painfully, we weed through the mass of photos, determining which ones are important enough to save in the album and which will be stored for safekeeping in the attic trunk. (One hesitates to throw out even second-rate relics.) Eventually, we forget the other pictures, and, as we are unable to recall every detail of the trip, the journey is restricted by our imagination to the set of photos in the album.

Suppose one day we read that when Sadat visited Jerusalem, he stayed in a special house that once had significance for Moslem-Jewish relations. Staring at the blurry black-and-white newspaper photograph, we remember seeing it, without, of course, knowing what it was at the time. A quick search in the trunk turns up the photo, and, smiling broadly, we hasten downstairs to show the family that, indeed, Sadat's house was part of our Israel itinerary.

Naturally, the picture is now no longer trunk-material; it deserves space in the album. We leaf through the pages to find room, and eventually, come across a picture of a cactus. Why we photographed a cactus is no longer clear. At the time, perhaps, the lonely desert cactus symbolized the rugged terrain of the biblical landscape, but now, thousands of miles and several years away from that wilderness, it is only a cactus. So out goes the cactus, and in goes Sadat's house.

When friends now ask about our trip, we point proudly at the picture of Sadat's house, which suddenly looms as the trip's highlight, even though it was barely even part of consciousness before. The cactus, that magnificent plant which used to be pointed out to guests as a gorgeous natural phenomenon, now goes unmentioned and, eventually, unremembered as well.

What actually was the trip to Israel? The album with the cactus, or the album with Sadat's house? The answer is, "Neither—yet both." We did see the things in the album, so to some extent they parallel our trip. But because the real trip is much larger than any recollection can contain, neither album really does the journey justice. The point is that any journey we make necessarily contains far more experience than our consciousness can assimilate. We select what we wish to retain in active memory and what we do not. Journeys are viewed with selective perception.

The journey of a people through its history is not dissimilar. It would be impossible for Jews of any generation to recall perfectly all the facts of their heritage. But we know that we dare not lose touch with our history, for only our history tells us who we are. In every age, we determine what to remember by constructing in our group memory a living photo album of our sacred trek from the beginning to the present.

These pictures of our history are recalled in many ways. Through education, for example, we impart them to our children. In movies or books about our past, we recollect them ourselves. *But perhaps the single most significant means of retaining them in group consciousness is through our rites and rituals, our liturgical celebration of our people's existence.* The rabbi reads the Torah, for instance, and expounds on biblical origins. At every Purim, we remember not only Haman but Hitler, along with all the other "Hamans" who would have destroyed us. And on Yom Kippur, ever since the fourth century or so, we have had the *Avoda*, an entire rubric dedicated to retelling the story of our history.

Like our photo albums, the story told in the *Avoda* is both true and untrue. Though we recall as honestly as possible what really happened, our account cannot possibly tally exactly with the immensity of actual experience. An objective historian might charge that we give too much weight to one period and not enough to another; or that we build heroes out of ordinary mortals, attributing military greatness to King David, for example, even though ancient Israel's might pales into insignificance when compared with the truly powerful armies of Greece, Rome, Babylonia, or Assyria. Our history, it would be said, is severely biased.

This charge would be accurate, but misleading. Every historical account is biased to some extent. Even the best historians are limited in their reconstructions to evidence previous ages leave behind, and what they themselves are lucky enough to read and understand; they must guess at the gaps. The history that we remember religiously is different primarily not in kind, but in the emotive appeal it has for us. Unlike the events recorded in textbooks, historical moments such as standing at Sinai and covenanting with God are sacred to us. What we have is a sacred history for which we learn to live and, if necessary, to die.

The Temple's destruction in 70 C.E. created a wrenching disjunction in that sacred history. Until that time, the Exodus had been seen as the first step leading without fail to occupation of the Land of Israel and the consequent establishment of a Temple and cult within its capital, the City of David. When the Temple proved less than eternal, the people who worshiped in it were forced to re-examine their past.

That such a re-evaluation occurred at all should not be taken lightly. Had the Jewish people failed to re-examine its sacred history until it was compatible with its most recent historical reality, it would have disappeared. By way of analogy, we might consider the case of normally healthy human beings who are beset by an overwhelming crisis. Their continued mental health depends on their ability to integrate the reality of their new situation into their composite picture of who they are. Their parents die, for example, and they must rebuild an identity as independent adults in their own right. A whole people is no different. That we Jews are still here testifies to our ability to readjust our sacred history to the changing tide of experience.

The redrawing of Jewish history occasioned by the Temple's demise was neither the first nor the only historical revision that occurred, but it lasted until modern times. For that reason alone it deserves our attention. In sum, the account of our past that was fashioned after the Temple was destroyed denied the reality of historical time. Its Rabbinic authors ignored ordinary historical data such as the details of dynastic reigns or the dates of plagues, battles, and wars. Instead, they divided the totality of time into three epochs, extending from the beginning of Creation to the coming of the Messiah. Within these epochs, the details of specific events paled into insignificance.

The first era, which we can call Time-Past, was said to have lasted until the Temple's fall. It was a halcyon time of peace and quietude, when the fulfillment of all the Torah's commandments, even those dependent on the Temple, was possible. The second epoch, Time-Now, is the one in which we now live. It began with the Temple's destruction and will last until the coming of the Messiah. During Time-Now, we are challenged to work to bring about the final epoch, Time-to-Come, when all enemies of Israel will disappear, and the whole world will recognize Israel's God. Then, said the Rabbis, the Temple will be reconstituted, and its sacrificial demands reinstituted, just as they were in Time-Past.

This emphasis on broad semi-historical eras with a concomitant denigration of the specific events of which the eras are made characterizes the perspective on time held by the Byzantine Jewish poets of whom we spoke (see above, pp. 76–77). Thus, even four or five centuries after the Temple's fall, they remained relatively oblivious to the events of their day; but they remembered the Temple as the central institution of Time-Past, and also as the predominant feature of Time-to-Come. To preserve its memory, they introduced a new sort of poem to the liturgy, a lengthy epic dedicated to describing the cult. Known as the *Avoda*, it found a ready place in the Yom Kippur liturgy. It told, as no other piece of liturgy, the medieval version of Jewish sacred history.

The *Avoda*'s account was simple. The single image of the Temple was believed to symbolize everything worth knowing about Time-Past (i.e., up to the Temple's destruction in 70 C.E.), and the events of Time-Now (i.e., after 70 C.E.) were considered insignificant enough that they could be omitted altogether. So the poem chronicled Jewish history from the story of Creation until the selection of Aaron and his progeny to be priests in the Temple. Then the story skipped to the cult's actual operation during the time of the Second Temple, which it described in great detail. But the Temple's fall was symptomatic of Jewish suffering, so the *Avoda* concluded with a martyrology, the favorite illustration being a gruesome account of how Hadrian had tortured the rabbinic rebels of the Bar Kochba revolt. This was followed by prayers for pardon, *Selichot* (see above, p. 123), since sin in Time-Past had caused the Temple's demise, and pardon for our sins in Time-Now would bring about the Temple's rebuilding in Time-to-Come.

In this way, the Rabbis replaced the data of history with a moral of history which went as follows: 1. We once had a Temple (Time-Past), but we sinned. 2. The Temple was destroyed, and we were sent into exile, a state of limbo (Time-Now) in which we work to bring about Time-to-Come. 3. To do so, we repent of our sins and are pardoned. In other words, sin is inevitable and leads to suffering; but we repent and are forgiven; until we sin again. Sacred history was, thus, forced into a cyclical mold of sin, suffering, atonement, and pardon. This moral dominated Jewish thinking for centuries.

In the 19th century, however, Europeans discovered the modern study of history. Dominating their view was their faith in two allied concepts: the steadiness of change and the inevitability of progress; a happy marriage of Darwin's theory of biological evolution and the heady optimism born of the industrial revolution. Into this milieu, Reform Judaism was born, so that its formulators transformed their age-old cyclical moral of history into a developmental model in which specific events had meaning. Armed with new scientific methods, they unveiled Time-Now as a progression of periods with natural causes and consequences. The age of visualizing history as a homogeneous marking of time until the Messiah arrived was over.

On the other hand, there seemed still to be a certain sameness to much of Jewish history. The Dark Ages still seemed all too dark, compared with the modern era in which these historians found themselves. Thus, there emerged a new sacred history that contrasted the pre-modern period, when Jews were frequently condemned to second-class status in a world dominated by superstition and injustice, with the new age that appeared to usher in the long-awaited epoch of Time-to-Come. Reform Jews thereby abandoned the traditionalistic equation of history with the moral of sin, punishment, atonement, and pardon, without, however, denying Judaism's inherent promise of a better time. They believed, no less than the Rabbis of old, that we are partners with God in creation, entrusted with the ethical task of exercising the Jewish Mission to humanity, and bringing about the culmination of the new age—which they sensed had already begun in their own lifetime—when all humanity would finally know only peace and harmony. This new historically conscious vision was recorded in the *Avoda* of early Reform services.

But the promise of inevitable progress proved illusory. In our time, we have witnessed greater evil than the historians of the 19th century could have imagined, despite all their unearthing of the individual instances of medieval darkness. So once again, our sacred history has necessitated alteration. From our Reform forebears we learned to appreciate the events of Time-Now as significant data that cannot be obscured from consciousness. We may well judge as false their anticipation of an immediate end to history's evil excesses; Time-to-Come, apparently, did not dawn with the advent of modern age. But we do not deny the hope they shared with the Rabbinic tradition as a whole. We too keep faith with the ancient promise encapsulated in the blessing after the *"Shema"* (see pp. 38–40 above), and the last unit of the *Shofar* Ritual (see pp. 99–100 above): now, as in Egyptian bondage so long ago, God works through history. We affirm the grim reality of our time, all the while awaiting the redemption of Time-to-Come, and convinced, as before, of our own mandate to labor patiently for its realization.

The sacred history for our time is abundantly clear from the *Avoda* of *Gates of Repentance* (pp. 410–449). Stylistically, it juxtaposes prose and poetry from every epoch of Jewish history, all the way from the Bible through the Rabbinic writings, the Middle Ages and today; and it incorporates poetry and prose written in three of the major languages of 20th-century Jewry: Hebrew, Yiddish, and English. The full impact of this poetic *Avoda* assumes that worshipers are familiar with the sources for the readings that make it up, to which end we supply the notes at the end of this book. We can suggest the most important sources here, however, so as to provide at least a feeling of the way in which the old and the new, the glorious and the sorrowful, are woven together for us to recapture the meaning of Jewish history now, in the closing decades of the 20th century.

The *Avoda* begins, as it always has, with a celebration of Creation—first in a section drawn from a traditional *Avoda* poem (p. 410), and then with the first verse of the biblical account: "In the beginning, God created the heavens and the earth" (p. 411). Our own poetry follows next, as we introduce the modern theme of evolution (pp. 412–416), but interspersed are psalms expressing our awe of the universe and of God who created it (pp. 413 and 415). Not all is sublime, however, and a hint of life's essential tension between good and evil enters with the tale of Cain's murder of Abel; we wonder aloud, "How long shall the curse of Cain / continue to haunt the human race? / . . . Cannot those whose mind and will / have brought them to the moon / do equal wonders on their native soil?" (pp. 416–417).

Recollections of revelation follow, before we trace our history through the First Temple, Babylonian exile, the Second Temple, and its destruction, too. But now, where the Rabbinic sacred history ended, ours still continues. Our martyrology contains not only a version of the traditional martyrology, i.e., the Hadrianic persecutions (pp. 432–434), but an account drawn from the chronicles of those who suffered in the Crusades (p. 434), and, of course, the Holocaust, which is represented on several pages. It is in this context that we looked at the powerful Confessions on pages 438–440. "Perhaps some of the blame falls on me," we consider, softly to ourselves; and then, aloud, we ask atonement: "For the sin of silence, / For the sin of indifference, / . . . For all that was done, / For all that was not done. . . . "

If the dismal line from Cain to the Holocaust is clear for all to see, so, too, is the buoyant connection between Creation and human creativity. Ezekiel's vision of the dry bones rising like a phoenix from the ashes is juxtaposed with an image of Zion redeemed (pp. 442–443), of "Jerusalem . . . the joy of all the world" (p. 444). We find Bialik's touching recollection of the synagogue, the study house in Eastern Europe, and the Jew's insistence on knowing Torah, our heritage (pp. 426–427). And we envision, finally, an age of redemption, when prophetic visions of reconciliation, peace, and justice will be realized (pp. 445–449).

The final song, "All the world" (p. 448), is testimony to the resolve of "This People Israel," as Leo Baeck called us. Composed by an unknown poet in the early Middle Ages, it expresses a vision of Time-to-Come. Even now—with the rediscovery of history and with the inclusion in our sacred account of both medieval and modern times, up to and including the Holocaust, the modern State of Israel, and our lot as free people in a Diaspora which we affirm—even now, that vision is a fitting conclusion for the Jewish dream. Its translation was bequeathed us by early Reform Judaism; its author was Israel Zangwill (1864–1926), known for his faith that Jewish life in the Diaspora would flourish.

144

Service for the Reading of the Torah (pp. 450–469)

For the general character of the rubric involving the Torah reading, see above, pages 84–90.

The traditional reading for the Afternoon Service of Yom Kippur is taken from Leviticus 18, and constitutes the Torah's categorization of those men and women between whom sexual relations are prohibited. Why this should have become the reading for Yom Kippur is unclear, but a traditional view, offered, for example, in 1917 by J. D. Eisenstein, is this: "On Yom Kippur even the most profligate sinners come to synagogue, those who do not come again all year round, so that they must be warned against illicit sexual relations."

We saw above that Reform practice prefers Torah and *Haftara* readings with themes appropriate to the spiritual expectations of modern worshipers. On Yom Kippur morning, for example, we read Deuteronomy 29–30, on human responsibility, rather than the traditional selection, Leviticus 16, which describes sacrifice (see above, p. 129). Here, too, it has been customary for us to replace the traditional reading of Leviticus 18 with selections from Leviticus 19, which is part of what Bible scholars call the Holiness Code. It details a series of ethical actions entailed in our striving for holiness.

Leviticus 19 has always occupied an exalted place in Jewish tradition, explicitly comparable to the Ten Commandments. On this fact, medieval commentators are almost unanimously in agreement. Rashi tells us, "Moses spoke this section of the Torah while all the people were assembled, since *"rov gufei haTorah teluyin bah,"* "most of the Torah is dependent upon it." Ibn Ezra adds that our reading (Chapter 19) is deliberately arranged so as to follow the listing of forbidden sexual relations in Chapter 18, since "the purpose [of both addresses] was to admit converts, and they had to be informed about forbidden sexual relations. The reason Chapter 19 comes immediately afterward is so that they do not think that by observing the sexual taboos alone, they would merit inclusion among those who were in the Land [i.e., among Israelites by birth]. . . . There are other *mitzvot* also, these being the Ten Commandments [to which our passage is likened], and failure to keep them entails banishment from the Land." The 16th-century Italian commentator, Obadiah Sforno, summarizes:

> God says now that the intention behind both warnings [proscribed sexual relations and prescribed ethical obligations] is that they [the Israelites] should be holy, in order that they may be as similar to their Creator as possible; this similarity is the whole point

behind the creation of human beings, as God said [at the time], "Let us make a person *in our image*." Now God adds: "Since I, the Lord your God, am holy, it is fitting for you to be like Me as much as possible in thought and in action, and in order to achieve this likeness to Me, it is necessary to keep the Ten Commandments [to which our passage alludes]."

The theme of achieving holiness through just acts is extended at the end of this rubric (pp. 469–471), where we add a concluding reading on the Torah portion's moral theme.

For the *Haftara* reading from the Book of Jonah (pp. 457–463), see above, pages 94–95.

We end our Afternoon Service (pp. 471–474) with five stanzas from yet another poem by Judah Halevi (see above, p. 105). The poet has inscribed his name in the first letters of each stanza, which, taken together, read "Judah." His theme is the rapturous awe of God brought on by a consideration of what God has wrought.

Memorial Service (pp. 477–494)

Overview

Like the Additional Prayers (pp. 361–391), the Memorial Service is not really a service. Technically, the word "service" should be reserved for liturgical offerings that once corresponded to cultic ones; these are constructed around the core of a *Tefila*, which the Rabbis regarded as the offering of our lips (see above, p. 9).

But the Additional Prayers are, at least theoretically, derived from a service, in that we include them in place of the traditional *Musaf* service. This Memorial Service is not derived from any traditional service at all. Instead, it represents one of two places where Reform liturgy excerpted selected prayers that were "buried" in another service, gave them independent status, and reconstructed the newly constituted whole so that it could stand alone. Since we have abandoned the traditionalist principle of indelibly tying the word "service" to the calendar of cultic events in the Temple of old, we feel free to look at our novel liturgical creation and call it a service, if in today's synagogues it seems to function like one.

Another example of the same process at which we looked (above, pp. 138–144) is the *Avoda* (410–449). Though that rubric is not labeled officially as "service," it is laid out typographically as if it were a separate service, and it definitely stands alone as one. There is this important difference, however. Regardless of the immense novelty represented by the *Avoda* offered in this *Machzor*, we are not the first liturgical poets to

146

turn the *Avoda* into the elaborate prayer that it is. The *Avoda* was our legacy from as early as, perhaps, the fourth or fifth century; we simply modernized it. But the Memorial Service is distinctively ours.

Though rooted in memorial prayers that reach back a few centuries, "*Yizkor*" (as it was known) was at best a tiny interlude at the end of the Morning Service, by the time the Reform Movement was born. But Reform Jews were convinced of the merit of a deeper experience of memorializing the dead on Yom Kippur. So they granted the Memorial Service its own structural autonomy, an idea that has since been adopted by Conservative and Orthodox Jews as well.

People who spent their childhood in traditional synagogues may still recall what "*Yizkor*" was like. It came in the middle of the day. Many in the congregation had come early and stayed through hours of prayer, but many more dropped in and out, some spending lengthy periods in rooms adjacent to the sanctuary, others whiling away the time outside or at home. By "*Yizkor*" time, however, the seats were full again, since people generally made sure to be there for "*Yizkor*."

But before "*Yizkor*" could begin, children with living parents were dismissed from the room. In 1917, J. D. Eisenstein collected the customs he had seen, and described the scene accurately: "It is customary to send outside or into the hall those children who have living parents, and even adults whose mothers and fathers are still alive." He offers several explanations for the dismissal, including the possibility that children will see their parents crying, and be moved themselves to tears—an unnecessary response, in his opinion, for people who themselves are not mourners. But the preferred reason, says Eisenstein, is "so as not to tempt Satan, or on account of the evil eye."

After the children had left, the mourners who remained said three prayers.

First came the "*Yizkor*" prayer itself, a short paragraph, which we have reproduced on page 491. The prayer asks God to remember the soul of one's father or mother, and leaves space for the name of the deceased to be filled in. There are many versions of this paragraph, some with special references to martyrs, others for whole families that have perished and can be remembered together. Mourners select the alternatives appropriate to their circumstances, and say them silently.

The second prayer is the "*Av Harachamim*," which we mentioned above (pp. 85–86). Both "*Yizkor*" and "*Av Harachamim*" go back to the Crusades (see above, pp. 76 and 85–86). "*Yizkor*" was at first not actually a prayer, but the first line of a martyrology list, comparable to memorial tablets on synagogue walls today. The word "*Yizkor* . . . " ("May [God] remember . . . ") introduced a community's list of the Crusaders' victims. Eventually, the original names in the *"Yizkor"* list were lost, but the idea remained, so that we now insert our own names there. The *"Av Harachamim"* consists of an angry outcry for divine vengeance against the soldiers who committed the massacre. We noted above (pp. 85–86) that in traditional services, *"Av Harachamim"* is recited also as part of the Shabbat liturgy surrounding the reading of the Torah. *Gates of Repentance* omits it there, and here, in the Memorial Service, too. Instead, it appears within the martyrology section of the *Avoda* (pp. 434–435), where it follows an eye-witness account of the actual massacre that prompted its composition in the first place.

The third prayer in the traditional *"Yizkor"* service derives from another tragedy. By the 17th century, Jews had been living in Poland for almost 400 years. Originally invited from Western Europe to build a modern economy for the Polish Crown and landed nobility, Jews had slowly moved into specific industries, one of them being the nobility's financial agents who dealt with the peasants, particularly in the Ukraine, whose native population was treated no better than serfs by their upper-class Polish overlords. The 17th century proved difficult for Poland, as it became embroiled in outside wars and internal economic decay. The Jewish community, never really financially solvent even during the more heady times of the century before, now became a convenient scapegoat for society's collapse.

The leader of the pogrom that followed was the infamous Bogdan Chmielnicki. He had already become politically estranged from the Polish monarch and had spent a year fomenting revolt among the Ukrainian peasantry. With the Ukrainian Cossack nationalist army behind him, he attacked Poland in 1648, where he sought the added support of the dis-affected peasantry there. This he achieved by supporting their wholesale slaughter of the Jews, who were readily perceived as the immediate agents of the economic and social subjugation of the lower class.

For two years, extensive massacres occurred, as Cossack armies entered one town after another, killing Jews. Chronicles from the time estimate the number of dead around 100,000. Even as late as 1654, new waves of slaughter were occurring, as Jews now found themselves caught in the middle between rampaging armies representing Poland, the Cossacks of the Ukraine, and Russia—all of whom were fighting for political control of the area. In our time, Hitler's Holocaust has replaced the Chmielnicki massacres in our consciousness. But there was an age, and not long ago, when the name Chmielnicki, not Hitler, conjured up the image of evil incarnate. To this day, tourists in Kiev can visit a national monument to Bogdan Chmielnicki, who is depicted as a general riding a horse; he has not ceased to be seen there as a Ukrainian national hero.

One liturgical reaction by Polish Jewry after this decimation was the creation of a new memorial prayer: *"El Malei Rachamim."* It, too, was added to the traditional *"Yizkor"* liturgy. (It appears in the middle of page 492.)

So when Reform Jews looked anew at the possibility of creating an independent Memorial Service, they had only three traditional prayers before them: *"Yizkor," "Av Harachamim,"* and *"El Malei Rachamim."* But these were adapted and augmented, until a complete order of memorial prayers was fashioned. The first such modern Memorial Service seems to have been the creation of the Hamburg Reform prayerbook of 1819. Since then, these services have been basic to our Reform Yom Kippur worship.

The service offered here is based largely on the previous Memorial Service from the *Union Prayer Book*, with some additions drawn from the British *Gate of Repentance*. It is rich in psalms, particularly those already popularly associated with death, such as Psalm 23 (pp. 488–489). We move from a general consideration of human fallibility (see, e.g., "We are feeble . . . " on pp. 479–480) to a sustained consideration of life and death themselves (e.g., pp. 482–486). Our thoughts then turn to our martyrs, those many who have left no one to remember them (pp. 487–490); then, to those who have died in our community during the past year (p. 490); and finally, through silent meditation, to the departed whom each mourner singly recalls in the *"Yizkor"* prayer itself (p. 491). But in the end, every single man and woman is reunited in the comfort of the community as a whole, as all rise, for the Cantor's chant of *"El Malei Rachamim"* and a communal recitation of the *Kaddish*.

Concluding Service (Ne-ila) (pp. 497–528)

Overview

According to a folk tradition passed on orally through the hillsides surrounding Jerusalem in the years that followed the Temple's demise, there had once been an enormous gate that opened into the Temple court. It was said that when the gate was opened and closed, it could be heard as far away as Jericho. Observers today might well wonder about the literal veracity of this tale. Even in the quietude of early morning or late evening, it must have taken quite a gate to echo so far through the hills. But the image of a gate opening and closing on the Temple cult, the most sacred ritual then devised by the Jewish people, has remained with us.

Through gates we enter; through gates we leave. Our new liturgy is termed the *Gates*: portals to prayer, repentance, forgiveness, and understanding. The Bible speaks of the gates to heaven.

All of these images come together in the final service for Yom Kippur, the *Ne-ila*, literally, "the locking" of the gates. The *Gates* we have been holding since Rosh Hashana began will be put back on shelves or locked away in closets for yet another year. The doors to our synagogues may be locked behind us as we leave for home in just a few minutes; just as the massive gates of the Temple once used to be shut against the backdrop of the sinking desert sun behind Jerusalem. And the gates to heaven? Those gates, the ones that open to God's presence, are never locked to us, says our tradition. Still—this is the time expressly set aside for our prayers to rise, and it is tonight that our fate is said to be sealed in the Book of Life.

"Sealed"—there is such finality in that word. "On Rosh Hashana," we read, "it is written, and on Yom Kippur it is sealed: . . . who shall live and who shall die" (*"Unetaneh Tokef,"* pp. 108, 177–178, and 313; on which see above, pp. 75–78). Is our fate really sealed today? Is it really known for certain who shall live and who shall die? Most of us will accept this image with as little narrow-minded literal precision as we do the report about the Temple's booming door. But, on a symbolic level, both images have something to say. The closing of the door was heard psychologically not just as far as Jericho, but wherever Jews gathered to come to terms with their lives before God. They now faced the fact that the annual opportunity to renew their lives was ending. As for living and dying, some of us will, indeed, have determined our fate by Yom Kippur's conclusion: if we have not opened ourselves to the possibility of change, if we have not seriously atoned, if we have not turned in repentance to God and to those we love, then we have determined the fact that next year will be sadly similar to the one just ending. Even if we are still physically alive twelve months from now, something in us will have died; and we will have sealed ourselves in spiritless coffins already at the close of *Ne-ila* this year.

The mood of *Ne-ila* is like no other time in the sanctuary. Traditionally, the Ark doors are left open for the whole service, symbolizing the Temple gates that have not been shut yet. The congregation, however, may be weak from fasting and is not required to stand before the open Ark. But, listen to the stern words of caution that the 20th-century mystic and seer Rav Kook offered those with whom he worshiped: "Even if you are weak from fasting, strengthen yourselves, and say the *Ne-ila* prayers with minds made absolutely pure, so that you will have taken upon yourself the fullness of repentance."

The cumulative effect of twenty-four hours of worship now takes its toll. When the worship service began, the rabbis may have been concerned about the sermons they had yet to give; both rabbi and cantor worried about the conduct of the service, hoping all would go well this year; congregants entered with their own expectations and anxieties—with such petty things as getting a good seat or worrying whether they are dressed appropriately, and with such serious matters as facing the fact that a father or mother, a husband or wife, even a son or daughter had passed away and would not share the High Holy Day services this year, or ever again. But *Ne-ila* has a leveling effect that convinces us we are all equal before God; it puts our personal concerns into perspective. A mood of passive stoicism has settled over laity and clergy alike: petty needs have disappeared; great concerns have faded into the background. Alike in the recognition of our human frailty, we all face the mystery of this final hour of awe. Weak from fasting, tired from praying, edgy from sitting, we begin to anticipate the setting of the sun and the chance to resume our normal lives. If we are fortunate, we collect our thoughts from the day almost over and dedicate these last few minutes of prayer to guaranteeing that those normal lives we resume will be alive again with the knowledge that we have been summoned to make a spiritual accounting and have emerged with the incredible opportunity to try again! Not only can we be cleansed from the inevitable squandering of our better selves that marks human failing, but we can rise again to the challenge of finding meaning in this mystery we call life.

As in all traditionally constructed services, we move from Preparatory Prayers to the *Tefila* (here omitting the "*Shema*" and its blessings, since this service is neither a morning nor an evening one), and then conclude our worship with the "*Aleinu,*" *Kaddish*, and perhaps another song or hymn. This basic structure holds in *Ne-ila*, but a few points of uniqueness remind us of the twin master-image: closing the gates, and sealing our fate.

Preparatory Prayers (pp. 497–501)

We have seen how every service commences with Preparatory Prayers. Here we alternate the offerings between novel readings and ancient material, which, however, is not traditionally used here.

"Grant us peace ..." (p. 498) is a slightly reworked version of one of the most popular prayers from the *Union Prayer Book*. It is found in *Gates of Prayer* as the blessing for peace in Shabbat Morning Service III (p. 345), Evening Service V (p. 202), and as an optional reading on the theme of peace (p. 695).

The advice, "Forgive your neighbors ... " (p. 500), with which we conclude the Preparatory Prayers, though sounding modern at times, actually goes back to the second or third century B.C.E.—we are not sure which—to a gentleman-farmer named Ben Sirah. He composed a lengthy book of proverbial aphorisms, which was not canonized in our Bible, but which remained as favored reading by Jews for many centuries, nonetheless. How little things change; wisdom then, and wisdom now! The last paragraph recapitulates the Mishna's advice for Yom Kippur with which we began (p. 251). (See above, pp. 109–110.)

The *Kaddish* which follows is sung to a special tune, and is known as the *Ne-ila Kaddish*.

The Tefila (pp. 501–507)

On the *Tefila* generally, see above, pages 18–23.

On the special insertions for the first and last two benedictions, which utilize the imagery of being inscribed in a Book of Life, see above, page 21. A subtle change in the traditional insertion on page 502 reminds worshipers of *Ne-ila*'s special mood. Normally, this petition says, "Remember us . . . and *inscribe* us in the Book of Life." In this service, the word *inscribe* is changed to *seal*.

Concluding Prayers

Concluding prayers for this Concluding Service are expanded, as we anticipate the final moment when the gates shall really be closed. Having said our last *Tefila*, equivalent to making our last offering to God, we now recite *piyutim*.

"*El Nora Alila*" ("God of awesome deeds. . . ," p. 509) is a Sefardic poem by Moses ibn Ezra (1055–1135)—not to be confused with the biblical commentator whom we have cited on occasion, Abraham ibn Ezra (1089–1164). Like many poets of the Spanish school, Moses was at home in secular and religious works. His early poems celebrate life and love, but his later works display a penchant for reflective consideration of the human situation, particularly the grand mysteries of life and death, and he is often said to have composed our finest *Selichot* (on which, see above, pp. 123–124). "God of awesome deeds . . . " is one such magnificent example.

"Avinu Malkenu" (pp. 511–512)

For extended discussion, see above, pages 23–25.

Here, as in the *Tefila* insertion (p. 502), the word "inscribe" is changed to "seal" (seventh line of "*Avinu Malkenu*," p. 511).

For the translation of the last line, which changes the usual "*for we* have little merit" into *"even when we have little merit,"* see above, page 25.

Traditionally, it will be recalled, the Ark remains open throughout the *Ne-ila* service. Those congregations preferring not to open it at the outset of *Ne-ila* will have opened it whenever the service instructions explicitly state that they are to do so; the final such occasion occurs now.

Confession (pp. 512–514)

On the Confessions generally, see above, pages 119–123.

The Confession here is not complete, however. Following traditional practice, our *Ne-ila* service utilizes only the Short Confession, not the Long one. Just as we expect the *"Al Chet,"* we arrive instead at a prayer beginning, "You hold out Your hand ... " (pp. 514–516). This prayer is composed of two separate poetic units written before the ninth century and included together in the first prayerbook, *Seder Rav Amram* (on which, see p. 56 above). Together, the two pieces express the paradox that marks Judaism's conceptualization of the human condition. On the one hand, we say over and over again that we are sinners; that no one dare enter the High Holy Day season without acknowledging the strikingly poor state of the world; that immense evil exists; that we each have responsibility for creating it, for abiding it, for failing to end it. Our efforts to change the universe are so puny, so doomed to disappointment. And, in the end, we die—and are forgotten. Yet, on the other hand, we say also that we are created in God's image, that we must dare to have great expectations. We stand in covenant with our Maker and are charged with a Jewish Mission to rectify the universe, and so, have every reason for optimism in our state.

Both views are possible; in fact, they are mutual correctives against sinful bravado, on the one hand, and morose self-pity, on the other. Our first composition emphasizes the negative perspective. "We end in dust," says the English on page 515 (the Hebrew actually says "worms"). Knowing that all forms of life meet the same dismal end, we ask, "Since all our achievements are as insubstantial as mist, how can we look upon ourselves as higher than the beasts?"

That question is not mere rhetoric. It receives an answer in the following paragraph: human beings were set aside from other forms of life from the very beginning. How so? We alone were given free will to effect moral judgments. Yom Kippur, then, signifies the very essence of human uniqueness. Only we humans are expected to make atonement, because sin, the greatest evil of all, is technically possible only for humans, the highest creation of all.

Open the Gate (p. 517)

In this traditional *piyut*, we now expand the theme of opening gates. The root metaphor is the Temple gate, which we wish to leave open longer, lest it close before we have atoned sufficiently. But even as that gate inevitably begins to shut, other gates in our lives will open. So we pray for gates of blessing, of righteousness, of kindness, and of love.

Stylistically, the Hebrew poet has listed a different gate for each letter of the Hebrew alphabet, thus presenting us with an alphabetic acrostic. Our English version does the same thing with our alphabet.

Kaddish (pp. 522–523)

For a fuller discussion of the *Kaddish*, see above, pages 47–50.

This *Kaddish* differs somewhat from the others in our *Machzor* in that it is the full Reader's *Kaddish*, rather than the shortened version used normally to divide rubrics from one another. This longer form signals that the service as a whole has reached its end.

The Sefardic custom is to blow the *shofar* before the word *Titkabel* ("O Maker of heaven and earth . . . ," p. 523), and our original manuscript suggested that practice, but the final decision was to follow Ashkenazic precedent by sounding the *shofar* at the end of the three statements of faith made on pages 523–524.

Havdala (pp. 526–528)

Since we provide the option of concluding the service with *Havdala*, we should say a brief word about this colorful and ancient ceremony. There can be no more beautiful ritual. It is brief but replete with imagery and objects which draw on all the senses.

Havdala is so old that tradition simply ascribes it to "The Great Assembly," this being a name invented for the authorities—whoever they were—who functioned before the dawn of Rabbinic memory. It is with *Havdala* that we declare the end of Shabbat and Holy Days. Many interpretations of the symbols have been given, and several may be consulted in the *Havdala* liturgies in *Gates of Prayer* (pp. 633–642).

The word *Havdala* itself means "separation," and as such, it evokes a fitting conclusion for this commentary.

First, we should say a word about the *Havdala*'s placement. In *Gates of Repentance*, it is appended to the end of the concluding benediction (p. 525); a note before that benediction informs us that *Havdala* is optional, but that congregations who include it may do so *before* the benediction on page 525. They would thus technically conclude Yom Kippur with the three-fold statement of faith (pp. 523–524) and the *shofar* blast (p. 524); then "separate" Yom Kippur from the next day, with *Havdala* (pp. 526–527); and, finally, bring the service of the Days of Awe to a suitably satisfying end, with the final benediction (p. 525).

Congregations for whom a strict interpretation of Halacha is decisive might feel constrained to follow this pattern, in that they would not want to recite *Havdala* until the *shofar* is blown. Aesthetically, however, interrupting the liturgical flow from the statement of faith and *shofar* blast (p. 524) to the benediction (p. 525) by skipping in the middle to the *Havdala* (pp. 526–527) creates a disturbing disjunction in the service. The final creed and benediction go together, in that they are congregational affirmations of faith and hope.

Congregations may wish, therefore, to say the *Havdala before* the creed (after the *Kaddish*, p. 523); or even earlier—before the *Kaddish* begins (p. 522), for example; just before the congregation rises (p. 520); or at the end of the paragraph on page 522 which begins (appropriately), "Now, as evening falls. . . ." Arrangements such as these would give the congregation the opportunity to sit, appreciate *Havdala*, and then rise for a climactic uninterrupted conclusion to the service.

There is no single "right" way of including *Havdala* here. Again, as we have observed so frequently in these pages, we encounter the classical Jewish emphasis on creativity within structural bounds. Here, as elsewhere, congregations need to study the service so that with the help of their rabbis, they may utilize their *Machzor* to its fullest advantage.

Finally, let us look more closely at the critical paragraph in *Havdala* which speaks of separation (pp. 526–527), to see if there might be one final message within the *Gates* that uniquely sums up the experience of these Days of Awe.

That paragraph is readily identifiable as a benediction praising God for devising four specific separations:

1. light from darkness,
2. the House of Israel from other peoples,
3. the seventh day of rest from the six days of labor, and
4. the sacred from the profane.

The fourth dichotomy is mentioned first, but is the synopsis of the entire benediction, being cited as the final eulogy that both terminates the blessing and summarizes its intent.

The distinction between light and darkness is not new to us (see above, pp. 36–37). Living in a Hellenistic world, Jews borrowed the imagery common to all peoples then, according to which light represented the world of goodness, while darkness stood for its opposite, i.e., evil.

But whence did we derive the other three divisions, and why should our ancient prayer have chosen exactly these? The answer is remarkably simple. All three exemplify the single essential contrast in the Jewish world-view that goes back even beyond the light/darkness distinction. It is none other than holiness and the profane. We Jews were given the Torah and charged with a Holy Mission; we, thus, have a history uniquely our own, as the "*Aleinu*" tells us (see above, pp. 42–46), and as the historical sidelights throughout this commentary must demonstrate again and again. We have a Holy Mission, as David Einhorn's priestly people (see above, pp. 42–43 and 81–82). "Merely to have survived is not an index of excellence," we read (p. 331). The Yom Kippur readings told us to be holy, because God is holy (see above, pp. 145–146). So we are the holy people.

This candid theological affirmation of Israel's potential holiness shares with the "*Aleinu*" a boldness in particularistic claims. The *Havdala* rituals in *Gates of Prayer*, in fact, eliminated this line. But we have restored it to the text in *Gates of Repentance*. We make no invidious contrast to other peoples; but we assert that we are recipients of Torah, with a God-given mission to rectify the world's evil, even at the price of great personal sacrifice. That others are part of God's plan is undoubtedly true. That we remain convinced of our role in the divine scheme of things is no less evident and deserves inclusion in that most ancient of blessings which says so. Jews who do not strive for holiness fail as Jews.

So the message of the *Havdala* is the distinction between holiness and the profane. It is a reminder to Jews of what should count in this life, of what distinctions we ought really to care about; for life is full of opposites, after all—rich and poor, success and failure, tall and short, weak and strong. But these opposites were not canonized in Jewish liturgy. They remain accidents of creation—opposites to be overcome, ignored if they hurt no one, corrected if they cause pain. The only lasting division intended from the time of creation, says the *Havdala*, the only separation intrinsic to life as a Jew, is the division between holy and profane.

That, surely, is Yom Kippur's lasting message. We who are charged to be a holy people prepare now to take leave of our holy time, these Days of Awe. But knowing that for most of the year ahead, we must inhabit the real world where profanation occurs daily round about us, we are instructed by the *Havdala* to remain firm in our resolve to strive after holiness. Holiness—through thought and action, study and *mitzva*—that is life's promise.

Part Two

On SHAAREI TESHUVAH— *Companion Notes to* GATES OF REPENTANCE

NOTES
TO *SHAAREI TESHUVAH*

Introduction

The Introduction to "Notes to *Shaarei Tefillah*" (*Gates of Understanding*, Volume I, pp. 177–179) gives a thumbnail sketch of the history of Jewish liturgy and explains the purpose of the Notes. That Introduction serves as well for these "Notes to *Shaarei Teshuvah*."

The immediate predecessor-volume to *Shaarei Teshuvah, Gates of Repentance*, was *Gate of Repentance*, edited by Rabbis John D. Rayner and Chaim Stern for the Union of Liberal and Progressive Synagogues, London, and published in 1973.

Rabbi Rayner wrote the Notes to that volume, and the Notes that follow owe much to him. Rabbi A. Stanley Dreyfus and Rabbi Lawrence A. Hoffman are, as with "Notes to *Shaarei Tefillah*," responsible for many corrections and improvements in the text of "Notes to *Shaarei Teshuvah*."

Rabbi Chaim Stern

Abbreviations

BOOKS OF THE BIBLE

N.B.   The references are to the Hebrew (Masoretic) division into chapters and verses, as maintained in Jewish translations of the Bible; Christian translations differ slightly in this respect.

Chron.	Chronicles	Lam.	Lamentations
Dan.	Daniel	Lev.	Leviticus
Deut.	Deuteronomy	Mal.	Malachi
Eccles.	Ecclesiastes	Mic.	Micah
Exod.	Exodus	Neh.	Nehemiah
Ezek.	Ezekiel	Num.	Numbers
Gen.	Genesis	Prov.	Proverbs
Hos.	Hosea	Ps., Pss.	Psalm, Psalms
Isa.	Isaiah	Sam.	Samuel
Jer.	Jeremiah	Zech.	Zechariah

159

OTHER ABBREVIATIONS

Abrahams   Dr. Israel Abrahams (1858–1935), *A Companion to the Authorised Prayerbook*, Hermon Press, N.Y., 1966 (first published 1922).

AF   Rabbi Albert H. Friedlander.

ASD   Rabbi A. Stanley Dreyfus.

B.   Babylonian Talmud.

b.   *ben, bar* (son of).

Bab.   Babylonia, Babylonian.

B.C.E.   Before the Common Era.

Ber.   Berachot (tractate of Mishna, Tosefta, or Talmud).

Buber   *Tales of the Hasidim*, ed. by Martin Buber (Schocken Books, Inc., N.Y., 1947; two volumes). Our references are to volume I, unless otherwise specified.

C.   century, centuries (Common Era, unless otherwise stated).

c.   *circa*.

CCAR   Central Conference of American Rabbis.

C.E.   Common Era.

ch.   chapter.

CS   Rabbi Chaim Stern.

E   English.

ed.   edited, edition, editor.

EG   Cantor Edward Graham.

Elbogen   Dr. Ismar Elbogen (1874–1943), *Der juedische Gottesdienst in seiner geschichtlichen Entwicklung*, Georg Olms Verlagsbuchhandlung, Hildesheim, 1967 (first published 1913).

GOH   *Gates of the House* (CCAR, N.Y., 1977), edited by CS.

Goldschmidt   *Machzor Leyamim Nora-im*, edited by Daniel Goldschmidt (appropriate volume), Koren, Jerusalem, 1970.

GOR   *Gate of Repentance* (Union of Liberal and Progressive Synagogues, London, 1973). High Holy Day prayerbook edited by Chaim Stern and John D. Rayner.

H   Hebrew.

Harlow   *Machzor for Rosh Hashanah and Yom Kippur*, edited by Jules Harlow (The Rabbinical Assembly, N.Y., 1972).

HB   Rabbi Herbert Bronstein.

ABBREVIATIONS

Idelsohn	Dr. Abraham Z. Idelsohn (1882–1938), *Jewish Liturgy and Its Development* (Schocken Books, Inc., N.Y., 1967; first published 1932).
IIM	Rabbi Israel I. Mattuck (1883–1954), editor of *Liberal Jewish Prayer Book*.
J.	"Jerusalem" ("Palestinian") Talmud.
JE	*The Jewish Encyclopedia*, Funk and Wagnalls Company, N.Y. and London, 1907.
JPS	Jewish Publication Society, Philadelphia.
JR	Rabbi John D. Rayner.
Levi	Eliezer Levi, *Yesodot Hatefila* (1961 edition).
LH	Rabbi Lawrence A. Hoffman.
lit.	literal, literally.
LJPB	*Liberal Jewish Prayer Book* (appropriate volume). Predecessor in Great Britain of *Service of the Heart* and *Gate of Repentance*.
M.	Mishna.
Meg.	Megila (tractate of Mishna, Tosefta, or Talmud).
MT	*Mishneh Torah*, by Moses b. Maimon (Maimonides, 1135–1204, Spain-Egypt), an important codification of Jewish law.
MV	*Machzor Vitry*, generally regarded as the first French Machzor, 11th century.
Newman	*The Hasidic Anthology*, edited by Louis I. Newman and Samuel Spitz (Bloch Publishing Co., N.Y., 1944).
O. Ch.	*Orach Chayim* (Part I of the *Shulchan Aruch* of Joseph Caro, 1488–1575, Turkey and Palestine), an important codification of Jewish law.
p., pp.	page, pages.
Pal.	Palestine, Palestinian.
PB	prayerbook.
q.	quotation, quoting, quoted by, quotes.
R.	Rabbi, Rav.
RH	Rosh Hashana (day or tractate).
RIK	Rabbi Robert I. Kahn.
RL	Rabbi Richard N. Levy.
RLK	Rabbi Robert L. Katz.

Rosenfeld	*The Authorised Selichot for the Whole Year*, translated and annotated by Rev. Abraham Rosenfeld, London, 1962.
RPB	*High Holiday Prayer Book* of the Jewish Reconstructionist Foundation, Inc., N.Y., 1948 (appropriate volume).
Soferim	"Minor Tractate" Soferim.
SOH	*Service of the Heart* (Union of Liberal and Progressive Synagogues, London, 1967), edited by Chaim Stern and John D. Rayner.
SRA	*Seder Rav Amram Gaon*, edited by Daniel Goldschmidt, Hotsaat Harav Kook, Jerusalem, 1971.
ST	*Shaarei Tefillah* (*Gates of Prayer*, the New Union Prayerbook), CCAR, N.Y., 1975, edited by Chaim Stern.
s.v.	*sub voce.*
trad.	tradition, traditional, traditionally.
trsl.	translated by, translation, translator.
UAHC	Union of American Hebrew Congregations.
ULPS	Union of Liberal and Progressive Synagogues (London).
UPB	*The Union Prayerbook for Jewish Worship* (appropriate volume).
v., vv.	verse, verses.
vol.	volume.
Yearnings	*Yearnings*, edited by Jules Harlow (The Rabbinical Assembly, N.Y., 1968).
YK	Yom Kippur.

Rosh Hashana

MEDITATIONS

No.   Page

         pecially during the Nazi period, coming thereafter to the U.S.A. and Great Britain; his dates are 1874–1956). The essay is called "Perfection and Tension." See *Leo Baeck, Teacher of Theresienstadt,* by AF (Holt, Rinehart and Winston, N.Y., 1968), p. 174.

13   6   *An ancient Jewish word* . . . *Ibid.,* p. 175.

14   7   *Free will is given* . . . MT, *Hilchot Teshuva* 5.1.

15   7   *All is foreseen* . . . M. Avot 3.19. A saying of R. Akiva b. Joseph (see no. 4). The 2nd sentence ("Everything is . . . ") is from B. Ber. 33b. It is a saying of the Pal. Amora (teacher) R. Chanina b. Chama, 3rd C.

16   7   *If you choose* . . . B. Yoma 38b. A saying of the Pal. Amora (teacher) Resh Lakish (R. Shimon b. Lakish), 3rd C.

17   7   *Do not imagine* . . . MT, *Hilchot Teshuva* 5.1f.

18   7   *In connection* . . . *Hilchot Dei-ot,* 1.5.

19   8   *With regard* . . . MT, *ibid.,* 1.4.

20   8   *How do we fix* . . . *Ibid.,* 1.7.

21   8   *Smooth speech* . . . *Ibid.,* 2.6.

22   9   *If you see* . . . *Ibid.,* 6.7.

23   9   *Our sages taught* . . . *Ibid.,* 6.8.

24   9   *This fragile life* . . . From *The Way of Response: Martin Buber,* ed. by Nahum N. Glatzer (Schocken Books, N.Y., 1966), p. 19.

25   10   *Ethical life* . . . *Ibid.,* p. 21.

26   10   *We shall accomplish* . . . *Ibid.,* p. 34.

27   10   *It was the favorite saying* . . . B. Ber. 17a (q. B. Ber. 5b). Yavneh is the location of the Academy established by R. Yochanan b. Zakkai (Pal. 1st C.) following the destruction of the Temple in 70 C.E.

28   10   *"The Lord loves* . . . " Num. Rabba 8.2, q. Ps. 146:8.

29   11   *"And an angel of the Lord* . . . " Gen. Rabba 56.7, q. Gen. 22:11.

30   11   *Every human being* . . . MT, *Hilchot Teshuva* 3.1.

31   11   *Rabbi Shimon ben Elazar said* . . . Avot deRabbi Natan 16.

32   11   *Rabbi Bunam said* . . . Adapted by CS from *A Jewish Reader,* ed. by Nahum N. Glatzer (Schocken Books, N.Y., 1946, 1961), p. 108. Rabbi Simcha Bunam of Pzhysha (1765–1827) was an important Hasidic master.

33   11   *Though the Torah warns* . . . J. Makkot 2.6, q. Ps. 25:8; Prov. 13:21; Ezek. 18:4; Lev. 1:4; 5:6,16. The introductory sentence is our own, following a suggestion by RLK.

34   12   *Who is truly repentant?* . . . B. Yoma 86b, where it is attributed to R. Judah.

35   12   *Do not think* . . . MT, *Hilchot Teshuva* 7.3, q. Isa. 55:7.

No. Page

36   12   *There are many reasons* ... Abridged and adapted by CS from a passage by Saadia Gaon (Egypt/Babylonia, 882–942) in *Days of Awe*, ed. by S. Y. Agnon (Schocken Books, N.Y., 1948), pp. 70ff.

37   13   *From year to year* ... New, by JR. The q. and allusions are: Ezek. 33:11; Amos 5:4; Deut. 30:19; M. Sanhedrin 4.5; Isa. 2:4; *Survival for What?*, by Zvi Kolitz (Philosophical Library, N.Y., 1969), p. 183; Gen. 22; and the trad. insertion for the Ten Days of Repentance (see no. 59).

38   13   *Glory to those who hope.* ... A poem by David Rokeach (Israel, 1914-), called *Kana-ei Erga*, in *Mo-adei Erga* (Hotsa-at Sifrei Tarshish, Jerusalem, 1958). Trsl. CS. Cf. his slightly different trsl. in GOR, pp. 11f.

39   14   *There is a grace* ... Adapted and abridged by CS from GOR, p. 18, where it was new, by CS.

EVENING SERVICE I

40   17   *Creator of beginnings* ... From Harlow, p. 39, where it is adapted from a prayer in *Sha-arei Tsiyon*, Prague, 1662. The 2nd sentence alludes to *Ahava Rabba* (p. 169) and Ps. 36:10.

41   17   *Blessed is the Lord* ... *Yom Tov*. The custom of kindling lights on the eve of a festival (as well as on the eve of Shabbat) is taken for granted in the Talmud (B. Pesachim 102b), but the text of the festival benediction is not attested earlier than the Middle Ages (Cf. *Shulchan Aruch*, O. Ch. 514.11). In some Reform congregations the lights are kindled as the service begins; in others, the lights are kindled earlier, and the service begins with the recitation of the benediction only.

42   17   *Blessed is the Lord* ... *this season*. This benediction, known as "*Shehecheyanu*," is found in various places in the Talmud (e.g., B. Pesachim 7b). It is trad. recited at the commencement of festivals and on other happy occasions. According to a 19th-C. legal commentary, it was common for women to say this blessing when they finished lighting festival lights (*Aruch Hashulchan*, O. Ch. 514.17).

43   19   *Behold me* ... A meditation for the Reader or Cantor dating from medieval times, of unknown origin. Trad. placed before the *Musaf* (Additional Service) on RH morning. Trsl. CS. Our text is abridged by ASD, to blunt the impact of overly humiliating language which the medieval author applies to himself, a d to avoid the theological notion of angels interceding between us a..d God.

No. *Page*

44　20　*Hear Me, Jacob* . . . A reading arranged, adapted, and trsl. by CS from Isa. 48:12d; 42:5ff; 45:18,19b; 65:17f. The concluding sentence is new, by CS.

45　21　*I lift up my eyes* . . . Ps. 121. The present trsl., by CS, is very slightly revised from his trsl. in ST, p. 547.

46　21　*God of our people* . . . Slightly adapted and abridged from a poem by Hilary Mindlin (contemporary, U.S.A.). Cf. GOR, pp. 10f.

47　23　*In the seventh month* . . . Lev. 23:24.

48　23　*Sound the Shofar* . . . Ps. 81:4f. The Ashkenazi liturgy places this after *"Hashkivenu"* (no. 56). These vv. are associated with RH already in the B. Talmud (RH 8a-b). UPB II (p. 17) adds Ps. 81:2. As does GOR (p. 16), we use these vv. as part of the introductory prayers.

49　23　*The Ark is opened.* The opening of the Ark at this point of the service is an innovation of the present PB. It adds weight to the proclamation of the New Year and the call to worship (nos. 50 and 51), which follow.

50　24　*May it be Your will* . . . Adapted from the trad. Rosh Chodesh (New Month) prayer, which can be traced back partly to SRA, p. 88, and partly to the Talmud (B. Ber. 16b), where it is mentioned as a daily private prayer in the name of the 3rd C. Bab. Amora (teacher), Rav. It comes here from GOR, p. 16, where its use in the present context, suitably adapted, was an innovation.

51　24　*Praise the Lord* . . . Based on Neh. 9:5 and cited in M. Ber. 7.3, this invocation trad. introduces the recitation of the *"Shema"* (see no. 54). The *"Barechu,"* as this invocation is called from its opening word, is followed by a congregational response that is first attested in *Sifrei* to Deut. 32:3.

52　25　*There was silence* . . . The first major section of the service is the recitation of the *"Shema,"* introduced by the *"Barechu"* and comprising, apart from the *"Shema"* itself, a series of benedictions which, in the Evening Service, number four: two before the *"Shema"* and two after it. So the Mishna ordains (see M. Ber. 1.4). The present H benediction, whose theme is "Creation of Light" is the 1st of the series and is known as *"Ma-ariv Aravim"* ("makes evening fall"). It is partly cited in B. Ber. 11b. The E text is from ST, p. 208, where it was new, by CS. For a trsl. of the H see Service II, pp. 54f.

53　25　*And how unyielding* . . . The H text is the 2nd of the 2 benedictions preceding the *"Shema"* in the Evening Service, known from its opening words as *"Ahavat Olam"* (cf. Jer. 31:2), and having as its theme "Revelation." It is cited in B. Ber. 11b. The E text is from ST, p.

No. Page

209, where it was new, by CS. For a trsl. of the H, see Service II, p. 55.

54 26 *Hear, O Israel* ... Trad., the *"Shema"* consists of 3 Scriptural passages: Deut. 6:4–9 (to which the term primarily refers), Deut. 11:13–21, and Num. 15:37–41. The antiquity of its liturgical use, at any rate of the 1st paragraph, is attested by the Nash Papyrus, 2nd–1st C. B.C.E., and as regards all 3 paragraphs, by Josephus (37–100 C.E.), *Antiquities* IV, 8.13. M. Tamid asserts that it was recited already in the days of the Second Temple, and in the Temple itself (see M. Tamid 5.1, which also refers to the Morning Service *Ge-ula*—nos. 55 and 157—as well as the *Avoda*—no. 75—and the *Birkat Kohanim*—nos. 75 and 176). According to M. Ber. 2.2, the 3rd paragraph was originally recited in the morning only. The *"Shema"* was intended as a daily Scripture lesson, to be recited evening and morning in accordance with the phrase "when you lie down and when you rise up." It is a solemn affirmation of the unity and uniqueness of God, and of the Jew's duty to study Torah and to obey God's commandments. The *"Shema"* remains what it has always been: the central statement of Jewish faith. In Reform PBs, the 2nd and 3rd paragraphs are generally omitted, wholly or in part. We, following ST (pp. 33f), include Num. 15:40f (see GOR, p. 23), extending this somewhat further than UPB II, p. 13. The congregational response, "Blessed is His glorious kingdom . . . . ," is not Scriptural, though reminiscent of Pss. 72:19 and 89:53. It apparently goes back to the Second Temple (cf. M. Yoma 3.8), and may be related to the response to the *Kaddish* (see no. 58), "Let His great name be blessed for ever and ever."

55 27 *What does it mean* . . . The 1st of the 2 benedictions that follow the *"Shema"* in the Evening Service reaffirms the unity of God proclaimed in the *"Shema"* and alludes to the Exodus from Egypt. For the latter reason it is known as *Ge-ula*, "Redemption." The Talmud alludes to it (B. Ber. 9b, 12a), and the Mishna alludes to the *Ge-ula* of the Morning Service (M. Tamid 5.1). M. Ber. 1.4 speaks of 2 benedictions that follow the *"Shema"* in the Evening Service, without naming them. Both B. Ber. 11b and 12a name the evening *Ge-ula* as the benediction following the *"Shema,"* and doubtless both forms of the *Ge-ula* were developed at about the same time. For the trad. H text and its trsl. (which we abridge), see Service II, pp. 57f. In the present service, we include only the concluding portion of the trad. H, all of it Scriptural: Exod. 15:11,18; Jer. 31:10. The present E is new, by CS. It is based on a thought by Abraham J.

No. Page

Heschel (1907–1972). The Scriptural allusions are to Lev. 19:2a and Exod. 19:6. The concluding E paragraph is freely adapted from the H.

56   29   *May we lie down* ... The 2nd of the 2 benedictions that follow the *"Shema"* in the Evening Service is known from its opening word as *"Hashkivenu,"* "Cause us to lie down." The Mishna (M. Ber. 1.4) refers to the 2 benedictions that follow the *"Shema,"* and we may safely assume that *"Hashkivenu"* is the 2nd one. The Talmud alludes to it specifically (e.g., B. Ber. 4b). Its theme is Divine Providence, although it is referred to in the Talmud, *ibid.,* as an extension of the *Ge-ula* (see no. 55). The E text is from ST, p. 212, where it was new, by CS. For a trsl. of the H, see Service II, p. 59. In regard to the H, we may observe that though most Reform PBs abridge or emend this benediction (see UPB II, p. 17, and GOR, pp. 24f), we follow ST (p. 133) and retain the classical text.

57   29   *Veshameru* ... Exod. 31:16f. Trad. this passage follows the *"Hashkivenu"* (see preceding note) in the Sabbath Evening Service and the festival Evening Service when the festival coincides with the Sabbath. It also introduces the *Kedushat Hayom* (see no. 69) in the Sabbath Morning Service. Its theme is the Sabbath, the observance of which constitutes Israel's recognition of its covenant with God and the divine creative activity. For this reason we have, following ST (p. 133), but unlike UPB I (pp. 18–19) and GOR (p. 30), retained the 2nd half of v. 17 ("for in six days ..."), holding this to be a poetical expression celebrating Creation, not a literal assertion that the world came into being in six days. UPB II omits this passage altogether. For a trsl. of the H, see Service II, p. 59.

58   29   *Yitgadal veyitkadash* ... The name *Kaddish,* Aramaic for "holy," is first found in Soferim 10.7, but the doxology itself is believed to date from early Rabbinic times, possibly from before the destruction of the Second Temple. There are allusions to it in the Talmud (e.g., B. Ber. 3a and J. Ta-anit 1.3; in the latter instance some of its phrases occur in a prayer of thanksgiving for rain). Its central response is reminiscent of Dan. 2:20 and Ps. 113:2. There may be a connection between this response, "Let His great name be blessed ... ," and the response to the *"Shema,"* "Blessed is His glorious kingdom ..." (see no. 54). It is generally thought that the *Kaddish* originated in the *Beit Hamidrash* (House of Study) rather than the synagogue, as a way of concluding a public discourse on a messianic note. Then it entered the synagogue liturgy as a concluding prayer marking the end of a service, or of a section of a service. Later still

it became also a mourner's prayer (Soferim 19.12), on the principle that one should praise God in sorrow as well as in joy (Job 1:21). Ultimately several versions of the *Kaddish* developed for different occasions and purposes. The version used in this PB at the end of services is the *Kaddish Yatom*, "Orphan's *Kaddish*," and is intended to serve both as a mourner's prayer for those recently bereaved or observing the anniversary *(Yahrzeit)* of a near relative's death, and as a concluding prayer for all. Apart from the last paragraph (based on Job 25:2b), the *Kaddish* was written in Aramaic "so that all might understand it, for this was their vernacular" (*Tosafot* to B. Ber. 3a). Here, however, we offer not the *Kaddish Yatom*, but a shorter version known as *Chatsi Kaddish*, "Reader's (lit. 'half') *Kaddish*," which is trad. recited at the end of a section of the service. Since it is not intended to be recited by mourners, it may be sung rather than spoken. Our use of the *Chatsi Kaddish* follows ST, where its use marked a return to the older Reform practice which, in this respect, followed the trad. liturgy. More recent Reform liturgy, through its exclusive use of the *Kaddish* as a memorial prayer, had obscured the messianic significance of this prayer. By its use of the *Chatsi Kaddish*, therefore, ST and the present volume emphasize its message of the coming of the divine realm, the essential point of all the forms of the *Kaddish*. It is worth noting that the *Kaddish* has no reference to death, for it looks forward to the messianic time when "death will be swallowed up for ever" (Isa. 25:8). It may be pointed out that the opening sentences of the "Lord's Prayer" (Matthew 6:9; cf. Luke 11:2) show close affinity to the *Kaddish*. For the trsl., see Service II, p. 60. For other forms of the *Kaddish*, see nos. 85 and 793.

59   30   *Eternal God, open my lips* . . . Ps. 51:17 trad. introduces the next major section of the service, the *Tefila* ("Prayer," i.e., par excellence) or *Amida* ("Standing"), a custom going back to the 3rd C. Amora, R. Yochanan b. Nappacha, B. Ber. 9b. The *Tefila* originated in the days of the Second Temple but continued to develop thereafter. According to B. Meg. 17b, its text was fixed under the authority of Rabban Gamaliel II, around 100 C.E. For weekdays it consisted for some time of 18 benedictions (hence its other name, *Shemoneh Esrei*, "Eighteen") but, perhaps in 3rd C. Bab., one benediction was divided into 2 separate ones, thus making a total of 19. On Sabbaths and festivals only the first 3 and the last 3 are recited, and the intermediate ones are replaced by a single peculiar to the day. Along with the "*Shema*" and its accompanying benedictions, the *Tefila* is

No. Page

the chief constituent of the daily liturgy. However, the *"Shema"* and its benedictions are recited only twice daily, in the morning and evening, while the *Tefila* is recited 3 times daily—morning, afternoon, and evening. The practice of praying three times a day is already alluded to in Dan. 6:11 and Ps. 55:18. Some of the blessings of the *Tefila* are paralleled by a psalm included in the H text of ch. 51 of Sirach (Ecclesiasticus, c. 200 B.C.E.). But the H may belong to a later time.

60 30 *We praise You, ... Shield of Abraham.* The first benediction of the *Tefila*, known as *Avot*, "Fathers" or "Ancestors" (M. RH 4.5). Like all the benedictions of the *Tefila*, it borrows much of its language from Scriptural phrases. It praises the God of all generations for the loving and redemptive acts we have experienced. Following ST, we trsl. the H אֲבוֹתֵינוּ, "our fathers," somewhat freely, here and elsewhere, to avoid excessive use of the masculine. Following ST and many Reform PBs in Europe and America, including Isaac Mayer Wise's *Minhag America*, 1866, and David Einhorn's *Olat Tamid*, 1856–1858, in its later eds., we emend the H word גּוֹאֵל "a redeemer," to read גְּאֻלָּה "redemption." Such, too, is the practice of UPB, SOH, and GOR. The paragraph beginning "Remember us unto life" is an insertion peculiar to the Ten Days of Repentance, 1st found in SRA, pp. 135. See Soferim 19.7.

61 31 *Great is Your might ...* The 2nd benediction of the *Tefila*, known as *Gevurot*, "Powers [of God]" (M. RH 4.5). Originally, the trad. text emphasized God's power in the physical and moral realms, but its main theme came to be the Resurrection of the Dead, a doctrine not accepted by Liberal Judaism. Some Reform PBs (e.g., LJPB) retained the trad. text but interpreted it in terms of spiritual immortality. Others (e.g., UPB, SOH, and GOR) follow Einhorn's *Olat Tamid* to emend the body of the text from מְחַיֵּה מֵתִים "You revive the dead," to מְחַיֵּה הַכֹּל "You are the Source of all life," or similar language. ST follows these precedents, as does the present volume, in regard to the body of the text. The earlier Reform PBs go on to emend the concluding eulogy by borrowing the words of the benediction after the reading of the Torah, praising God who has "implanted within us eternal life." Following ST, we have preferred to remain within the trad. liturgical form, and have retained the emendation utilized in the body of the text, מְחַיֵּה הַכֹּל, trsl. here as "Source of all life." The sentence beginning "Who is like You, Source of mercy" is another insertion peculiar to the Ten Days of Repen-

No. *Page*

tance, first found in SRA, p. 135. The present trsl. of the H text derives from ST (cf. ST, p. 38), but differs substantially from it in some respects.

62   32   *You are holy* . . . This begins the 3rd benediction of the *Tefila*, known as *Kedushat Hashem*, "The Holiness of God" (M. RH 4.5). The H that we have rendered by "those who strive to be holy" (so already in ST) might be more lit. rendered as "holy beings" (i.e., the angels). GOR (and SOH, which it follows) emends the text to say (in H and E), "and every day we will praise Your holiness." UPB retains the trad. H text (as we do, following ST), but renders it by "Thy worshipers."

63   32   *Lord our God, cause all Your works* . . . The first of the 3 paragraphs trad. inserted in the 3rd benediction of the *Tefila* on RH and YK, each beginning "*Uvechen*" (lit. "And so"). They are 1st found in SRA, pp. 135f, but are generally believed to be much older, owing to their affinity to the *Malchuyot* ("Kingship verses" of the *Shofar* Ritual) which are already mentioned in the M. (RH 4.5), and where a discussion is recorded between R. Yochanan b. Nuri and R. Akiva. (2nd C.). According to R. Yochanan, the *Malchuyot* were to be inserted in the 3rd benediction of the *Tefila*; according to R. Akiva, in the 4th. R. Akiva's view prevailed, although the whole custom of reciting the *Malchuyot*, as well as the *Zichronot* ("Remembrance verses") and *Shofarot* ("*Shofar* verses"), in association with the sounding of the *shofar*, became ultimately confined to the RH *Musaf* (Additional Service). It has therefore been conjectured that the presence of the "*Uvechen*" paragraphs in the 3rd benediction of the *Tefila* may be a survival of, or a concession to, the view represented by R. Yochanan b. Nuri, and thus may point to their antiquity.

64   32   *Grant honor, Lord* . . . The second of the 3 "*Uvechen*" paragraphs. Following GOR, from which our trsl. comes with some adaptation by CS, we have, in place of the trad. conclusion ("a flourishing horn to Your servant David, and a constant light to the son of Jesse, Your Anointed One, speedily in our days"), substituted (in H and E) "and cause the light of redemption to dawn for all who dwell on earth."

65   33   *Then the just shall see* . . . The 3rd of the "*Uvechen*" paragraphs, concluding with Ps. 146:10. Following GOR, we have abridged the text, omitting the phrase (which follows ". . . over all Your works"), "on Mount Zion, the dwelling-place of Your glory, and in Jerusalem, Your holy city."

66   33   *You are holy; awesome is Your name* . . . A continuation of the *Ke-*

No. Page

dushat Hashem, now confined to RH and YK. In ancient Palestine it was recited also on weekdays. So Elbogen, p. 45, on the basis of *Sifrei* to Deut.

67   33   *The Lord of Hosts* . . . Isa. 5:16. Interpolated in the *Kedushat Hashem* on RH and YK, a custom that originated in Bab., according to Elbogen, *loc. cit.*

68   33   *Blessed is the Lord, the holy King.* The concluding eulogy of the *Kedushat Hashem* during the Ten Days of Repentance, as prescribed by Rav (B. Ber. 12b). Rav was a 3rd C. Bab. Amora (teacher). During the rest of the year it ends "the holy God."

69   34   *In love and favor* . . . This begins the benediction known as *Kedushat Hayom*, "The Holiness of the Day," which, on Sabbaths and Festivals, replaces the 13 (originally 12) "Intermediate Benedictions" of the *Tefila*. It is mentioned in the Talmud (e.g., B. Yoma 87b) and in the Tosefta (Ber. 3.14). Our version is slightly abridged and somewhat freely trsl.

70   34   *Our God . . . be mindful* . . . This continues the *Kedushat Hayom*. Our version is abridged and comes from ST (e.g., p. 43), except, of course, for the reference to RH, which replaces the references there. This passage is alluded to in B. Ber. 29b, Tosefta Ber. 3.10, Soferim 19.7. As in ST, we trsl. the H אֲבוֹתֵינוּ, "our fathers," somewhat freely, to avoid exclusive use of the masculine. Our E text is very slightly different from that of ST.

71   35   *Our God . . . may You rule* . . . This paragraph is trad. inserted in the *Kedushat Hayom* for RH; so already SRA, p. 136, where it 1st appears, though it may well be as old as the "*Uvechen*" paragraphs (see no. 63). It may have been placed here at the same time the "*Uvechen*" paragraphs were placed in the *Kedushat Hashem*, in order to satisfy both of the conflicting opinions recorded in the M. Unlike LJPB II and GOR (p. 29), which place this passage in the *Kedushat Hayom* "for the sake of greater thematic unity," we keep it in its trad. place because, together with the paragraph that follows, it sounds the distinctive trad. note which holds universalism and particularism in creative tension.

72   35   *Our God . . . the Day of Remembrance.* This continues and concludes the *Kedushat Hayom*. Unlike GOR (p. 32), we retain the complete trad. text, thus keeping its fuller reference to Shabbat. The concluding eulogy is specific to RH, as are some phrases in the antecedent text, and is 1st found in SRA, p. 136. Once again (see, e.g., no. 70), we trsl. the H אֲבוֹתֵינוּ, "our fathers," somewhat freely, to avoid

No. Page

exclusive use of the masculine. This applies as well to our trsl. of no. 71.

73   36   *Be gracious* ... The 1st of the last 3 benedictions of the *Tefila*, known as *Avoda*, "Worship" (M. Tamid 5.1; M. RH 4.5). Following UPB, SOH, GOR, and many other Reform PBs, we have omitted the trad. references to sacrificial worship, substituting (an innovation of ST) a thought (based on Pss. 145:18; 25:16) on the theme of God's nearness to all who seek God with sincerity. The H for "Let our eyes behold Your presence in our midst" also comes from ST, where it is new in the present benediction, but based on phrases occurring in such Scriptural vv. as Ezek. 39:29 and Joel 3:2. From ST, too, is the restoration of the trad. concluding eulogy, trsl. rather broadly to carry out the more universal theme we wish to convey, i.e., God's presence in Zion *and* wherever our people worship Him in truth. Unlike ST, we add here, at the beginning of the last sentence in Roman type, the words "Pour out Your spirit upon us"; these appear already in the H of ST (p. 43). For another H text, with E trsl., see RH Morning Service I, p. 115.

74   37   *We gratefully acknowledge* ... The penultimate benediction of the *Tefila*, known as *Hoda-a*, "Thanksgiving" (M. Ber. 5.2,3; M. RH 4.5). Unlike UPB and GOR, but following ST, we give the complete text here, but we trsl. the H אֲבוֹתֵינוּ, "our fathers," somewhat freely, to avoid exclusive use of the masculine. The passage "let life abundant ... Your covenant" is an insertion peculiar to the Ten Days of Repentance, 1st found in SRA, p. 137. Our trsl. is very slightly adapted from ST (p. 44).

75   38   *Grant us peace* ... The H text is the evening version of the last benediction of the *Tefila*, known as *Birkat Kohanim*, "The Priestly Benediction" (and called by us, already in ST, *Birkat Shalom*, "The Benediction Concerning Peace"), in reference to Num. 6:24ff, on which this benediction (especially the longer morning version) is based, and which is trad. recited here in the Morning Service. This shorter evening version has been traced back only to the 11th C., though it is probably older. Here we retain the trad. text (cf. ST, p. 46), unlike those Reform liturgies that universalize this benediction by emendation. In this we agree with UPB II, p. 26, unlike UPB I, pp. 22f and GOR, p. 34. The penultimate sentence ("Teach us, O God, to labor ... ") is an insertion (somewhat freely rendered in the E) peculiar to the Ten Days of Repentance, 1st found in SRA, p. 137, with some variation. The concluding eulogy, trad. during

No. Page

these days, is found in some Reform liturgies throughout the year. The E text comes from ST, p. 202, and is based on the UPB I (p. 22) prayer on the theme of peace. Cf. UPB II, p. 26.

76 38 *O God, keep my tongue* ... A meditation that trad. follows the *Tefila*, composed by the Bab. Amora (teacher), Mar b. Rabina, c. 400 C.E., and cited in B. Ber. 17a. Our trsl. (which is very slightly adapted from ST, p. 47) is somewhat compressed, with the effect of slightly abridging the H.

77 39 *May the words* ... Ps. 19:15, from the trad. meditation following the *Tefila* attributed to Mar b. Rabina (see preceding note). It is cited in B. Ber. 17a, where it is called suitable for recital either at the beginning or the end of the *Tefila*. Its placement at the end is there explained on the ground that it comes at the end of the 1st 18 chapters of Psalms (counting Pss. 1 and 2 as a single Psalm), and therefore it appropriately follows the 18 (weekday) benedictions of the *Tefila* (see no. 59).

78 39 *May the One who causes peace* ... This verse, 1st found as the conclusion of the *Kaddish* (see no. 58), in SRA, p. 39, trad. forms the conclusion of the meditation that follows the *Tefila*. It is based on Job 25:2b. Following ST (p. 47), from which our text differs very slightly, we have added the E words "and all the world." (Cf. GOR, p. 43, note 83.) There those words are added in H as well, and trsl. "and to all mankind."

79 40 *Our Father, our King* ... A penitential litany, known from its opening words as *"Avinu Malkenu,"* generally attributed to R. Akiva on the basis of a story in the Talmud (B. Ta-anit 25b) that once, during a drought, he prayed successfully for rain, in words corresponding to the 1st and last vv. of this litany. On the one hand, however, Akiva may have used an already established formula; on the other hand, it is certain that many vv. were added after his time. SRA (pp. 138f) has 25; the German Ritual has 38; the Polish Ritual has 44. Ours, in the present service, follows UPB II in its selection, but includes 2 additional vv.—the last 2. See UPB, p. 29. In the RH Morning Service, we again provide 9 vv., one of which, the penultimate one, differs from the one in the Evening Service (see Morning Service I, pp. 121f.; cf. UPB, pp. 62–63, where again the same 7 vv. are provided). Trad., the *"Avinu Malkenu"* is recited, after the *Tefila*, throughout the Ten Days of Repentance, but only in the Morning and Afternoon Services; and at the end of YK Eve service. Following UPB II, LJPB II, and GOR, we have included it also in the RH Evening Services, because of its relevant and powerful character.

No. Page

Unlike those PBs, however, we have also included it in the YK Concluding Service (*Ne-ila*), following in this respect the trad. rituals. We also depart from tradition in that we do not omit it on Shabbat. Since there are many vv. from which to select, our versions of "*Avinu Malkenu*" will differ to a greater or lesser degree from those of RH. This is true of UPB II (cf. pp. 158–159), though our selections are more extensive and venturesome than are those of UPB II. GOR utilizes 12 vv. of "*Avinu Malkenu*" throughout, but provides them without variation (pp. 37f, 74f, 167ff, 232f).

80   42   *Kiddush.* Although *Kiddush* is essentially a domestic ritual, preceding the meal on the eve of Sabbaths and Festivals, the practice of reciting it also in the synagogue, before the "*Aleinu*" (no. 83), is ancient, being mentioned in the Talmud (B. Pesachim 101a) and referred to approvingly by Rav Amram in the name of his predecessor, Natronai Gaon (SRA, p. 65). It is, however, not essential, and some authorities have actually opposed it on the ground that *Kiddush* should be recited only where one eats. It may therefore be omitted, in which case the service would proceed with the "*Aleinu*" (pp. 43f or pp. 72f).

81   42   *Blessed is the Lord . . . the fruit of the vine.* The benediction is to be recited before drinking wine (M. Ber. 6.1). Wine is a symbol of joy (Ps. 104:15), and the beginning of the New Year is an occasion for rejoicing, as well as solemnity (Neh. 8:9–12).

82   42   *Blessed is the Lord . . . who has chosen us . . . the Day of Remembrance.* The RH *Kiddush*, largely identical with the version for other festivals that is already mentioned in the Talmud (B. Pesachim 105a). The earliest reference specifically to the RH version is Soferim 19.7. Our text is virtually the trad. one, omitting 2 words that are trad. inserted when RH coincides with Shabbat. On the "*Shehecheyanu*," which follows, see no. 42.

83   43   *We must praise the Lord of all . . .* This prayer is known from its opening word as "*Aleinu*" (lit., "It is our duty"). The Scriptural q. in it are Deut. 4:39; Exod. 15:18; Zech. 14:9. It is commonly attributed to Rav (Bab., 3rd C.) as the reputed redactor of the section of the RH liturgy relating to the sounding of the *shofar* (see nos. 63, 115), for it is in that context, introducing the *Malchuyot* ("Kingship verses" of the *Shofar* Ritual), that the "*Aleinu*" is 1st found. Only in the 10th or 11th C. did it also become a concluding prayer for all services throughout the year. J. Heinemann (*Hatefila Bitekufat Hatana-im Veha-amora-im*, pp. 173ff) has conjectured that the 1st half of the "*Aleinu*" (up to "*Al ken nekaveh*," "We therefore hope")

No. Page

may be a good deal older than Rav, going back to Temple times. See also Abrahams, p. 87. The 1st paragraph contains a passage that we trsl. *ad sensum,* " . . . who has set us apart . . . among the nations." Most Reform PBs have omitted or replaced this passage with a substitute (see Petuchowski, *Prayerbook Reform in Europe* [The World Union for Progressive Judaism, N.Y., 1968], ch. 12). With this version of *"Aleinu,"* we attempt to restore its classical balance of particularism and universalism, and we offer elsewhere 2 other versions (see pp. 72f and 282f), which are closer to the UPB version, whose emphasis is exclusively universal.

84   45   *At this sacred moment* . . . Abridged and slightly adapted from ST, p. 626, where it was adapted by CS from a meditation by Solomon B. Freehof, in UPB I, pp. 366f.

85   46   *Let the glory of God* . . . see no. 58. The present text is the *Kaddish Yatom,* "Orphan's (Mourner's) *Kaddish."* Our trsl. of the last sentence adds the words "and all the world" (see no. 78). This form of the *Kaddish* is longer than the "Reader's *Kaddish,"* the last 2 sentences being additional. *May the Source* . . . see no. 747.

86   47   *Adon Olam (He is the eternal Lord)* . . . This doctrinal hymn, emphasizing the transcendence, unity, and immanence of God, is known from its opening words as *"Adon Olam,"* "The Eternal Lord." Its author is unknown, but it is generally believed to date from the 11th or 12th C.

87   48   *The Lord of all.* Very slightly adapted from a metrical version of *"Adon Olam"* (see preceding note), by F. De Sola Mendes. *Union Hymnal,* p. 77.

EVENING SERVICE II

88   49   *With the setting* . . . Adapted by CS from GOR, p. 15, where it was new, by Malcolm Stern and CS. It alludes, in the 2nd sentence, to Ps. 43:3.

89   49   *Blessed is the eternal Power* . . . For the H text, see no. 41. The E is slightly adapted from ST, p. 204, where it was based on a passage in *A Common Service,* by T. G. Falcon and H. B. Zyskind, revised and ed. by Alvin J. Reines.

90   49   *Blessed is . . . this season.* For the H text, see no. 42. The E is adapted.

91   50   *Lord, I cry out* . . . From a new trsl. by CS of Pss. 3 and 5 in GOH, pp. 89f. The vv. here offered are Pss. 3:5–7a,8a,9; 5:8,12f.

No.   Page

Kedushat Hayom, "The Holiness of the Day," which this passage begins. On the H text, see no. 69.

116   65   *On this Day of Remembrance* . . . The H text continues the *Kedushat Hayom*. See no. 70. The E is new, by CS.

117   65   *You transcend* . . . New, by CS. On the H text, which continues the *Kedushat Hayom*, see no. 71.

118   65   *The kingdom of law* . . . On the H text, which concludes the *Kedushat Hayom*, see no. 72. The E is new, by CS.

119   66   *Let our thoughts* . . . New, by CS, on the theme of *Avoda* (see no. 73). The H text used here differs from the one discussed in no. 73. It is, rather, the *Avoda* text used *throughout* UPB I (p. 139), UPB II (p. 25), SOH (p. 53), and GOR (p. 33), and *occasionally* used in ST (pp. 200f). The present text omits one passage from the trad. text (a supplication for the restorations of the Temple and the sacrificial cult), and substitutes, for the concluding eulogy, a version, "whom alone we serve in reverence," which is recorded in J. Sota 7.6, and which is trad. recited in the Reader's repetition of the *Tefila* in the Festival *Musaf*. (This substitution goes back to the Hamburg Temple, 1841—see Petuchowski, *Prayerbook Reform in Europe*, p. 231—and was followed thereafter by most Reform PBs.) For a trsl. of the present H see RH Morning Service I, p. 115.

120   66   *O world, where miracles* . . . New, by CS, on the theme of *Hoda-a* (see no. 74), and partly based on a passage by CS in ST, p. 386. The H text used here differs from the one discussed in no. 74. It is the shorter form of the *Hoda-a*, known as *Modim Derabbanan*, "Thanksgiving of the Rabbis" (B. Sota 40a), and is trad. recited during the repetition of the *Tefila*. The concluding eulogy is cited in J. Ber. 1.5. The use of this text as an occasional alternative to the trad. *Hoda-a* (no. 74) began in SOH (p. 101), and was continued in GOR (pp. 357f) and ST (p. 155). We have substituted (already in SOH), in the H, "give us strength" for "gather our exiles to Your holy courts" and made one slight omission. For a slightly free trsl. of this text, see the YK Afternoon Service, p. 407. The H preceding the concluding eulogy is the trad. insertion for the Ten Days of Repentance (see no. 74). The present occasion is the only one in which we include that insertion in this particular version of the *Hoda-a*.

121   67   *Words there are and prayers* . . . From ST, pp. 275f, where it was new, by RL (somewhat revised by CS), on the theme of *Birkat Shalom* (see no. 75), whose H text we here omit. The present version of the E text is abridged. The q. are Isa. 2:4; Ps. 34:15b.

No. Page

122   68   *Rabbi Eliezer said* ... Midrash Tehillim to Ps. 90:16. R. Eliezer b. Hyrcanus was a Pal. Tanna (teacher) of the 1st-2nd C. His comment follows one by R. Joshua, his contemporary, based on Ps. 90:12, that if we knew the number of our days, we would repent before we died. The statement we have attributed to R. Eliezer may well have been said by his equally distinguished contemporary, R. Elazar b. Azariah.

123   68   *Yihyu leratson* ... See no. 77.

124   68   *Oseh Shalom* ... See no. 78.

125   69   *Our Father, our King* ... See no. 79.

126   71   *Kiddush.* See no. 80.

127   71   *Blessed is the Lord* ... *the fruit of the vine.* See no. 81.

128   71   *Blessed is the Lord* ... *the Day of Remembrance.* See no. 82.

129   72   *Let us adore* ... This is the UPB version of *"Aleinu"* (see no. 83), somewhat adapted (already in ST, p. 617), and provided with the H extract from the *"Aleinu"* used in UPB II, p. 261.

130   73   *The light of life* ... Slightly adapted from ST, p. 627, where it was slightly revised by CS from a passage in *A Common Service* (see no. 89).

131   74   *Let the glory of God* ... See no. 85. *May the Source* ... See no. 747.

132   75   *Adon Olam.* See no. 86.

MORNING SERVICE I

133   79   *Praise the Lord* ... *like a curtain.* Pss. 104:1f. The wearing of a *talit* at a morning service (and by the leader at every service) is attested often in the Talmud and Midrash (e.g., B. Shabbat 147a; B. Menachot 41a, b). It is derived from the Scriptural injunction to attach fringes to the corners of one's outer garment as a reminder of the *mitzvot.* See Num. 15:38ff; Deut. 22:12.

134   79   *Blessed is the Lord* ... *in the fringed Tallit.* B. Menachot 43a. We trsl. *vetsivanu* (lit., "commands") as "teaches."

135   80   *How lovely are Your tents* ... This, the *"Ma Tovu,"* is a mosaic of Scripture vv.: Num. 24:5; Pss. 5:8, 26:8, 95:6 (with a change from plural to singular), and 69:14, trad. recited on entering the synagogue. Early PBs vary with regard to their selection of vv. Our trsl., by CS, derives from ST (p. 283). At the suggestion of EG, we have altered the trsl. of the penultimate sentence.

136   80   *Shout joyfully* ... Ps. 100. Trad. recited in the Morning Service on weekdays only. It appears in many ancient rites, but not in the oldest

No. Page

(e.g., SRA). It was associated, in Temple times, with thank-offerings (Lev. 7:2). It was the practice at times during the Middle Ages to recite this Ps. on Sabbaths and Festivals, and following UPB II (p. 39), we offer it for RH, even as SOH (p. 140) and ST (p. 318) offer it for the Sabbath.

137 82 *Lord, who may abide* . . . Ps. 15, adapted by changes from singular to plural; so already in ST (p. 177). This Ps. does not appear in the trad. liturgy, but it is found in many Reform liturgies. "Who give their word . . . retract" is an attempt to make sense of an unclear H text.

138 82 *Great and holy Maker* . . . Slightly adapted by CS from his trsl. in GOR (pp. 51f) of a poem by Hillel Zeitlin (Russia, 1871–1942). Zeitlin was a writer, thinker, and mystic who died on the way to Treblinka.

139 85 *Blessed is the Eternal . . . who has implanted* . . . A series of benedictions found (except for the 5th one, which is not attested earlier than MV) in B. Ber. 60b and incorporated in the *Birchot Hashachar* ("Morning Blessings"). Of the original 15 benedictions, we include 12, following ST (pp. 286f), but have changed the order, which there followed the trad., which itself does not quite follow the Talmudic order. Following a variant medieval tradition, our 10th benediction has *"she-asani Yisra-el,"* "who has made me a Jew," in place of *"shelo asani goi,"* "who has not made me a gentile." We also have, in our 8th benediction, *"she-asani ben chorin,"* "who has made me to be free," in place of *"shelo asani eved,"* "who has not made me a slave." (Cf. *Sabbath and Festival PB*, Rabbinical Assembly [Conservative], p. 45).

140 87 *Blessed . . . who has made* . . . An appreciation of the wondrous complexity of the human body. Cited in B. Ber. 60b; SRA, p. 2. Our trsl. comes from ST, pp. 51f, with one small stylistic change.

141 87 *The soul that You have given me* . . . Another selection from *Birchot Hashachar* ("Morning Blessings"). It goes back to B. Ber. 60b. Our version is slightly abridged and, with one slight stylistic change, derives from ST, p. 53. We have changed the concluding eulogy (in H and E) from "who restores souls to dead bodies" to "in whose hands are the souls of all the living and the spirits of all flesh (Job 12:10)." Cf. UPB II, p. 40, and SOH, p. 141.

142 88 *Master of all the worlds* . . . A prayer cited in the Talmud, B. Yoma 87b, as intended for the YK Concluding Service, where it still appears in part (see no. 780), but which also became a part of the *Birchot Hashachar* ("Morning Blessings"). Our text is abridged, and we

No. *Page*

have inserted (in H and E) the words "and called to Your service" at the end of the penultimate sentence in the italic type. Our trsl. derives from ST, pp. 288f, but the concluding sentence of the 1st paragraph in ST is replaced by the one in UPB II, pp. 40f. Cf. GOR, pp. 49f.

143   89   *You raised up a vine* . . . The use of this passage is an innovation of the present PB, suggested by LH and trsl. by CS. It is found in an article by Jacob Mann, "Genizah Fragments of the Palestinian Order of Service," in *Hebrew Union College Annual*, Vol. II, 1925, reprinted in *Contributions to the Scientific Study of Jewish Liturgy*, ed. by Jakob J. Petuchowski (Ktav Publishing House, Inc., N.Y., 1970), p. 405. It is an old Palestinian parallel to *"Ahava Rabba"* (see no. 240). Since its theme is Revelation, it is appropriately placed here as the introduction to the section on Torah which is trad. found in the *Birchot Hashachar* ("Morning Blessings"). The 1st v. of this passage is based on Ps. 80:9.

144   89   *Blessed is the Eternal* . . . *the study of Torah.* Cited in B. Ber. 11b, in the name of Samuel (Bab., 3rd C.). Cf. ST, p. 52.

145   90   *These are obligations* . . . B. Shabbat 127a, an elaboration upon M. Pe-a 1.1. (See also B. Kiddushin 39b.) Trad. found, along with the preceding and following benedictions, in the *Birchot Hashachar* ("Morning Blessings"). Our trsl. derives from ST, pp. 52f, but with some adaptation.

146   91   *Eternal our God, make the words* . . . This passage trad. precedes the one above it. It is cited in B. Ber. 11b, in the name of R. Yochanan b. Nappacha (3rd C.), as a benediction to be recited before the reading of the Torah, but trad. found only here, in the *Birchot Hashachar* ("Morning Blessings"). But, see SOH, p. 450, where, with a different concluding eulogy, it is offered as an alternative benediction to *follow* the reading of the Torah. (And in SOH, p. 449, no. 144 above is offered as an alternative benediction before the reading.) Our trsl. differs in some respects from that in ST, p. 52, whence it derives.

147   91   *Praised be the One* . . . This benediction, the *"Baruch she-amar,"* trad. introduces the 2nd section of the Morning Service, known as *Pesukei Dezimra* (lit., "Verses of Song"), and consists mainly of Pss. It is first attested in SRA, p. 7. Our version, which is very slightly adapted from ST, pp. 53f, is abridged.

148   92   *The heavens declare* . . . Pss. 19:2–5b. Our trsl. is adapted from ST, pp. 290f.

149   93   *Let all who are righteous* . . . Pss. 33:1–6,9,11,15,20ff. Our text is

No. Page

slightly abridged from the one in ST, pp. 291f, where vv. 16f are also included.

150 94 *Halleluyah! Praise God* ... Ps. 150. Our trsl. comes from ST, p. 297, where it was trsl. by CS.

151 95 *Let every living soul* ... A somewhat abridged version of the "*Nishmat kol chai*," which is trad. added to the *Pesukei Dezimra* (see no. 91) on Sabbaths and Festivals. According to R. Yochanan, in B. Pesachim 118a, the words "the benediction over song" in M. Pesachim 10.7 are a reference to this prayer. It is partly cited in B. Ber. 59b and B. Ta-anit 6b. It contains many Scriptural allusions and q. Ps. 35:10. Starting with the words "supreme and exalted," it q. Isa. 57:15 and Ps. 33:1. On the last paragraph, cf. M. Pesachim 10.5. Our trsl. follows that of ST, pp. 297–300, but with some changes from 3rd to 2nd person, and a change in word order on pp. 97f (ST, p. 299).

152 98 *Let the glory of God* ... See no. 58.

153 99 *Praise the Lord* ... See no. 51.

154 99 *Blessed is the grace* ... New, by CS, on the theme of *Yotser*. On the H text, see no. 239.

155 100 *The Law has been* ... New, by CS, on the theme of "*Ahava Rabba.*" On the H text, see no. 240.

156 101 *Hear, O Israel* ... See no. 54.

157 102 *We worship the power* ... *Redeemer of Israel.* From ST, pp. 210f, where it was new, by CS, on the theme of *Ge-ula* ("Redemption"). The H is an abridged version of the *Ge-ula*, the one benediction that follows the "*Shema*" in the Morning Service (for the corresponding evening version, see no. 55). According to M. Tamid 5.1, a version of it was recited already in the Second Temple. It includes Exod. 15:11,18. The 3 benedictions surrounding the "*Shema*" in both the Evening and Morning Services emphasize respectively these 3 basic themes of Jewish theology: Creation, Revelation, Redemption. The concluding passages (beginning "Who is like You .... ") we give in trsl. For a trsl. of the preceding H, see Service II, pp. 171f.

158 104 *Eternal God, open my lips* ... See no. 59.

159 104 *We praise You* ... *Shield of Abraham.* See no. 60.

160 105 *Great is Your might* ... See no. 61.

161 106 *It is said* ... New, by CS. Suggested by a meditation by JR in GOR, pp. 92f.

162 107 *Let us proclaim* ... *the everlasting God!* A famous *piyut* (liturgical poem) known from its opening words as "*Unetaneh Tokef.*" Its au-

No. *Page*

thor is unknown. Legend associates it with one R. Amnon of Mayence, who is said to have recited it on RH as he died a martyr's
death, or to have transmitted it after his death in a dream to its
transcriber. At one time it was attributed to Kalonymos b. Me-
shullam of Mayence (11th C.). More recently it has been dated as
early as Byzantine times by Eric Werner, *The Sacred Bridge* (Den-
nis Dobson and Columbia University Press, N.Y., 1959), pp. 252–255.
Much of it has a strongly fatalistic ring, yet our ability to change
our ways, and therefore our destinies, is emphatically maintained,
especially in the affirmation that "repentance, prayer, and charity
temper judgment's severe decree." That affirmation is based on Gen.
Rabba 44.12, and the poem is replete with allusions to biblical and
rabbinic sources. See Goldschmidt, Vol. I., pp. 169ff, for an analysis
of these allusions. This poem trad. precedes the *Kedusha* (see no.
163) in the Reader's repetition of the *Musaf Tefila* for RH. Since
we have no *Musaf* ("Additional Service"), we place it before the
Kedusha in our Morning Service *Tefila*. UPB II (pp. 256–259) provides an abridged version of *"Unetaneh Tokef"* in the Afternoon
Service for YK, but none at all for RH. GOR does provide it for RH
(pp. 93f, within the *Shofar* Ritual), but even more sharply abridged
than in UPB II. Our text is complete.

163   110   *We sanctify Your name* . . . This is the *Kedusha* ("Sanctification"),
a doxology built around Isa. 6:3, which expands the *Kedushat Hashem* (see no. 62) of the Evening Service. It is trad. recited during
the Reader's repetition of the *Tefila* in the Morning, Afternoon, and
Additional Services on weekdays, Sabbaths, and Festivals. It dates
to Tannaitic times (before 200 C.E.), and is mentioned already in
the Talmud (B. Ber. 21b). The present text includes Isa. 6:3; Ps.
8:10; Ezek. 3:12; Num. 15:41; Ps. 146:10. The various liturgical
rituals (e.g., the Ashkenazi, Sefardi, and Yemenite rituals) have
differing versions of the *Kedusha*. Ours comes from ST, pp. 307f.
It incorporates elements from the Ashkenazi Morning and Additional Services, and omits some portions of both. The UPB II (pp.
52–55) version is almost identical to ours in the H, but our trsls.
differ markedly. GOR uses a somewhat different H text (pp. 62f),
and therefore a different E text. Our text, like that of UPB II, is
uniform. GOR has a somewhat more elaborate *Kedusha* in the YK
Morning Service (pp. 203–205), which is repeated in the YK Concluding Service (pp. 394f).

164   111   *Lord our God, cause all Your works* . . . See no. 63.

165   112   *Grant honor, Lord* . . . See no. 64

171   114   *Those who keep the Sabbath* ... A passage alluding to Isa. 58:13; Gen. 2:3; Exod. 20:11, 31:17. It occurs in the *Kedushat Hayom* (see no. 69) of the *Musaf* ("Additional Service") both on the Sabbath and on a festival when it falls on a Sabbath. Except for its opening words, it also occurs in the *Kedushat Hayom* of the Sabbath Morning Service. It is found, substantially as now, in SRA, p. 72. The E of the present version comes from ST, p. 154. It is based on a rendering by Samuel S. Cohon in UPB I (p. 32), its second half is not a trsl., but a variation on the theme of the H. It does not appear in UPB II. Like the present volume, GOR uses it only in the Morning Service (p. 66). SOH (p. 99), UPB I (p. 32), and ST (p. 154) use it occasionally in the Evening Service as well, as does the Sefardi ritual.

172   114   *Our God ... be mindful* ... See no. 70.

173   115   *Our God ... the Day of Remembrance.* See no. 72.

174   115   *Look with favor* ... From ST, pp. 200f, where it comes from UPB I, pp. 138–139 (UPB II, pp. 24–25). Cf. GOR, p. 33. This is the UPB form of the *Avoda* (see no. 73). On the H text, which differs from the trad. one, see no. 119.

175   115   *We gratefully acknowledge* ... The E text is slightly abridged from ST, pp. 201f, where it was slightly adapted from UPB I, pp. 138–139. This version of the *Hoda-a* provides an abridged form of the trad. H text (see no. 74), but includes the insertion peculiar to the Ten Days of Repentance. UPB II (pp. 144–145) follows UPB I on YK, but on RH (p. 24) offers another E version, which introduces the theme of thanksgiving for "our land, and for the blessings of liberty and the ideals of righteousness which our nation cherishes." In the 1st ed. (1894) of UPB II, the *Hoda-a* appears only in the RH and YK Morning Services. In both instances (pp. 54, 166) the text is substantially the one presented here.

176   116   *Our God and God of all generations* ... The Priestly Benediction (Num. 6:24ff) was recited daily in the Temple (M. Tamid 5.1). In the synagogue service, the Reader continued to recite the Priestly Blessing during the public repetition of the *Tefila*, prefaced with the words that form our 1st paragraph (these are already attested in MV, p. 67). *Grant peace and happiness* ... This version of *Birkat Shalom* (see no. 75) is freely adapted from ST, p. 313. It is a fairly

No. Page

close rendering of the trad. H provided here, except that it universalizes the text (by including "all the world") and in some degree abridges it. It also renders the H אָבִינוּ, "our Father," as "our God." There are references to the H text in the Talmud (e.g., B. Meg. 18a). The penultimate sentence and the concluding eulogy are trad. for the Ten Days of Repentance, first found in SRA, p. 137. This concluding eulogy is used by some Reform PBs (e.g., UPB I and SOH) throughout the year.

177 118 *We pause in reverence* . . . Adapted by CS, incorporating some suggestions by HB, from GOR, pp. 71f, where it was new, by AF, who used the first line of a poem by Jacob Trapp, in *Intimations of Grandeur* (Lindsey Press, 1968), p. 10.

178 118 *May the words* . . . See no. 77. *May the One who causes peace* . . . See no. 78.

179 120 *There is none like You* . . . From the trad. introduction to the reading of the Torah on Sabbaths, Festivals, and the Days of Awe. These 2 paragraphs, an abridged version of the introduction, are cited in Soferim 14.8. They embody Pss. 86:8; 145:13; 29:11. The trsl., slightly adapted by changes in paragraph 2 from 3rd person singular to 2nd person singular, comes from ST, p. 417 (which also provides the trad. 3rd paragraph, here omitted).

180 120 *Avinu, Malkeinu: A hundred generations* . . . Adapted by CS from his prayer in GOR, pp. 73f.

181 121 *Our Father, our King* . . . See no. 79. Here, however, we have replaced the penultimate v. with another from the trad. litany.

182 122 *The Lord, the Lord God* . . . Exod. 34:6f. Known as the "Thirteen Attributes [of God]." This designation, and the liturgical use of this passage, are attested in B. RH 17b in the name of the 3rd C. Pal. Amora (teacher), R. Yochanan ben Nappacha. See SRA, p. 147. Trad., it is here recited 3 times. Our text, following ST, p. 392, is trad. UPB II (p. 65) and GOR (p. 76) cut the text short by one word. The biblical text, from which this passage is extracted, concludes with the words: "*Venakei lo yenakeh*," "yet [God] will not fully pardon the guilty." The Rabbis reversed the meaning of this Scriptural passage by omitting the last 2 words, thus yielding, as in our text, "and granting pardon." We consider this a salutory instance of Rabbinic independence of thought, and therefore retain the omission mentioned above.

183 122 *O House of Jacob* . . . Isa. 2:5.

184 123 *Praised by the One* . . . Trad. at this point. First alluded to in MV, p. 157.

COMPANION NOTES TO *GATES OF REPENTANCE*

No.   Page

185   123   *Hear, O Israel* . . . Deut. 6:4. *Our God is One* . . . Not Scriptural.

186   123   *Yours, Lord* . . . I Chron. 29:11. The congregational response to the preceding.

187   125   *Praise the Lord* . . . *Giver of the Torah.* The practice of reciting a benediction before (and after) the reading of the Torah is mentioned already in the M. (Meg. 4.1). The present version is cited in B. Ber. 11b in the name of R. Hamnuna, a 3rd-4th C. Bab. Amora (teacher).

188   125   *There came a time* . . . Gen. 22:1-19. The public reading of the Torah is very ancient and mentioned already in the Bible itself; cf. Deut. 31:10-13; Neh. 8:1-8. The custom arose of reading from the Torah on the following occasions: Sabbaths and Festivals, Fast Days, Mondays and Thursdays, New Moons, Chanuka, Purim, and the intermediate days of Pesach and Sukkot. This goes back to the early days of the synagogue. The M. takes it for granted; cf., e.g., M. Meg. 3.6; 4.1f. But a fixed lectionary for the Sabbaths and Festivals emerged only gradually with important alterations occurring as late as the 8th C. As regards the portion to be read on RH, the M. (Meg. 3.5) ordains Lev. 23:23-25. The Tosefta (Meg. 4.6) proposes Gen. 21, but mentions that some favor Lev. 23:23-25. The Talmud (B. Meg. 31a) also gives 2 opinions: (a) a passage beginning "in the seventh month" which the commentators take to refer to Num. 29:1-6 but which probably refers to the Lev. passage mentioned in the M. and Tosefta; (b) Gen. 21. But it then goes on to say that on the 2nd day of RH (instituted because of a calendrical uncertainty at a time when the beginning of the month depended on visual observation of the New Moon but continued even after that uncertainty ceased to exist, and observed by Orthodox and Conservative Jews still, as well as by a limited number of Reform Jews) the reading is to be Gen. 22. The current trad. practice is to read Gen. 21 on the 1st day, Gen. 22 on the 2nd, and Num. 29:1-6, additionally, on both days. It will be evident, in the light of the foregoing, that in most Reform congregations the 2nd day is not observed, and the reading on the 1st day is Gen. 22, i.e., the story of the *Akeda*, the "Binding" of Isaac. So it is in UPB II (pp. 66-71) and GOR (pp. 78-81); GOR, however, provides an alternative reading: Deut. 10:12-21a. We provide an alternative reading (Gen. 1:1-2:3) in Morning Service II (pp. 192-197).

189   129   *Praised be the Lord* . . . *Giver of the Torah.* The benediction trad. recited after the reading of the Torah. It is first cited in Soferim 13.8, but no doubt is much older.

190   129   *This is the Torah* . . . Deut. 4:44; Num. 4:37. Trad. recited as the

No. Page

Torah is lifted up after the reading. The Sefardim, however, do this *before* the reading. On the practice, see Soferim 14.14 and Nahmanides on Deut. 27:26.

191 129 *Praised be the Lord . . . truth and righteousness.* The benediction trad. recited before the reading of the *Haftara.* It is 1st cited in Soferim 13.9.

192 129 *There was a man . . .* I Sam. 1:1–5, 9–28 (1–28 in the E). This is an abridged version of the trad. *Haftara* for the 1st day of RH. The word *Haftara* means "Conclusion" or "Dismissal," and it is likely that at one time the *Haftara* (also called אשלמתא, "Completion") ended the service itself. The practice of "concluding" the public reading of the Torah on Sabbaths and Festivals by reading, additionally, a portion from the prophets, is ancient, though not as ancient as the former. It is well attested in the M. (e.g., Meg. 4.1f). However, a fixed lectionary established itself only in the course of the centuries. As regards RH, the Talmud (B. Meg. 31a) ordains for the 1st day the story of Hannah (I Sam. 1 onwards) and for the 2nd day a section of Jeremiah beginning with or including the v. "O Ephraim, are you not my precious child . . . ?" (31:19). Such became the trad. practice, and we provide both these passages, and an alternative to each. Other Reform liturgies have chosen various passages: UPB II offers a choice of I Sam. 2:1–10 or Neh. 8 (which we also make available). GOR, following LJPB II, offers Isa. 55:6–13 only (which we also make available). In v. 20 of the present passage, the parenthetical conclusion is added by CS as a speculative solution to the word-play which in the H would otherwise remain either a very weak pun or a puzzle.

193 133 *At the coming of the seventh month . . .* Neh. 7:73–8:3a, 9f. We offer this as an alternative *Haftara.* Cf. UPB II, pp. 75f.

194 135 *Praised be the Lord . . . just and true.* The first sentence of the 4 trad. benedictions that follow the reading of the *Haftara.* It is 1st cited in Soferim 13.10.

195 135 *For the Torah . . .* The Festival version of the last of the 4 benedictions trad. recited after the reading of the *Haftara.* The text is first cited in Soferim 13.14.

196 135 *Praised be the Lord . . . just and true.* See no. 194. Here it begins the complete set of benedictions that follow the reading of the *Haftara.*

197 137 *You are the Faithful One . . . the Shield of David.* Soferim 13.11–13. These are excluded from UPB II and GOR, but following ST (p. 421), we include them as optional readings. Their antiquity is made clear

No. Page

by their close relationship to the prayers of the High Priest when reading the Scriptures on YK (see M. Yoma 7.1; M. Sota 7.2). We understand the references to Elijah and David to be metaphors of the coming of the messianic age.

198 137 *For the Torah* ... See no. 195.

199 138 *The Sounding of the Shofar.* From M. RH 4.5 it seems that in ancient times the *shofar* was sounded during the *Shacharit* (Morning Service) *Tefila.* It was then postponed to the *Musaf* (Additional Service), possibly on account of an incident related in J. RH 4.8, when the Romans, mistaking the *shofar* sounds as a signal of revolt, massacred a whole Jewish community. This modified practice is, indeed, already reflected in another paragraph of the same chapter of the M. (RH 4.7). Later still, perhaps in order not to delay the "great moment" so long, it became customary to sound the *shofar* at *two* points in the service: after the reading of the Torah (in the Morning Service) and during the Additional Service (*Musaf*). Since we have no Additional Service, we place them here together, with some modification: the former, which became known as *Teki-ot Meyushav* ("the blasts sounded while sitting"), we provide as an introduction, but without the actual *shofar* blasts, to the latter, which in our service follows immediately, and which came to be called *Teki-ot Me-umad* ("the blasts sounded while standing"). The number and nature of the blasts are minutely discussed and regulated in the Rabbinic sources (e.g., M. RH 4.9; Tosefta RH 2.12; B. RH 34a). Trad., each series of blasts is sounded 3 times, and the final blast (of each of the 2 series) is prolonged. Our version of the *Teki-ot Meyushav* omits several trad. passages: Ps. 47 (trad. recited 7 times), and a passage composed of Scriptural vv. called *Kera Satan* ("cut off the accuser"), after the acrostic made up by the initial letters of these vv., and it contains passages not found in the trad. version. See below.

200 138 *Note: In ancient Israel* ... Based on GOR, p. 90, where it is part of a longer passage by JR, partly adapted from LJPB II (p. 53) and UPB II (p. 77).

201 138 *In the seventh month* ... Num. 29:1.

202 138 *Hear now the Shofar* ... New, by CS. This passage alludes to a number of Rabbinic and Scriptural passages which interpret the meaning of RH in general and the sounding of the *shofar* in particular. For a convenient summary, see the passage by Saadia Gaon on pp. 12–13 (Meditation no. 36).

203 139 *Awake, you sleepers* ... MT, *Hilchot Teshuva*, 3.4.

204 140 *We must praise the Lord of all* ... See no. 83. This is the *"Aleinu,"*

No. Page

with which the *Teki-ot Me-umad* (see no. 199) begin. According to trad., the RH *Musaf* (Additional Service) consists essentially of a repetition of the *Shacharit* (Morning Service) *Tefila*, but with many elaborations, especially in the Reader's repetition. The *"Unetaneh Tokef"* (see no. 162) is one such elaboration, trad. inserted in the 3rd benediction. More particularly, the 4th benediction (*Kedushat Hayom*; see nos. 68–71) is expanded to accommodate the *Malchuyot* (passages about God's Sovereignty), and followed by 2 additional benedictions, embodying the *Zichronot* ("Remembrance passages") and the *Shofarot* ("*Shofar* passages"). The earliest reference to this schema is M. RH 4.5ff. In common with most Reform liturgies, we do not repeat the *Tefila* as a whole. But we do include a somewhat abridged version of the trad. *Malchuyot, Zichronot,* and *Shofarot*. In regard to *"Aleinu,"* we provide part of each of its 2 paragraphs. For an alternative *Shofar* Ritual, see Morning Service II, p. 208ff.

205   141   *The Torah proclaims* ... The M. (RH 4.6) speaks of 10 Scriptural vv. to be recited in each of the 3 sections of the *Shofar* Ritual. The trad. selection for *Malchuyot* (see no. 204) is Exod. 15:18; Num. 23:21; Deut. 33:5; Pss. 22:29, 93:1, 24:7–10; Isa. 44:6; Obadiah 1:21; Zech. 14:9; Deut. 6:4. It will be seen that the trad. selections divide into 3 groupings, i.e., from Torah, Prophets, and Writings, with a concluding v. from Torah. From these vv., we have selected Num. 23:21 (adapted); Ps. 24:7,10; Isa. 44:6; Deut. 6:4.

206   142   *Our God ... may You rule ... the Day of Remembrance.* See no. 71. To this passage we add the concluding eulogy from no. 72, the remainder of which we here omit.

207   142   *Blessed is the Lord ... the sound of the Shofar.* The benediction trad. recited before the sounding of the *shofar*. The obligation to recite such a benediction is mentioned in the Talmud (B. Pesachim 7b), but the text is 1st found in late Geonic and early medieval law codes (e.g., MT, *Hilchot Shofar* 3.10).

208   142   *Blessed is the Lord ... this season.* See no. 42.

209   143   *This is the day* ... Trad. recited after the sounding of the *shofar* at the end of each of the 3 sections, *Malchuyot, Zichronot,* and *Shofarot* (see no. 204). First found in SRA, p. 142. Cf. B. RH 10b: "Rabbi Elazar says that the world was created in Tishri."

210   143   *O God Supreme* ... Trad. follows the preceding passage at the end of the 3 sections mentioned in no. 209. In each appearance the conclusion of this passage refers to its particular section. Here, therefore, the reference is to *Malchuyot*. First found in SRA, p. 142.

211   144   *You remember* ... This passage, first found in SRA, pp. 142f, trad.

No. Page

begins the 2nd section, *Zichronot* ("Remembrance passages"). As the theme of the 1st section is Divine Sovereignty (Creation is its secondary theme), so the theme of *Zichronot* is Divine Remembrance.

212 144 *This is the day . . . shall not be ashamed.* A continuation of the preceding, but somewhat abridged.

213 145 *The Torah proclaims: God heard . . .* The trad. 10 Scripture vv. for *Zichronot* are Gen. 8:1; Exod. 2:24; Lev. 26:42; Pss. 111:4, 5; 106:45; Jer. 2:2; Ezek. 16:60; Jer. 31:19; Lev. 26:45. Our selection of 4 vv. from the trad. includes Exod. 2:24; Ps. 106:45 (adapted); Ezek. 16:60; Lev. 26:45. See no. 205.

214 146 *Our God . . . remember us with favor . . . who remembers the covenant.* A slightly abridged version of the concluding passage of *Zichronot*. The passage is 1st found in SRA, p. 143. An earlier version of concluding eulogy is preserved in M. Ta-anit 2.4.

215 147 *This is the day . . .* See no. 209.

216 147 *O God Supreme . . .* See no. 210. Here, of course, the concluding reference is to *Zichronot*.

217 148 *In a cloud of glory . . . manifest to us.* This passage, 1st found in SRA, pp. 143f, trad. begins the 3rd section of the *Shofar* Ritual, *Shofarot* ("*Shofar* passages"). Its primary theme is Revelation, its secondary theme Redemption. A number of the Scripture vv. included (see no. 218) have no connection with these themes, and seem to have been chosen solely because they refer to the *shofar*.

218 149 *The Torah proclaims: As the third day . . .* The trad. 10 Scripture vv. for *Shofarot* are Exod. 19:16,19; 20:10; Pss. 47:6; 98:6; 81:4; Isa. 18:3; 27:13; Zech. 9:14f; Num. 10:10. Our selection of 4 of these vv. includes Exod. 19:16; Ps. 47:6; Isa. 18:3; Zech. 9:14 (a departure from the pattern of returning to the Pentateuch for the final v.). The concluding sentence is not Scriptural. See no. 205.

219 150 *Our God . . . Sound the great Shofar . . .* This is the concluding passage of *Shofarot*. First found in SRA, in a somewhat different form, on p. 144. Our version is abridged and emended by CS. It retains the references to Zion (here understood by us as expressions of hope for both Jewish and universal redemption) and, in place of the references to the sacrificial cult, substitutes the passage "raise the banner . . . in exile," on which see ST, p. 41. The phrases inserted as substitutes for the trad. text are based on Ps. 119:134 and Lev. 25:10. The passage in ST goes back to SOH, p. 50, but the Lev. passage was 1st utilized in this manner by R. Manuel Joel in his *Israelitisches Gebetbuch*, Breslau, 1872, an example followed in

No. Page

several subsequent German Reform PBs (see Petuchowski, *Prayerbook Reform in Europe*, pp. 218ff). Its use in the present passage, however, is an innovation of this PB. An earlier version of the concluding eulogy is preserved in M. Ta-anit 2.4.

220 150 *This is the day* . . . See no. 209.

221 151 *O God Supreme* . . . See no. 210. Here, of course, the concluding reference is to *Shofarot.*

222 152 *Lord, we pray to You* . . . The custom of reciting a prayer for the congregation, and for the Community of Israel generally, after the reading of the Torah, can be traced back to the earliest PBs (see SRA, p. 59). The trad. Ashkenazi PB has 2 such prayers, one in H and one in Aramaic. The present version is freely adapted by CS from GOR, pp. 85f, where it is based on 2 found in SOH (see GOR, note no. 119). The q. in paragraph 3 is Deut. 1:11.

223 152 *We pray for all* . . . The custom of reciting a prayer for the government has been traced back to the 14th, and possibly to the 12th, C. (Abrahams, p. 160; the earlier date is based on a report by A. L. Frumkin [see his ed. of SRA] who describes a ms. in his possession dated 1196). Its underlying concept derives from Jer. 29:7 and M. Avot 3.2. The present version is slightly abridged and adapted from GOR, p. 86, which adapted an earlier version still from LJPB (see GOR, note no. 120).

224 153 *We pray for the land* . . . The custom of praying, additionally, for the State of Israel and its people has become widespread in recent times. This prayer is slightly adapted from GOR, p. 86, where it was new, by CS.

225 154 *Let us praise* . . . Ps. 148:13ab. First found in SRA, p. 59, in its present liturgical use. We have (already in SOH, p. 156, and carrying through to GOR and ST, p. 422) trsl. the 1st word as 1st person plural (instead of "Let *them* praise") so that the Reader and congregation may be associated in praise of the Torah.

226 154 *God's splendor* . . . Ps. 148:13c–14. Cf. the preceding note.

227 154 *The law of the Lord* . . . Ps. 19:8–10; Prov. 4:2; 3:18; Lam. 5:21. Trad., Ps. 19:8f is recited *before* the reading of the Torah (there is an allusion to this in Soferim 14.14; cf. SRA, p. 59). The Prov. vv. are trad. recited in the present context, preceded by Num. 10:36 and Ps. 132:8ff, and followed by Lam. 5:21. Our trsl. of Ps. 19:10 assumes that the word יראת, "fear," should read אמרת, "word," in the light of the context. Cf. Ps. 119:38; Isa. 5:24; Dahood, *The Anchor Bible, Psalms* I (Doubleday and Company, Inc., Garden City, N.Y., 1966), pp. 123f.

No. Page

228 156 *We must praise the Lord of all* . . . See no. 83.

229 158 *Lord, You give us* . . . Adapted by CS from UPB II, p. 89.

230 159 *Let the glory of God* . . . See no. 85. *May the Source* . . . See no. 747.

231 160 *All the world.* An anonymous poem, found in MV, pp. 386f, and included in the *Musaf* (Additional Service) for the Days of Awe. Following ST (p. 710), we have slightly adapted Israel Zangwill's trsl. of stanzas 1, 2, and 4, and we omit stanza 3.

232 162 *And now, at the beginning* . . . New, by CS, based on Isa. 11:2 and concluding with a passage, freely rendered in the E, 1st found in *Sefer Maharil* (a compendium of laws and customs by R. Jacob Moellin, known from the abbreviation of his H name as the Maharil, who lived in the Rhineland 1365–1427), p. 38a, in connection with the custom of eating, after *Kiddush* on RH Eve, sweet apples with honey (cf. also Neh. 8:10). We continue to observe that custom. See GOH, p. 53.

MORNING SERVICE II

233 163 *Adat Yisra-el, Congregation Israel* . . . New, by HB and CS. The Rabbinic q. in the 1st paragraph is from Midrash Tehilim, on Ps. 123:2, where it is attributed to R. Shimon b. Yochai (2nd C.). The Scriptural passage on which it is based is Isa. 43:12.

234 165 *Sweet hymns* . . . The 1st 3 vv. and the last v. of a poem known as *Shir Hakavod* ("Hymn of Glory"), possibly by Judah b. Samuel of Regensburg (Yehuda Hechasid, d. 1217). The E is from ST, p. 364, where it was slightly adapted from UPB I, p. 111. This metrical version is not a literal trsl. but is intended to be sung.

235 165 *This Rosh Hashanah* . . . Adapted from ST, p. 333, where it was adapted by CS from a new meditation by RIK.

236 166 *O Source of light* . . . From ST, p. 143, where it was new, by CS.

237 167 *Let the glory of God* . . . See nos. 58, 104.

238 167 *Praise the Lord* . . . See no. 51.

239 168 *Praised be the Lord* . . . *the Maker of light.* This, known from its key word as *Yotser* ("Creator"), is the 1st of the 2 benedictions that precede the *"Shema"* in the Morning Service, corresponding to the *Ma-ariv Aravim* (see no. 52) in the Evening Service. The Talmud cites it partially (B. Chagiga 12b), and notes elsewhere (Ber. 116) that Isa. 45:7 "Creator of evil" has been changed euphemistically in the blessing to "Creator of all things." Also included is Ps. 104:24. This benediction, especially for Sabbaths and Festivals, contains

No. Page

mystical and angelological elements which we omit here. We include instead, as an innovation from GOR, a poem by Judah Halevi (Spain-Palestine, 1086–1141), "To You the stars . . . the breath of early light." That poem is used in another context in SOH (p. 222) and ST (p. 654). Its trsl. is slightly adapted from one by Olga Marx in *Language of Faith*, ed. by Nahum N. Glatzer (Schocken Books, Inc., N.Y., 1947, 1967), p. 54. The trsl. of the rest of this passage (i.e., the H of the *Yotser* itself) is a revised version of that in ST, p. 55.

240 169 *Great is Your love* . . . This, known from its opening words as *"Ahava Rabba"* (and also as *Birkat Torah*, "The Benediction Concerning Torah") is the 2nd of the 2 benedictions that precede the *"Shema"* in the Morning Service, corresponding to the *"Ahavat Olam"* (see no. 53) in the Evening Service. It is partly cited in B. Ber. 11b. Our version comes from ST (p. 56) and it omits one sentence of the trad. text, a petition for the Ingathering of the Exiles. Our trsl. is slightly adapted from the one in ST.

241 170 *Hear, O Israel* . . . See no. 54.

242 171 *True and enduring . . . Redeemer of Israel.* An abridged version of the one benediction that follows the *"Shema"* in the Morning Service, known as the *Ge-ula* ("Redemption"), see no. 157. Our text comes from ST, pp. 58f, and our trsl. is slightly adapted from the one in ST.

243 173 *Eternal God, open my lips* . . . See no. 59. *Each generation has its path* . . . (p. 174). New, by CS, on the theme of *Avot*. On the H text, see no. 60.

244 175 *Great is the eternal power* . . . New, by CS, on the theme of *Gevurot*. On the H text, see no. 61.

245 175 *It is said* . . . See no. 161.

246 176 *Let us proclaim . . . the everlasting God!* See no. 162.

247 180 *Holy is the dignity* . . . New, by CS. On the H text, the *Kedusha* ("Sanctification"), see no. 163.

248 180 *Why be concerned* . . . Slightly adapted by CS from *The Wisdom of Heschel: Writings of Abraham Joshua Heschel*, selected by Ruth Marcus Goodhill (Farrar, Straus and Giroux, N.Y., 1975), p. 8.

249 181 *It is not enough . . . Ibid.*, p. 4.

250 181 *What is the meaning . . . Ibid.*, p. 3.

251 181 *We stand in awe* . . . New, by CS. On the H text (the 1st of the 3 *"Uvechen"* passages in the *Kedushat Hashem*), see no. 63.

252 182 *We stand in awe of courage* . . . New, by CS. On the H text (the 2nd of the 3 *"Uvechen"* passages in the *Kedushat Hashem*), see no. 64.

No.	Page	
253	182	*Honor to those who endure!* ... New, by CS. On the H text (the 3rd of the 3 "*Uvechen*" passages in the *Kedushat Hashem*), see no. 65.
254	182	*For goodness shall reign* ... New, by CS. The H preceding this passage concludes the H of no. 253 and contains Ps. 146:10. The H following this passage begins with Isa. 5:16, followed by its trsl. The remaining H, for which the E is new, by CS, concludes the *Kedushat Hashem*. See nos. 66–68.
255	183	*Out of the mystery* ... New, by CS, on the theme of *Kedushat Hayom*. On the H text (the 1st paragraph of this benediction), see no. 69.
256	184	*Those who keep the Sabbath* ... See no. 171.
257	184	*As in the heart of matter* ... New, by CS. On the H text, which continues the *Kedushat Hayom*, see no. 70.
258	185	*We give thanks* ... New, by CS. On the H text, which concludes the *Kedushat Hayom*, see no. 72.
259	185	*O fill our minds* ... From ST, pp. 99f, where it was new, by CS. On the H text, the *Avoda* ("Worship"), see no. 119.
260	186	*Many are our blessings* ... Slightly adapted by CS from ST, p. 155, where it was new, by CS, based on a prayer by JR and CS on the theme of the *Hoda-a* in SOH, pp. 86. On the H, see no. 120 (here the H is without the trad. insertion for the Ten Days of Repentance—a version of which we give in the E).
261	187	*Peace, happiness, and blessing* ... A variation by CS on the trsl. of *Birkat Shalom*, in ST, p. 330. On the H, see no. 176.
262	187	*Be among those* ... New, by CS.
263	187	*Yihyu leratson* ... See no. 77.
264	187	*Oseh shalom* ... See no. 78.
265	188	*The earth is the Lord's* ... Ps. 24:1–6. Trad. recited before the returning of the Scroll to the Ark on weekdays and Festivals occurring on weekdays. On the correct interpretation of this Ps. (which has influenced our trsl.), see *The Problem of "Curse" in the Hebrew Bible*, by Herbert Chanan Brichto (*Journal of Biblical Literature* Monograph Series, Vol. XIII, Society of Biblical Literature and Exegesis, Philadelphia, 1963), pp. 64–67. On the trsl. of v. 6a, we follow the new JPS. The basic meaning of דּוֹר (usually "generation") in the present context is "type." For this suggestion we are indebted to Prof. Brichto (in an oral communication); cf. Pss. 12:8; 14:5. Another line of reasoning leads to its trsl. as "destiny" in SOH, pp. 191ff, which was followed in *The New English Bible* where it is trsl. as "fortune." Following most trsls. we add to the H of v. 6b the English words "O God of [Jacob]."

No. Page

292 210 *In the beginning* . . . Gen. 1:1; Pss. 33:6; 19:2; Job 26:14; Ps. 95:3; Isa. 44:6; Pss. 22:29; 96:10; 97:1; Exod. 15:18. For the 10 Scripture vv. trad. recited in *Malchuyot*, see no. 205. This is a new selection, 1st found in GOR, pp. 98f. Our trsl., which differs from that of GOR, in several vv. changes the H 3rd person to the E 2nd person.

293 211 *Blessed is the Eternal God . . . Day of Remembrance.* The concluding eulogy of the *Kedushat Hayom*'s last paragraph, the remainder of which we here omit. See no. 71.

294 211 *Blessed is the Lord . . . the sound of the Shofar.* See no. 207.

295 211 *Blessed is the Lord . . . this season.* See no. 42.

296 212 *The Lord reigns . . .* Ps. 93:1f.

297 212 *God of all lands and ages* . . . This is the introductory passage to the present version of *Zichronot*, whose theme is Remembrance (cf. no. 211). It is adapted by CS from GOR, p. 101, where is was new, by CS.

298 212 *We remember* . . . A continuation of the preceding. It is new, by CS, suggested by an unpublished passage by JR.

299 213 *We remember what You mean* . . . New, by CS. In this passage, and the Scripture vv. that follow it, we emphasize strongly the theme of human remembrance of God, as opposed to the traditional idea of God's remembering us.

300 213 *Lord, Your love is everlasting* . . . Pss. 103:17f; 119:93; Isa. 63:7; Ps. 105:8; Deut. 4:31; Pss. 119:52,15,16; Deut. 16:20; Amos 5:24. Some of these vv. are slightly adapted, by CS. This is a new selection, by CS. For the 10 Scripture vv. trad. recited in *Zichronot*, see no. 213.

301 214 *Blessed is . . . who remembers the covenant.* The concluding eulogy of the final passage of *Zichronot*. See no. 214.

302 214 *For the mountains* . . . Isa. 54:10.

303 215 *Now we call to mind* . . . This is the opening passage of the present version of *Shofarot*, whose dual theme is Revelation and Redemption (cf. no. 217). This 1st paragraph is freely adapted by CS from UPB II, pp. 83f. Paragraphs 2 and 3 are freely adapted by CS from his passage in GOR, pp. 101f. Paragraphs 4 and 5 are freely adapted by CS from GOR, p. 105, where it is new, by JR, q. Ps. 95:7b.

304 216 *On that day* . . . Isa. 27:13; Lev. 25:9f; Pss. 89:16a, 16b; Isa. 25:9a, 9b; 40:4f; Pss. 98:4,6. For the 10 Scripture vv. trad. recited in *Shofarot*, see no. 218. This is a new selection, 1st found in GOR, pp. 106f.

305 217 *We praise You, the merciful God* . . . The concluding eulogy of the final passage of *Shofarot*. See no. 217.

Yom Kippur

No. Page

359 239 *For transgressions against God* . . . M. Yoma 8.9. A saying of R. Elazar b. Azariah (Pal. 1st–2nd C.).

360 239 *If we are guilty* . . . B. Ta-anit 16a. An anonymous *baraita* (see no. 347).

361 240 *We do not ask* . . . By Claude G. Montefiore (see no. 356), in *Liberal Judaism* (Macmillan and Co., Ltd., London, 1903), p.164.

362 240 *When you talk* . . . Adapted by CS from a saying by R. Isaac Meir of Ger, the 1st "Gerer Rebbe" (Poland, 1799–1866), in *A Jewish Reader*, ed. by Nahum N. Glatzer (Schocken Books, N.Y., 1961), p. 111; suggested by RLK.

363 240 *After the flood* . . . Adapted by CS from a passage suggested by RLK from an unidentified midrashic source.

364 241 *"Return, O Israel . . ."* Pesikta DeRav Kahana 24.12, q. Hos. 14:2, 5. Cf. Harlow, p. 131.

365 241 *God says* . . . Midrash Tehillim, to Ps. 120:7. The q. is Isa. 57:19.

366 241 *Friends, what does it say* . . . M. Ta-anit 2.1, q. Jonah 3:10; Joel 2:13. These are the opening words of a fast-day sermon.

367 241 *Atonement with God* . . . By Hermann Cohen (German-Jewish philosopher, 1842–1918), in *Judische Schriften*, trsl. by William Wolff, in Harlow, p. 528.

368 242 *Our Rabbis have taught* . . . B. Yoma 23a, q. Judges 5:31.

369 242 *To act* . . . From "Prayer," by Henry M. Slonimsky, in *Essays* (Hebrew Union College Press, 1967), p. 128. Reprinted in *Gates of Understanding*, Vol. 1, p. 79.

370 242 *One can always find* . . . By Leo Baeck (see no. 12).

371 242 *One wears* . . . From *Basic Judaism*, by Milton Steinberg (Harcourt, Brace, & World, Inc., 1947).

372 243 *When we are dead* . . . By Jacob P. Rudin, q. in *A Treasury of Comfort*, ed. by Sidney Greenberg (Crown Publishers, Inc., N.Y. 1954), p. 183.

373 243 *There was a villager* . . . From *Kehal Chasidim Hechadash*, a collection of Hasidic stories published in Lwow in 1906, q. in *Days of Awe*, ed. by S. Y. Agnon (Schocken Books, Inc., N.Y., 1948), pp. 268ff.

374 244 *Rabbi Joshua* . . . B. Sanhedrin 98a. It contains an allusion to Ps. 95:7

375 244 *Rav Beroka of Bei Hozae* . . . B. Ta-anit 22a. The trsl. comes from *Hammer on the Rock: A Short Midrash Reader*, ed. by Nahum N. Glatzer (Schocken Books, Inc., N.Y., 1948), p. 66; suggested by RLK.

376 244 *Darkness is not the road* . . . By Hayyim Greenberg (Russia-U.S.A.,

No. *Page*

1889–1953), in *The Inner Eye: Selected Essays* (Jewish Frontier Association, Inc., N.Y., 1953), p. 256. Slightly adapted by CS.

377 245 *Everyone suddenly burst out singing* . . . "Everyone Sang," a poem by Siegfried Sassoon, from *Collected Poems* (©1948 by Siegfried Sassoon; reprinted by permission of The Viking Press, Inc.).

EVENING SERVICE

378 247 *Lord of the universe* . . . Adapted by CS from GOR, p. 130, where it was new, by JR. It q. Isa. 6:5; Pss. 24:3; 130:3; 22:4, and uses phrases from various medieval precentors' prayers and from the trad. prologue to the *"Kol Nidrei."* Cf. no. 43.

379 248 *Blessed is the Lord* . . . *the Day of Atonement.* The text of our blessing is rendered by R. Moses Isserles in his gloss to *Shulchan Aruch*, O. Ch. 610.1.

380 248 *Blessed is the Lord* . . . *this season.* See no. 42.

381 249 *In the beginning* . . . Adapted by CS from GOR, pp. 131ff, where it was new, by JR, though based in part on a prayer by CS in SOH, pp. 92f. It contains allusions to Gen. 1:1 and Ezek. 18:31.

382 249 *Once more Atonement Day* . . . New, by CS. Cf. GOR, pp. 134f, which influenced the present passage.

383 250 *Kol Nidrei is the prayer* . . . New, by CS.

384 251 *For transgressions* . . . See no. 359.

385 251 *Light is sown* . . . Ps. 97:11.

386 251 *In the sight of God* . . . By R. Meir of Rothenburg (Germany, 1220–1293; Talmudic commentator, halachist, and poet). It is difficult to ascertain who the "transgressors" mentioned in this passage may have been. It has been speculated that these were Jews returning to the Synagogue after having been forcibly converted to Christianity. At all events, the Talmudic basis for this passage is B. Keritot 6b: "A public fast in which Jewish transgressors do not participate is no fast. . . . "

387 251 *Kol Nidrei: a whisper of wings* . . . New, by CS. It is based on the preceding passage.

388 251 *Heart of all life* . . . Freely adapted by CS from GOR, p. 132, a passage which is slightly adapted from UPB II, p. 130 (see no. 389).

389 252 *Let all our vows* . . . The *"Kol Nidrei"* ("All the vows"), in its trad. form, is a legal declaration, in Aramaic, absolving those who have made a vow (to God, but not to a person) from fulfilling it, if unable to do so. It is 1st found, though, in H, in SRA, pp. 162f. But many leading rabbis, including Amram himself, both in the Geonic Age

201

No. Page

and in the Middle Ages, were opposed to it (cf. JE, s.v. "*Kol Nidre*"; Idelsohn, pp. 225–228; LH, *The Canonization of the Synagogue Service*, pp. 100–102, 215–216). It persisted, nevertheless, partly in defiance of Gentile denunciations (based on misrepresentations of its intent) and partly on account of the haunting melody, probably dating from the 16th C. (A. Z. Idelsohn, *Jewish Music in Its Historical Development*, Schocken Books, N.Y., 1967, pp. 159f), to which it came to be sung in the Ashkenazi communities. (See Eric Werner, *A Voice Still Heard* [Pennsylvania State University, 1976], pp. 35–38.) The text is found with many variations in different liturgical rituals. Our present text is prospective; it speaks of vows made between this YK and the next—a change instituted in the 12th C. by R. Jacob b. Meir (Rabbenu Tam, 1100–1171, grandson of Rashi and a great figure in his own right). The older version was retrospective, calling for the annulment of vows that had been made during the year beginning with last YK. Some rituals retain the older form; others have both. Trad., the "*Kol Nidrei*" is chanted 3 times, and, since vows may not be annulled on Sabbaths or Festivals, it is chanted before sunset. Most earlier Reform PBs replaced "*Kol Nidrei*" (UPB II, 1945, p. 130, refers to it without printing the text; its earlier eds. made no mention of it) either by a poem in the vernacular (notably R. Leopold Stein's *O Tag des Herrn*, written in 1840, E versions of which appeared in UPB II, p. 127, and LJPB II, p. 68) or by a new H text, beginning with the words "*Kol Nidrei*" but going on to ask for God's acceptance of the worshipers' vows of repentance. Of the latter, several examples are given in *Prayerbook Reform in Europe*, by Jakob J. Petuchowski, ch. 15. The E that precedes the Aramaic of "*Kol Nidrei*" is slightly adapted from UPB II, p. 130, where it was by Samuel S. Cohon. It is similar to the text introduced in Hanover in 1870 (see Petuchowski, *ibid.*, p. 343), as is the H "*Kol Nidrei*" of GOR, p. 132. We have restored the trad. Aramaic text, followed by an abridged trsl.

390 252 *Knowingly or not* ... Num. 15:26. First attested in SRA, p. 163.

391 252 *As, in Your love* ... Num. 14:19. Found in SRA, p. 56, in the *Tachanun* ("Supplications") for Mondays and Thursdays. According to Idelsohn (*Liturgy*, p. 228), its use here is first indicated by Pal. custom.

392 253 *And the Lord said* ... Num. 14:20. The preceding note applies.

393 253 *Blessed is the Lord* ... *this season.* See no. 42.

394 253 *Praise the Lord* ... See no. 51.

395 254 *O God, how can we know You?* ... From ST, p. 180, where it was

No. Page

416 265 *O Source of mercy ... Sanctify us with Your Mitzvot ... the Day of Atonement.* This continues and concludes the *Kedushat Hayom.* It is adapted by CS from UPB II, p. 58. It q. Isa. 43:25; 44:22; Lev. 16:30. It is partly cited in B. Yoma 68b; J. Yoma 7.1; Soferim 19.6; SRA, pp. 163f. Cf. no. 72.

417 266 *Be gracious ...* See no. 73.

418 267 *We gratefully acknowledge ...* From ST, p. 201, where it was slightly adapted from the UPB I version (p. 138) of the *Hoda-a.* Here, unlike UPB II (p. 144), we include the insertion trad. for the Ten Days of Repentance and the concluding eulogy. On the H text, see no. 74.

419 267 *Grant us peace ...* See no. 75.

420 268 *Do not say ...* Based on Midrash Tehillim, to Ps. 40:3.

421 268 *What is genuine repentance? ...* MT, *Hilchot Teshuva* 2.1; cf. B. Yoma 86b.

422 268 *May the words ...* See no. 77.

423 268 *May the One ...* See no. 78.

424 269 *Our God ... grant that our prayers ...* Opening paragraph of the *Vidui,* "Confession." As an established feature of the YK liturgy of the synagogue, the Confession is 1st alluded to in the Tosefta, Yom Hakippurim 5.14. The Talmud (B. Yoma 87b) mentions several versions, including a phrase from the present one. The full text is in SRA, p. 160. The last clause is based on I Kings 8:47. We trsl. אֱלֹהֵינוּ וֵאלֹהֵי אֲבוֹתֵינוּ (lit., "Our God and God of our fathers") somewhat freely, to avoid exclusive use of the masculine.

425 269 *We have all committed ...* Known from its opening word as "*Ashamnu*" or, by contrast with the "*Al Chet*" (no. 427), as the "Short Confession" (*Vidui Zuta*); this is an acrostic, listing the whole gamut of sins in alphabetic sequence. It is 1st mentioned in SRA, p. 161. Our 1st E sentence, by CS, is introductory. The E that follows is not a trsl., but an incomplete alphabetical acrostic by CS intended to convey the flavor of the H. Cf. Harlow, pp. 377–379, for a similar acrostic.

426 270 *We have turned aside ... concealed from Your sight.* Partly cited already in the Talmud, B. Yoma 87b (beginning with אַתָּה יוֹדֵעַ רָזֵי עוֹלָם ...). All of it is in SRA, p. 161.

427 271 *Now may it be Your will ...* This is the "Long Confession" (*Vidui Rabba*). It is found in SRA, p. 161. SRA had at most 30 vv. (the manuscripts differ). In the Middle Ages it was greatly elaborated and arranged alphabetically. The Birnbaum High Holy Day PB has 44 vv. (i.e., a double alphabetical acrostic); UPB II has 10; GOR

No.   Page

text, which appears in GOR, pp. 169f. The beginning H is listed as no. 129. The concluding passage ("Blessed be the name . . . ") is Pss. 113:2; 72:19b.

439   283   *Birth is a beginning* . . . By Alvin I. Fine. Very slightly adapted.

440   285   *Let the glory of God* . . . See no. 85.

441   286   *"Yigdal."* This hymn has been attributed to Daniel b. Judah of Rome, 14th C. It is a brief summary in v. of the "Thirteen Principles of the Jewish Faith" as expounded by Moses Maimonides in his commentary on the M. (to Sanhedrin 10.1). In v. 12 we have (following UPB) changed the 1st half ("He will send our Messiah at the end of days") to "At the end of days He will send an everlasting redemption," in the H. In the last v. we have followed UPB, GOR, etc. in changing (H and E) "In His great love God will resurrect the dead" to "He has implanted eternal life within us." Cf. the benediction after the reading of the Torah, no. 189.

442   287   *We praise the living God* . . . This is a metrical version of *"Yigdal"* (see no. 441), by Newton Mann, *Union Hymnal*, p. 56, here revised by Malcolm H. Stern.

MORNING SERVICE

443   291   *Praise the Lord* . . . *like a curtain.* See no. 133.

444   291   *Blessed is the Lord* . . . *in the fringed Tallit.* See no. 134.

445   292   *Hear the word* . . . An arrangement by CS of the following Scriptural passages: Isa. 1:10a,12a,13,15ff; Amos 5:14,24.

446   293   *Early will I seek You* . . . By Solomon ibn Gabirol (Spain, c. 1021–c. 1058, poet and philosopher), found in the *Birchot Hashachar* ("Morning Blessings") in many PBs. The E is a metrical version by Gustav Gottheil (1827–1903, rabbi in Berlin, Manchester, and New York), and is meant to be sung. We have slightly revised the text of UPB I, p. 103.

447   293   *This is the day* . . . adapted by CS from a prayer in UPB II, p. 170. Cf. GOR, pp. 181f.

448   294   *We are tenants* . . . Adapted by CS from GOR, pp. 183f, where it was new, by CS, incorporating material from a prayer by IIM in LJPB II, pp. 40f, and q. Ps. 36:10

449   295   *Not for ourselves alone* . . . New, by CS. Suggested by a prayer in UPB II, p. 171.

450   295   *God of pity and love* . . . From Sonnet XIII, by Robert Nathan (American Jewish poet and novelist, born 1894), in *Selected Poems* (Knopf, N.Y., 1935). Already in GOR, p. 182.

No. Page

507　340　*Hear, O Israel . . . Our God is One!* See no. 185.

508　341　*Let us declare . . .* The 1st half of the v. is based on Deut. 32:3. Its use in the Torah Ritual is trad.; cf. Soferim 14:11, SRA, p. 58.

509　341　*Yours, Lord . . .* See no. 186.

510　343　*Praise the Lord . . .* See no. 187.

511　343　*You stand this day . . .* Deut. 29:9-14; 30:11-20. On the public reading of the Torah, see no. 188. The trad. reading for YK morning is Lev. 16, about the ritual of the scapegoat (already mentioned in M. Meg. 3.5), with the addition of Num. 29:7-11, about the YK sacrifices (mentioned in the Tosefta, Meg. 4.7). Reform liturgies have generally chosen, instead, other passages especially from Deut. 29 and 30. See LJPB II, UPB II, and GOR, whose precedent we follow.

512　345　*Praised be the Lord . . . Giver of the Torah.* See no. 189.

513　345　*This is the Torah . . .* See no. 190.

514　347　*Praised be the Lord . . . truth and righteousness.* See no. 191.

515　347　*God says: Cry aloud . . .* Isa. 58:1-14. On the reading of the *Haftara* generally, see no. 192. For YK morning the Talmud (B. Meg. 31a) ordains a passage beginning with, or including, "For thus says the High and Lofty One . . . " (Isa. 57:15). The trad. is to read Isa. 57:14-58:14. So, too, LJPB II and UPB II. Following GOR, we begin with Isa. 58:1. We supply the 1st 2 words of the reading, "God says," which are not carried in the H, for the sake of clarity.

516　351　*Praised be the Lord . . . just and true.* See no. 194.

517　351　*For the Torah . . .* See no. 195.

518　351　*Praised be the Lord . . .* See no. 196.

519　351　*You are the Faithful One . . . the Shield of David.* See no. 197.

520　353　*For the Torah . . .* See no. 195.

521　354　*Lord, we pray . . .* See no. 222.

522　354　*We pray for all . . .* See no. 223.

523　355　*We pray for the land . . .* See no. 224.

524　356　*Let us praise . . .* See no. 225.

525　356　*God's splendor . . .* See no. 226.

526　356　*This is the covenant . . .* Jer. 31:33f. Cf. ST, p. 429; GOR, p. 246; SOH, pp. 175f; LJPB I, p. 401.

527　357　*Behold, a good doctrine . . .* Prov. 4:2; 3:18; Lam. 5:21. See no. 227.

528　357　*This day, strengthen us! . . .* From a medieval *piyut* (liturgical poem). The earliest printed PB in which this appears seems to be *Machzor Sabionetta,* 1557, p. 248. The second letter of the second H word in each line indicates an incomplete H acrostic. Abudarham (14th C. Spain) knew of additional lines.

No. Page

ADDITIONAL PRAYERS

529 361 *Listen to Me* . . . A composite passage trsl. and arranged by CS, incorporating the following Scriptural vv.: Isa. 41:1; 42:10; 43:15f, 18f,20f,25; 44:3,23; 55:3b; 66:22; 9:1.

530 362 *This is a day* . . . New, by CS. The responses are Scriptural: Ps. 34:13ff; Gen. 17:1; Lev. 19:2; Hos. 2:21f; Ps. 104:33.

531 363 *There are moments* . . . From ST, p. 102, where it was new, by CS.

532 363 *You shall be holy* . . . Lev. 19:2.

533 363 *We cannot pray to You* . . . Freely adapted by CS from a prayer by Jack Riemer, in *New Prayers for the High Holy Days* (©1970, 1971, Prayer Book Press of Media Judaica, Inc.). Paragraphs 4-6 are new, by CS. The concluding paragraph is based on Ps. 19:15.

534 365 *'When you pray . . .'* From *Man's Quest for God*, by Abraham J. Heschel (Charles Scribner's Sons, N.Y., 1954), pp. 33ff. The q. is B. Ber. 28b.

535 365 *We are God's own creation* . . . A somewhat free trsl. of Gen. 1:27.

536 365 *Our tradition says* . . . M. Sanhedrin 4.5; Seder Eliyahu Rabba, ch. 10, beginning. As regards the 1st paragraph, some manuscripts of the M. speak of the destruction or salvation of one human soul "in Israel," but following other ancient versions we omit "in Israel," thus extending the scope of this passage to all humanity.

537 366 *God of the beginning* . . . From ST, p. 362, where it was new, by Henry Butler and CS.

538 366 *In a place* . . . M. Avot 2.6.

539 366 *How greatly* . . . M. Avot 3.18.

540 367 *Then Isaac asked* . . . By Edmond Fleg, from a midrashic source.

541 367 *'You are My witnesses . . .'* Midrash Tehillim, to Ps. 123:2. Attributed to R. Shimon b. Yochai (2nd C.). The q. is Isa. 43:12.

542 367 *The stars of heaven* . . . From ST, pp. 238f, where it was new, by CS. The conclusion alludes to Ps. 8:6. Cf. RPB, Vol. 1, pp. 122–125, by Eugene Kohn.

543 368 *Glory and honor* . . . From ST, p. 239, where it was new, by CS.

544 368 *Whither can I go* . . . Ps. 139:7ff.

545 368 *Our rabbis taught* . . . B. Makkot 23b-24a (q. Mic. 6:8; Isa. 56:1; Amos 5:4; Habakkuk 2:4); Sifra 89b (q. Lev. 19:18 and Gen. 5:1); B. Shabbat 31a.

546 369 *The luckless* . . . Slightly adapted from *Days of Awe*, ed. by CS (Ktav Publishing House, Inc., N.Y., 1971), p. 40, where it was new, by CS.

547 369 *We have learned* . . . Slightly adapted from Newman, p. 62.

No. Page
548 370 *And it has been written* . . . *Ibid.*, pp. 173f. The q. is Lev. 6:6.
549 370 *Raba said* . . . B. Shabbat 31a. Our version is abridged.
550 370 *The greatest victory* . . . Compiled by CS from various (mainly Hasidic) sources.
551 370 *In days to come* . . . B. Sukka 52a. The q. is Zech. 8:6. The passage is attributed to R. Judah b. Ilai (Pal., 2nd C.).
552 371 *Lord, we are not so arrogant* . . . Adapted from GOH, where it was new, by Norman Hirsh.
553 372 *Now is the time* . . . By Jack Riemer, in *New Prayers* (see no. 533).
554 372 *As for us* . . . Adapted by CS from a somewhat free trsl. by HB of "*Enosh Ma Yizkeh*," a *piyut* (liturgical poem) from the trad. YK Morning Service. It is in the form of an unrhymed alphabetical acrostic inserted in the 2nd benediction of the Reader's repetition of the *Tefila*. Cf. the paraphrase of this poem in UPB II, pp. 210f.
555 373 *Rabbi Chama bar Chanina said* . . . Adapted by CS from a composite passage compiled by JR from B. Yoma 86a–b; M. Avot 4.17; B. Ber. 34b. The Scriptural q. are Hos. 14:5, 2a; Isa. 59:20; Hos. 14:2 (again, this time in full).
556 374 *Repentance and the Day of Atonement* . . . MT, *Hilchot Teshuva* 2.9f.
557 374 *Eternal God, what can we say* . . . New, by CS. Based on his prayer in GOR, p. 31.
558 374 *Your power, O God* . . . Adapted by CS from GOR, p. 36, where it was new, by CS. It begins with a paraphrase of a saying by Alfred North Whitehead, in *Science and the Modern World* (Cambridge Univ. Press, 1926, 1933 ed.), p. 239.
559 375 *Help us to return* . . . Lam. 5:21.
560 375 *Come, let us consider* . . . Slightly adapted by CS from a poem, "Atonement," by Ruth Brin, in *Interpretations for the Weekly Torah Reading* (Lerner Publications Co., Minneapolis, 1965), pp. 157f.
561 376 *Yes, it is true* . . . An alphabetical acrostic for the YK Evening Service in the Polish ritual, attributed to R. Yom Tov of York (died 1190).
562 377 *Praise the Lord, O my soul* . . . Pss. 103:1–8,13–19. Some of these vv. are adapted by changes in person (from 3rd to 2nd), or in number (to plural).
563 378 *"Behold, I have set . . ."* Slightly adapted by CS from a meditation in *Confessions of the Heart*, ed. by HB, p. 9. The q. is Deut. 30:19.
564 379 *For all we sought* . . . "The Road," a poem by Humbert Wolfe, in *This Blind Rose* (Doubleday and Co., Inc., N.Y., 1929).
565 380 *Once Rabbi Yochanan ben Zakkai* . . . From Avot DeRabbi Natan, ch. 4. The q. is Hos. 6:6.

No.   Page

MacIntyre of a poem by Rainer Maria Rilke, "Solemn Hour," in *Rilke: Selected Poems* (©1940, University of California Press).

577   389   *They list for me* ... An anonymous sonnet in *Lyra Mystica*, ed. by Charles C. Albertson, p. 210.

578   390   *Slowly now the evening* ... A poem by Rainer Maria Rilke, trsl. by C. F. MacIntyre in *Rilke: Selected Poems* (see no. 576).

579   390   *Create in me* ... Ps. 51:12, followed by a poem attributed to Bachya ibn Pakuda (Spain, c. 1050–1120), included in *The Language of Faith*, ed. by Nahum N. Glatzer (Schocken Books, Inc., N.Y., 1967). The passage ends with Ps. 73:26. Trsl. by CS, slightly adapted here from his trsl. in GOR, pp. 153f, where it first appeared.

580   391   *Wait for the Lord* ... Ps. 27:14.

AFTERNOON SERVICE

581   394   *At this hour* ... New, by HB and CS. The congregational response is based on Isa. 43:21.

582   395   *O that I might be* ... A poem by Judah Halevi (Spain-Palestine, c. 1075–1141). The metrical trsl. is from UPB II, p. 248.

583   396   *O Sovereign Source of salvation* ... A *piyut* (liturgical poem) in the form of a nominal acrostic, by Mordechai b. Shabtai (Italy or Greece, 13th C.), found in the trad. *Selichot* for the YK *Musaf* (Additional Service). Following UPB II (pp. 281ff), we include 6 of the original 12 stanzas. Our trsl. is new, by CS.

584   398   *You who hold fast* ... Deut. 4:4.

585   398   *Eternal God, open my lips* ... See no. 59.

586   398   *God of the past* ... Slightly adapted from ST, p. 236, where it was new, by Molly Cone and CS. Here we add the trad. insertion for the Ten Days of Repentance, in a somewhat free rendition. On the H text (*Avot*), see no. 60.

587   399   *We pray that we might know* ... From ST, pp. 255f, where it was new, by RL, on the theme of *Gevurot* (see no. 61). The H text utilized here, however, is trad., without emendation (so already in ST). Thus, "*Mechayei Hametim,*" "Who revives the dead," is retained here because of its interpretive use. The text also includes a passage trad. inserted into the *Gevurot* from Simchat Torah until Pesach, i.e., "*Mashiv Haru-ach* ... ," "You cause the wind to blow ... " (this is also used figuratively here), first attested in M. Ta-anit 1.1. We do not include here the insertion trad. for the Ten Days of Repentance.

588   400   *God of holiness* ... The 1st sentence is new, by CS. On the remaining

No. Page

E which trsls. the 1st and last sentences of the H, see nos. 62, 68. On the H text, which forms part of the *Kedushat Hashem*, see nos. 62, 66–68.

589 401 *Now all acclaim* ... A *piyut* (liturgical poem), in the form of an alphabetical acrostic, sometimes attributed to R. Eliezer Hakalir (Pal., c. 6–7th C.), but probably older. Trad., it precedes the *Kedusha* (see no. 163) in the Reader's repetition of the *Tefila* in the RH and YK Morning Service.

590 403 *Let now an Infinite Presence* ... Slightly adapted by CS from GOR, pp. 354ff, where it was new, by CS.

591 404 *We have sinned against life* ... A free adaptation by CS of an unpublished reading by JR on the theme of "*Al Chet*" (see no. 427). Following a suggestion by RIK, CS has included the opening H words of "*Al Chet*."

592 405 *For all these* ... The concluding paragraph of "*Al Chet*" (see preceding note).

593 405 *God before whom* ... New, by CS, based on a meditation by John Baillie. The penultimate sentence is Ps. 51:12, slightly adapted by a change from 1st person singular to 1st person plural.

594 406 *Our God ... sanctify us with Your Mitzvot* ... See no. 406. Here the trsl. is abridged.

595 406 *Let me hear You* ... From ST, p. 232, where it was new, by CS. On the H text (*Avoda*), see no. 119.

596 407 *O God of Israel's past* ... A somewhat free trsl. of the *Modim Derabbanan* ("Thanksgiving of the Rabbis"; see no. 120). Here and elsewhere used as the *Hoda-a* (see no. 74). See ST, p. 232f, from which this trsl. comes. Here, however, we include in the E the trad. insertion for the Ten Days of Repentance.

597 407 *O Source of peace* ... Abridged from ST, p. 173. It is a prayer based on a poem by R. Nachman of Bratzlav (see no. 1) entitled "*Adon Hashalom*," "Lord of Peace," trsl. by CS, and adapted for use here for the theme of *Birkat Shalom*. Here we add, in E, the insertion trad. for the Ten Days of Repentance, in an abridged form. On the H text, see no. 176.

598 408 *Lord our God* ... From J. Ber. 4.2, where it is reported by R. Pedat in the name of R. Jacob b. Idi as one of the 3 prayers by R. Eliezer (2nd C.). See ST, p. 679; cf. GOR, p. 359.

599 408 *May the One who causes peace* ... See no. 78.

600 408 *May the One whose presence* ... The blessing which, according to the 4th C. Pal. Amora, R. Chelbo, was spoken in the Temple every Sabbath by the outgoing watch to the incoming watch (B. Ber. 12a).

No. *Page*

The trsl. which appears in GOR, p. 359, interprets it in a broader sense than originally intended. Ours adheres more closely to the text, but renders the H's 2nd person plural by a 1st person plural in the E.

601 409 *Let us adore* ... A portion of the *"Aleinu"* (see no. 83; cf. no. 129). Here, of course, it does not conclude a service. Rather, it augments the following passages. Cf. UPB II, pp. 260f.

602 410 *Author of life* ... Approximately half of *"Ata Konanta,"* an early (6th C.?) *piyut* (liturgical poem) in the form of an alphabetical acrostic by an unknown author (cf. Goldschmidt, *Machzor*, II, pp. 18ff). It is one of many introductions to the *Avoda* ("Temple Service" remembrance) which forms part of the YK *Musaf* (Additional Service). The present text is from the Sefardi ritual and may be the earliest poem of its kind. All such poems present a brief review of history from Creation to the selection of the family of Aaron for the priesthood. The role of the priest in the Temple cult is then extolled. The E, by CS, is not a trsl., but an alphabetical acrostic—*à la* the H—also of half the alphabet—which ponders the meaning of Creation and of creatureliness. It introduces a section which surveys the human universe "From Creation to Redemption." See also no. 624.

603 411 *I wait for God* ... A precentor's prayer from Geonic times, q. Pss. 51:17; 19:15.

604 411 *In the beginning* ... Gen. 1:1-3. Simple recitation of the story of Creation on YK is a novel practice in modern times, but was known to the Geonim. See *Otsar Hageonim*, Vol. 5, Megila, *Teshuva* no. 228.

605 412 *For countless ages* ... Abridged from GOR, p. 259, where it was adapted by CS from RPB, p. 366, where it was attributed to Eugene Kohn.

606 412 *Then God said* ... Gen. 1:20-24.

607 412 *Creatures were born* ... Abridged and adapted from GOR, p. 260, where it was adapted by CS from RPB, p. 366.

608 413 *Praise the Lord* ... Ps. 104:lf,4,10-11a,12,19,24.

609 414 *May the glory* ... Ps. 104:31.

610 414 *Every living creature* ... Slightly adapted from GOR, p. 264, where it was adapted by CS from RPB, pp. 367f.

611 414 *Then God said* ... Gen. 1:26ff.

612 415 *We were unlike* ... Adapted from GOR, p. 265, where it was adapted by CS from RPB, p. 368.

613 415 *Sovereign Lord* ... Ps. 8:2,4ff.

No. *Page*

614   416   *You gave us* . . . Adapted from GOR, pp. 267–269, where these passages were adapted by CS from RPB, p. 369.

615   416   *And the Lord saw* . . . Gen. 6:5.

616   416   *How long* . . . *Though our deeds* . . . *Long ago* . . . Adapted by CS from GOR, pp. 268f, where it was adapted from RPB, p. 371.

617   417   *Then the Lord said* . . . Gen. 12:1f,3b.

618   418   *Many generations later* . . . From GOR, p. 270, where it was new, by JR.

619   418   *When God revealed* . . . Exod. Rabba 29.9.

620   418   *I, the Lord* . . . Exod. 20:2–14. An abridged version of the Ten Commandments.

621   419   *Thus pledged* . . . Adapted by CS from GOR, pp. 271f, where it was new, by JR.

622   419   *But no city* . . . Freely adapted by CS from GOR, pp. 272f, where it was new, by JR. It alludes to Ps. 137, and q. Ps. 137:4.

623   420   *Take comfort* . . . Isa. 40:1–5. This is the trad. *Haftara* reading for Shabbat Nachamu, the Shabbat immediately after the Ninth of Av. It is the paradigmatic liturgical reading of consolation despite tragedy. The passage opens with a 2nd person plural imperative verb, which we render freely by "take comfort."

624   420   *How like a dream* . . . Freely adapted by CS from GOR, p. 274, where it was new, by JR. It alludes to Ps. 126.

625   421   *The ritual begins at dawn* . . . Adapted by CS from GOR, p. 274, where it was new, by JR. Here the trad. *Avoda* ("Worship") reaches its climax, recalling the YK ritual as performed by the High Priest in the ancient Temple; it is trad. interpolated in the *Kedushat Hayom* (see no. 68) of the Reader's repetition of the YK *Musaf Tefila*. The earliest mention of this practice is in the Talmud (B. Yoma 56b), relating to the 1st half of the 4th C. The oldest versions follow closely the account of the Temple ritual as given in the M., tractate Yoma. In the Middle Ages the *Avoda* was profusely elaborated with poetic compositions; the various rituals have widely differing selections. Some of them open with a composition describing the creation of the world and continue the story down to the institution of the priesthood (Elbogen, p. 277). That is the scheme adopted in this PB, as in GOR and RPB, but we carry it on (as does GOR) to the messianic future. For a historical view of the YK Temple ritual, which has influenced us, see *The Jewish Festivals*, by Hayyim Schauss (UAHC, 1938), ch. 15. See also no. 602.

626   421   *How glorious he is* . . . Inspired by classical description of the High Priest in Ben Sirach (Ecclesiasticus) 50. GOR (p. 275) has a much

No. Page

longer passage from Sirach at this point, following the precedent of IIM in LJPB II, pp. 191f.

627 422 *Three times the white-robed* ... Adapted by CS from GOR, p. 275, where it was new, by CS, suggested by RPB, p. 375.

628 422 *O Lord, pardon the sins* ... M. Yoma 3.8, q. Lev. 16:30.

629 422 *So, too, do we confess* ... Adapted by CS from GOR, p. 276, where it was new, by CS, suggested by RPB, p. 375.

630 422 *Having confessed* ... Slightly adapted from GOR, p. 277, where it was new, by CS, influenced by LJPB II, pp. 194f. Cf. UPB II, pp. 267f.

631 423 *O Lord, pardon the sins* ... M. Yoma 4.2, q. Lev. 16:30.

632 423 *Like the High Priest* ... Slightly adapted by CS from UPB II, p. 266, at the suggestion of ASD.

633 423 *Now the High Priest* ... New, by CS. Cf. GOR, p. 278.

634 423 *O Lord, pardon the sins* ... M. Yoma 6.2, q. Lev. 16:30.

635 424 *When the priests* ... M. Yoma 6.2.

636 424 *We, too, pray not only* ... From GOR, p. 277, where it was new, by CS, influenced by LJPB II, pp. 194f. Cf. UPB II, pp. 267f.

637 424 *Some have strayed* ... Adapted by CS from GOR, pp. 277f, where it was new, by CS, influenced by LJPB II, pp. 194f. Cf. UPB II, pp. 267f.

638 425 *For all these sins* ... See preceding note.

639 425 *The Second Temple* ... From GOR, p. 281, where it was new, by JR. Here adapted and abridged by CS.

640 426 *How lovely are your tents* ... Num. 24:5; cf. no. 135.

641 426 *If you wish to know* ... From a poem by Chaim Nachman Bialik (Russia-Palestine, 1873–1934, leading Hebrew poet of modern times). Trsl. by CS.

642 427 *Look back* ... New, by CS.

643 428 *Thus says the Lord God* ... Isa. 42:5–7. The inclusion of the so-called "Servant Poems" from Isa. 42, 49, 50, and 52f in the present context was a feature of LJPB II (pp. 198–202), carried on in GOR (beginning on p. 285), and continued here in abridged form. We have trsl. some of the passages relating to the "servant" in the plural (e.g., the present passage) to bring out their meaning, i.e., that the entire House of Israel is (intended to be) God's servant and witness. In some of the passages, of course, the plural is there already.

644 428 *You are My witnesses* ... Isa. 43:10f.

645 428 *Behold My servants* ... Isa. 42:1–5.

646 429 *God chose us* ... Adapted by CS from GOR, p. 282, where it was new, by JR, alluding to Isa. 6:8.

No.	Page	
647	429	*God's witnesses, God's servants!* ... Adapted by CS from GOR, p. 287, where it was new, by AF, q. Exod. 19:6. This passage introduces the *"Eleh Ezkera"* ("These things I remember"), or Martyrology. The custom of commemorating Jewish martyrs on Tish-a Be-Av, on YK, and on certain Sabbaths, grew up in the Middle Ages, especially from the time of the Crusades. Some communities kept lists of martyrs' names, known as *Memor* books. Also, Jewish poets composed elegies (*kinot*) recalling particular persecutions. One such composition, *Eleh Ezkera* (see no. 654), found its way into the YK *Musaf* (Additional Service) liturgy. It commemorated the *Asara Harugei Malchut*, 10 rabbis martyred by the Romans in the 2nd C. Some modern PBs (notably RPB and Harlow) have developed that theme into a more general commemoration of Jewish martyrdom, with special reference to the greatest calamity of all, the most recent: the Holocaust of the Nazi era. Until the present PB, which builds on GOR, the latter was the most extensive development of this theme.
648	429	*They had no outward grace* ... Isa. 53:2–5, 7–9. Again we trsl. the H into plural E (see no. 643).
649	430	*The earth's crust* ... Adapted by CS from GOR, p. 289, where it was new, by CS.
650	430	*Now, therefore, we honor* ... Adapted by CS from GOR, p. 290, where it was new, by CS.
651	430	*And especially do we remember* ... Adapted by CS from GOR, p. 290, where it was new, by CS.
652	430	*Look and remember* ... Part of "Travelogue for Exiles," from *Selected Poems*, by Karl Shapiro (American Jewish poet, born 1913), published by Random House, N.Y.
653	430	*Days and years of peace* ... Adapted by CS from GOR, p. 291, where it was new, by CS.
654	431	*These things do I remember* ... Opening sentence of *"Eleh Ezkera"* (see no. 647). The trsl. is free, by Nina Salomon (England, 1877–1925).
655	432	*For Zion and her cities* ... From one of the medieval "Zionide" *kinot* (elegies) inspired by Judah Halevi's *Ode to Zion*, trad. sung on Tish-a Be-Av (see A. Z. Idelsohn, *Jewish Music*, Schocken Books, N.Y., 1967, p. 171). For the full text, see *Seder Hakinot LeTish-a Be-Av*, by Daniel Goldschmidt (Mosad Harav Kook, Jerusalem, 1968), pp. 144f.
656	432	*I have taken an oath* ... Part of a poem, *"Neder"* ("Oath"), by Avraham Shlonsky (Russia-Palestine/Israel, 1900–1974), in *Avraham Shlonsky: Yalkut Shirim*, ed. by A. B. Yafeh, Yachdav, Tel Aviv, 1967. This trsl. is slightly adapted by CS from his trsl. in GOR, p.

No. Page

292; for another trsl., by HB, see ST, p. 573, and *A Passover Haggadah* (CCAR, 1974), p. 46.

657   432   *In the time of Hadrian* ... Adapted by CS from GOR, pp. 294f, where it was new, by CS and AF. It is based on "*Eleh Ezkera*" (see no. 654), which, in turn, draws on the medieval *Midrash Asara Harugei Malchut*, based on older midrashic and Talmudic sources. See JE, s.v. "Martyrs, the Ten," and Chanoch Albeck's Notes in his H edition of Leopold Zunz's *Die Gottesdienstlichen Vorträge der Juden (Haderashot BeYisra-el*, Hotsa-at Mosad Bialik, Jerusalem, 1954), pp. 312f. The use of the refrain here ("These things I remember. . . ") was suggested by Harlow, p. 555. The passage includes a number of Scriptural allusions and q. Prov. 3:18; Job 13:15a; Deut. 6:4f.

658   434   *In the days of the Crusades* ... Slightly adapted by CS from GOR, pp. 295f, a passage that combines several passages from *The Jew in the Medieval World: A Source Book*, ed. by Jacob R. Marcus (UAHC, Cincinnati, 1938). The concluding paragraph is adapted from GOR, p. 296, where it was new, by CS.

659   434   *A voice is heard in Ramah* ... Jer. 31:15.

660   435   *Merciful God* ... An elegy for martyrs dating from the period of the Crusades (12th C.), emanating from the Rhineland. Trad. recited on some Sabbaths after the reading of the *Haftara* in the Ashkenazi ritual. We provide it here in abridged form. The concluding q. is Deut. 32:43. There is an earlier allusion to II Sam. 1:23.

661   435   *How many there are* ... Slightly adapted by CS from GOR, p. 297, where it was new, by CS.

662   435   *All this has come* ... Ps. 44:18,23.

663   436   *We walk the world* ... From Harlow, pp. 557–559. It is an E adaptation of a trsl. by Helena Frank of the Yiddish version of part of a poem, "*Ir Haharega*" ("City of Slaughter"), written in H by Chaim Nachman Bialik (see no. 641).

664   436   *Lord our God, we have testified* ... Slightly adapted by CS from GOR, p. 298, where it was new, by CS. It q. Midrash Tehillim, to Ps. 123:2.

665   436   *Without Jews* ... A poem by Jacob Glatstein, trsl. by N. Halper, in *A Treasury of Yiddish Poetry*, ed. by Irving Howe and Eliezer Greenberg (Holt, Reinhart and Winston, N.Y., 1969), pp. 331f.

666   437   *Silence* ... Adapted by CS from GOR, pp. 299f, where it was new, by CS.

667   438   *Perhaps some of the blame* ... From "Perhaps," by Binem Heller

No.   *Page*

(Poland-Israel, born 1908; Yiddish poet), in *The Golden Peacock,* ed. by Joseph Leftwich (A. S. Barnes & Co., Inc., Thomas Yoseloff, N.Y., 1961), p. 495.

668 439 *Out of the depths* . . . Ps. 130:1.

669 439 *For the sin of silence* . . . From ST, p. 408, where it was new, by cs.

670 439 *And yet even in the inferno* . . . Freely adapted by cs from GOR, p. 301, where it was new, by cs.

671 440 *Is not a flower* . . . From GOR, p. 302, where it was new, by cs.

672 440 *When Leo Baeck* . . . Slightly adapted by cs from GOR, p. 303, where it was new, by AF. Rabbi Leo Baeck (1874–1956) was the heroic leader of German Jewry during the Nazi period as well as an outstanding theologian. AF is a leading interpreter of his writings.

673 441 *You must not say* . . . From *"Mir Zeynen Do,"* which became the battle song of the Vilna partisans, Yiddish by Hirsh Glick, slightly adapted by cs from a trsl. by AF, included in his anthology, *Out of the Whirlwind.*

674 442 *After the suffering* . . . Freely adapted by cs from GOR, p. 305, where it was new, by cs and JR. This begins a new section of the *Avoda,* "Rebirth."

675 442 *The Lord is my strength* . . . Ps. 118:14,17.

676 442 *In one land especially* . . . Freely adapted by cs from GOR, pp. 305f, where it was new, by cs.

677 443 *The hand of the Lord* . . . Ezek. 37:1–6,10–12,14.

678 444 *Judah shall abide for ever* . . . Joel 4:20.

679 444 *Jerusalem is the joy* . . . Freely adapted by cs from GOR, p. 310, where it was new, by JR. It alludes to Ps. 48:3 (and see the great poem by Judah Halevi which begins *"Yefeh nof, mesos tevel,"* "Beautiful prospect, joy of the world"); Ps. 24:1; B. Ber. 6a.

680 445 *The storm will end* . . . From a poem, "The Moon's Brightness," by Haim Lensky, a Russian Jewish poet, born in 1905, imprisoned in a Siberian labor camp in 1935, where he almost certainly perished, as did many Jewish poets, artists, and intellectuals during the Stalin and subsequent regimes. Text and trsl. by Robert Friend (copyright), from *Anthology of Modern Hebrew Poetry,* ed. by S. Y. Penueli and A. Ukhmani (Israel Universities Press, Jerusalem, 1966), Vol. 2, p. 353.

681 445 *Today let us remember* . . . Adapted by cs from GOR, p. 315, where it was new, by cs. The phrase "hammer of chaos" is from a poem, "Hammer of Chaos," by Edith Sitwell, q. in *A Year of Grace* (see no. 484), p. 14.

No. Page

682 446 *This is the vision* . . . By Karl Jaspers (German philosopher, 1883-1969), q. in *From Darkness to Light*, ed. by Victor Gollancz (Gollancz, 1956), p. 334.

683 446 *Lord, today we turn* . . . Slightly adapted by CS from GOR, pp. 315f, where it was new, by CS. It q. Deut. Rabba 2.12 and MT, *Hilchot Teshuva* 2.1.

684 446 *Lord, make us whole* . . . New, by CS, based on the conclusion of the preceding passage in GOR.

685 446 *Use us, Lord* . . . Slightly adapted by CS from GOR, p. 316, where it was new, by CS. It q. Amos 5:24.

686 447 *Our God . . . May You rule* . . . See no. 71.

687 448 *All the world* . . . See no. 231.

688 450 *It shall come to pass* . . . Isa. 2:2f (adapted). Cf. GOR, p. 336; UPB II, p. 233 (which utilizes the parallel passage from Mic. 4:1-4 in the Morning Service).

689 450 *There is none like You* . . . From the trad. introduction to the reading of the Torah on Sabbaths, Festivals, and High Holy Days. Cited in Soferim 14.8, these paragraphs embody Pss. 29:11; 86:8; 145:13. Here we omit the trad. 3rd paragraph (beginning "Source of mercy . . .") found in ST, p. 417.

690 451 *For out of Zion* . . . Isa. 2:3b. The use of this v. here is trad.

691 451 *Praised be the One* . . . Trad. at this point. First alluded to in MV, p. 157.

692 451 *O house of Jacob* . . . Isa. 2:5.

693 451 *Hear, O Isreal* . . . *Our God is One!* See no. 185.

694 451 *Yours, Lord* . . . See no. 186.

695 453 *Praise the Lord* . . . *Giver of the Torah.* See no. 187.

696 453 *The Lord spoke to Moses* . . . Lev. 19:1-4,9-18,32-37. On the public reading of the Torah generally, see no. 188. The passage trad. read on YK afternoon is Lev. 18, about the "Prohibited Degrees of Consanguinity." So already in B. Meg. 31a. Most Reform PBS have chosen, instead, selections from Lev. 19, the "Holiness Code." We follow that precedent.

697 455 *Praised be the Lord* . . . *Giver of the Torah.* See no. 189.

698 457 *This is the Torah* . . . See no. 190.

699 457 *Let us exalt* . . . See no. 502.

700 457 *Praised be the Lord* . . . *truth and righteousness.* See no. 191.

701 457 *The word of the Eternal* . . . The complete H text of Jonah; the E text is slightly abridged, consisting of Jonah 1:1-2:1; 2:11-4:11. Our trsl. is adapted by CS from the new JPS trsl., in *The Five Megillot and Jonah*, 1969. On the reading of the *Haftara* in general,

MEMORIAL SERVICE

No.   Page

it from LJPB II, pp. 252f, which took it from the then current ed. of UPB II. See UPB II, p. 309.

721   480   *Our days are few* ... Job 14:1 (adapted).

722   480   *The eye is never satisfied* ... Note 720 applies. And see UPB II, p. 310.

723   480   *Lord, what are we* ... Pss. 144:3f; 90:6,3; Deut. 32:29; Pss. 49:18; 37:37; 34:23. Cf. UPB II, pp. 306f; GOR, pp. 367f.

724   481   *We are strangers* ... Adapted by CS from UPB II, pp. 310f.

725   481   *Lord, You have been* ... Ps. 90:1f,4ff (adapted),10,12,16f.

726   482   *O God, Author of life and death* ... Adapted by CS from UPB II, p. 314. The responses are newly provided, and are Ps. 139:12 and the concluding v. from *"Adon Olam"* (see no. 86). The last paragraph also contains an allusion to Ps. 23:4.

727   483   *I lift up my eyes* ... Ps. 121.

728   484   *If some messenger* ... Very slightly adapted from GOR, p. 370, where it is from *Belief and Action, An Everyday Philosophy*, by Viscount (Herbert Louis) Samuel (1870–1963), Pan Books, 1953, pp. 67f.

729   484   *We shall not fear* ... Sirach (Ecclesiasticus) 41.3 (adapted).

730   484   *"Alas for those who cannot sing"* ... Abridged and adapted by CS from GOR, p. 371, where it was new, by JR, influenced by LJPB II, p. 253. Zvi Kolitz, in *Survival for What?* (Philosophical Library, N.Y., 1969), p. 114, attributes the q. to Oliver Wendell Holmes (1809–1894).

731   485   *Rabbi Tarfon says* ... M. Avot 2.15. R. Tarfon was a Pal. teacher of the 2nd C.

732   485   *All things pass away* ... Very slightly adapted by CS from GOR, p. 372, where it was new, by JR.

733   485   *The dust returns to the earth* ... Eccles. 12:7.

734   485   *The soul is Yours* ... This is the refrain of a *piyut* (liturgical poem) found in *Machzor Oholei Ya-akov*, ed. by R. Yaakov ibn Yitzchaki (Jerusalem, 1910), Vol. II, p. 37. Idelsohn (p. 235) attributed it to Abraham ibn Ezra (Spain, 1092–1167, poet and biblical exegete).

735   485   *In You, Lord, do I seek refuge* ... Pss. 71:1; 39:5–8; 73:26; 91:1 (adapted), 2.

736   486   *I have set the Eternal always* ... Ps. 16:8–11.

737   487   *Let us call to mind* ... Adapted by CS from UPB II, pp. 315f.

738   487   *I think continually* ... By Stephen Spender, in *Poems* (Random House, Inc., N.Y., 1934).

739   488   *O Lord of life, bless the memories* ... Adapted by CS from GOR, p. 376, where it was new, by JR.

740   489   *The Lord is my shepherd* ... Ps. 23.

CONCLUDING SERVICE

No.   Page

from LJPB II, p. 267, which is itself an adaptation of a UPB II (p. 325) version. The *Union Hymnal* (p. 196) calls its authorship "composite."

753   500   *Forgive your neighbors . . . commandments.* Sirach (Ecclesiasticus) 28.2–6 (adapted). Cf. GOR, p. 387.

754   500   *Let not the fierce sun . . .* From *The Voice of Silence* (an anthology compiled by Madame Blavatsky), q. in *From Darkness to Light*, ed. by Victor Gollancz (Gollancz, London, 1956), p. 531. Cf. GOR, p. 388.

755   500   *For transgressions against God . . .* See no. 359. Cf. GOR, p. 388.

756   501   *Let the glory of God . . .* See no. 58.

757   501   *Eternal God . . .* See no. 59.

758   502   *Source of all being . . .* From ST, pp. 152f, where it was new, by CS, on the theme of *Avot*. On the H text (*Avot*), see no. 60. Here, however, as is trad. in the *Ne-ila* (Concluding Service), there is a change in the H insertion for the Ten Days of Repentance: "*chotmenu*" ("seal, confirm us") replaces "*kotvenu*" ("inscribe us").

759   503   *Eternal God, the power of Your spirit . . .* From ST, pp. 356f, where it was new, by RIK and CS. On the H text (*Gevurot*), see no. 61.

760   503   *Hear now! . . .* This is the refrain from a *piyut* (liturgical poem) trad. at this point in the Reader's repetition of the *Ne-ila Tefila*, in the Ashkenazi ritual. It is attributed to R. Simeon b. Isaac b. Abun (Mayence, 11th C.).

761   503   *We sanctify Your name . . .* See no. 163.

762   504   *You are holy . . .* See no. 66.

763   505   *The Lord of Hosts . . .* See no. 67.

764   505   *Blessed is the Lord, who rules in holiness.* See no. 68.

765   505   *Our God . . . pardon our sins . . . the Day of Atonement.* See no. 416. Here we offer an abridged version of this, the concluding paragraph of *Kedushat Hayom*.

766   505   *O Lord our God, may we . . .* From ST, p. 187, where it was new, by HB and CS. It is a free trsl. of the H which combines (and abridges) several versions of the *Avoda*. On the H text, see no. 73, and, for the concluding eulogy, see no. 119.

767   506   *For the glory of life . . .* From ST, p. 187, where it was a free trsl. by CS of an abridgement of the *Hoda-a* (see no. 74).

768   506   *Our God, the Guide of humanity . . .* From ST, pp. 109f, where it was a composite prayer by CS, adapting SOH, p. 292, and influenced by UPB I, p. 349. In turn, the passage from SOH was slightly adapted from a prayer by IIM in LJPB I, p. 274. See, as well, "We humbly ask You . . ." in SOH, p. 292 (LJPB I, p. 275). On the H text (*Birkat*

No. Page

784 516 *It is Your way* . . . An ancient penitential prayer which Idelsohn (p. 236) attributes to Jose b. Jose (Pal., c. 6th C.).

785 517 *Now send forth* . . . From a *piyut* (liturgical poem) trad. interpolated into the *Kedusha* (see no. 163) in the Reader's repetition of the *Ne-ila Tefila*.

786 517 *Open for us the gates* . . . An alphabetical acrostic, listing various "gates." The present passage resembles closely one found in the trad. PB after the *Havdala* and following the post-Sabbath *Zemirot* ("Table Songs"). In turn, that passage comes from a *piyut* (liturgical poem) called *"Te-anu Vete-ateru,"* which, in the Sefardi YK ritual, comes at the end of *Ne-ila*. Another version of this acrostic is given in Goldschmidt, Vol. II, p. 731. Our H text follows that of Harlow, p. 724. Our E version is new, by CS. It is a double alphabetic acrostic, with several letters omitted.

787 518 *Restore us, O God* . . . Ps. 80:4.

788 518 *Open the gates* . . . A *piyut* (liturgical poem) trad. inserted in the Reader's repetition of the *Kedushat Hayom* (see no. 69) of the *Ne-ila Tefila*. The earliest references we have found to it are in the commentaries to O. Ch. 623.2.

789 518 *The day is fading* . . . Adapted by CS from GOR, pp. 407f, where it was adapted by CS from LJPB II, pp. 280f (cf. UPB II, pp. 344ff), where it was adapted by IIM from the then current ed. of UPB II, itself based on David Einhorn's *Olat Tamid* of 1858 (pp. 367–371). Cf. Emil G. Hirsch's E trsl. of *Olat Tamid*, published in 1896, pp. 262–267. The Scriptural allusions and q. are Deut 6:4; Isa. 56:7; Ps. 24:7,10.

790 520 *Lift up your heads* . . . Ps. 24:7,10.

791 520 *Lord, whither can I go* . . . Adapted by CS from GOR, pp. 409ff, where it was adapted by CS from UPB II, pp. 346ff, and LJPB II, pp. 282ff. The former goes back to David Einhorn's *Olat Tamid* (see Hirsch's trsl., pp. 274 *et seq.* and 789); the latter was written by IIM. The Scriptural allusions and q. are Pss. 139:7–12; 8:4–7; Ezek. 33:11; Ps. 30:12f.

792 522 *We therefore bow* . . . From the *"Aleinu"* (see no. 83). The recitation of this verse here does not seem to be trad., but it is found in some Reform PBS. See, e.g., David Einhorn's *Olat Tamid* (Hirsch's E ed.), p. 278; GOR, p. 412; UPB II, p. 349.

793 522 *We sanctify Your name* . . . This form of the *Kaddish* is known as *Kaddish Titkabel,* from the opening word of its interpolated sentence ("O Maker of heaven . . . *Titkabel [Accept]* . . . "). Trad. it *follows* the passages referred to in the next note. According to De Sola Pool,

No. Page

in *The Old Jewish-Aramaic Prayer, the Kaddish*, p. 66, this form of the *Kaddish* is "a closing formula for the end of a service." Our trsl. of this *Kaddish* is somewhat free, by CS, and intended for congregational reading. On the *Kaddish* in general, see no. 58.

794   523   *Hear, O Israel . . . Blessed is . . . The Eternal Lord . . .* Deut 6:4; the congregational response to the preceding; I Kings 18:39. The recitation of these vv. is 1st mentioned in MV. The trad. custom is to recite the 1st once, the 2nd 3 times, and the 3rd 7 times (O. Ch. 623.8). Moses Ribkes (1600–1660), in his commentary *Be-er Hagola*, cites as the authority for this practice the *Sefer Mitzvot Gadol*, by R. Moses of Coucy (France, 13th C.), basing itself on Rabbenu Judah b. Isaac (known as Sir Leon of Paris), 1166–1224. The practice in Reform synagogues varies, and we suggest following the trad. custom. UPB II and GOR are silent on this point.

795   524   *The Shofar is sounded . . .* The Sefardi custom of sounding the *shofar* with a series of blasts (*Teki-a, Shevarim, Teru-a, Teki-a*) within the *Kaddish Titkabel* (see no. 793) goes back to SRA, p. 171; we retain the Ashkenazi practice of a single blast (cf. O. Ch. 623.8). As to its length, trad. is silent. GOR, in note no. 558, p. 495, refers to the widespread custom of prolonging the single blast from *Teki-a* to *Teki-a Gedola*, and such is our recommendation.

796   525   *And now, at the close . . .* Slightly adapted by CS from UPB II, p. 350. The Scriptural references are to Mal. 3:24; Ps. 121:8.

HAVDALA

The word *Havdala* means "separation" or "differentiation," and refers especially to the ritual for "ushering out" the Sabbath or a festival. This custom seems to be as ancient as the *Kiddush*, going back to Pharisaic times (cf., e.g., M. Ber. 8.5 and Tosefta Ber. 6.7).

797   526   *Blessed is the Lord . . . fruit of the vine.* See no. 81. M. Ber. 8.5–8 refers to this and to the other *Havdala* benedictions; Tosefta Ber. 6.7 (cited in B. Ber. 52a) mentions all 3: wine, light, and spices.

798   526   *Blessed is the Lord . . . all the spices.* See preceding note. The text of the benediction is cited in B. Ber. 43a. The use of spices in this context may go back to an ancient domestic custom of bringing spices on burning coals into the room at the end of a meal (cf. M. Ber. 6.6); this, of course, could only be done hen the Sabbath was over (cf. Levi, p. 204); thus, it is trad. to recite this blessing on Saturday night only. But YK is called "The Sabbath of Sabbaths." Maimonides

No.   Page

explains the custom as intended to "cheer up" the "additional soul" which, according to Rabbinic legend, dwells within the Jew during the Sabbath (B. Beitsa 16a; B. Ta-anit 27b); that "additional soul" is saddened when the Sabbath departs, for it, in turn, must leave the Jew (MT, *Hilchot Shabbat* 29.29).

799   526   *Blessed is the Lord . . . the light of fire.* Lit., "lights." Because of the plural, it is customary to use a twisted candle, with 2 or more wicks (cf. B. Pesachim 103b). The benediction is cited in M. Ber. 8.5 as that recommended by the School of Hillel. The custom of lighting a candle at the conclusion of the Sabbath is probably due to the desire to kindle light as soon as the Sabbath, during which the kindling of fire was prohibited, was over. It has also been connected with the story of Creation; in this view, the blessing of light at the start of the first day commemorates the first day of Creation, whose feature was the creation of light (cf. Gen. Rabba 12.5; B. Pesachim 53b). It may also be connected with the legend that Adam was frightened when it grew dark at the end of the Sabbath, whereupon God taught him how to kindle a fire (B. Pesachim 54a; cf. Levi, p. 204).

800   526   *Blessed is the Lord . . . who separates the sacred from the profane.* This is the principal benediction of the *Havdala,* from which its name is derived. It is cited in B. Pesachim 103b. Scriptural allusions include Gen. 1:4 and 2:1-3.

801   528   *You separate sacred from profane* . . . An abridged version of a poem with an acrostic indicating that it was written by "Isaac the Little," whom it is, however, not possible to identify with certainty. It may have been R. Isaac ibn Giyyat (11th C. Spain; cf. F. L. Cohen in JE, Vol. VI, p. 187). It was probably intended originally for the Concluding Service of YK; hence its penitential tenor. Following GOR, p. 427, we have changed the trad. refrain, "*Shavua tov*" ("A good week"), to "*Shana tova*" ("A good year").

SONGS

802   531   *O Lord, where shall I find You?* Slightly adapted by CS from the trsl. by Solomon Solis-Cohen of a poem by Judah Halevi (cf. no 452). *Union Hymnal,* pp. 22f.

803   531   *O God, our help* . . . A metrical version of Ps. 90 by Isaac Watts. *Union Hymnal,* p. 50.

804   532   *America the Beautiful.* By Katherine Lee Bates.

YOM KIPPUR—SONGS

Part Three

Index

235

D

Daniel (Book of): written in Hasmonean revolt, 33.

Daniel ben Judah (Dayan): author of *"Yigdal,"* 125, 126.

Darwin, Charles: theory of evolution, and Reform Judaism, 142.

David: prophets spoke to, 32; and doctrine of messianism, 38; place in sacred myth, 140–141.

Day of Atonement: atoning power of, 110; *Ne-ila*, service unique to, 130. See also Atonement, Repentance.

Day of Judgment: name for RH, 41, 94; in *"Unetaneh Tokef,"* 75; in poetry of Kalir, 138. See also Judgment.

Day of the Lord: In Zechariah, and *"Aleinu,"* 44.

Day of Remembrance: referred to in *Tefila*, 20, 94; primary name for RH, 41, 94. See also Remembrance, Remembrance Verses.

Day of the *Shofar* Blast: name for RH, 41. See also *Shofar, Shofar* Verses.

"(The) Day the world was conceived": see *"Yom Harat Olam."*

"(The) Day of the World's Birth": see *"Yom Harat Olam."*

Days of Awe: penitential quality of, 15–16; introduced by *"Hineni,"* 16; themes of, reflected in *Tefila*, 18, 21–23; defined as RH and YK, 19; *"Avinu Malkenu"* recited on, 23; Creation as major theme of, 29, 102; as messianic, 40; normal concluding prayers said on, 41; petitions of *Tefila* omitted on, 51; spiritual renewal as theme of, 64, 156; *"Unetaneh Tokef"* expresses awesome nature of, 75, 77; as days of aspiration to our highest nature, 78; meditations for, described, 83; as days of return to God, 87; concreteness of imagery for, and problem of language of gender, 90; Remembrance as major theme of, 94–95, 98; 13 attributes of God recited on, 106;

themes appropriate to, in Additional Prayers for YK, 132; *Avoda* as spiritual climax of liturgy for, 138; *Havdala* for, 155–156.

Death: *Kaddish* and, 47, 50; white attire as reminder of, 113; Confession on deathbed, 119; resurrection of the dead, 136–137; prompts redefinition of personal identity, 141; Memorial Prayer for, 147–152. See also Mourning.

Demon(s): belief in, and origin of *"Ma Tovu,"* 63.

Deuteronomy: 11:3 as proof text for *Tefila* as "offering of the heart," 79; 29:9–14 and 30:11–20 as Torah reading for MS of YK, 129, 145.

Diaspora: and prayers for Zion, 22–23; 2nd day of holidays, 27–28, 93; Priestly Benediction in, 80–81; Mission of Israel in, 81; Israel Zangwill's faith in, 144.

Dreyfus, Alfred: Dreyfus Affair (1894–1906), 134.

Dualism: in Gnosticism, 36–37.

Duchan: platform for Priestly Benediction, 80.

Duchenen: name for Priestly Benediction, 80, 81.

E

"Early will I seek You . . ." **(*"Shachar avakeshcha"*)**, 127.

Eastern religions: monotheism of, 29–30.

Egypt: Judah Halevi dies in (1141), 105; Exodus from, 38–39, 125, 143. See also Cairo.

"*Ein banu ma-asim*": see "We have little merit."

"*Ein Keloheinu*": history and structure of, 107.

Einhorn, David: emphasizes Priestly Benediction, 81, 129; author of *Olat Tamid*, 81; emphasizes Mission of Israel, 81, 129, 156; liturgical expression